# Elizabeth Pewsey

Elizabeth Pewsey was born in Chile in 1948 and educated in Calcutta, London and at St Hilda's College, Oxford. She has worked as a civil servant and publisher, and now lives in Wells, Somerset, with her husband and two children. Her first novel, CHILDREN OF CHANCE, and her third, UNHOLY HARMONIES, are also published by Sceptre.

D1470806

SCEPTRE

# Divine Comedy

## ELIZABETH PEWSEY

SCEPTRE

Copyright © Elizabeth Pewsey 1995

First published in Great Britain in 1995 by Hodder and Stoughton
First published in paperback in 1996 by Hodder and Stoughton
A division of Hodder Headline PLC
A Sceptre Paperback

10 9 8 7 6 5 4 3 2

British Library C.I.P.

Pewsey, Elizabeth
    Divine Comedy
    I. Title
    823 [F]

ISBN 0 340 65420 1


Typeset by Hewer Text Composition Services, Edinburgh
Printed and bound in Great Britain by
Cox & Wyman Ltd, Reading, Berkshire

Hodder and Stoughton
A division of Hodder Headline PLC
338 Euston Road
London NW1 3BH

For James Hale

# Prologue

Where was this?

Quinta rubbed at the window. The coach was standing in a bay, with its engine off. Two tired-looking men in uniform conferred by a sign urging readers to Keep Up With *The Times*. A cigarette glowed briefly in the dark.

Quinta yawned, and stretched to ease her back. She looked at her watch. Quarter to twelve. They weren't in Scotland, that was hours away yet.

She went to the front of the coach and stood in the door, shivering slightly. The northern air was cool; she was used to southern warmth.

One of the uniformed men looked towards her.

'Where are we?' she asked.

'Eyot,' said the man. 'Didn't you notice the Cathedral when we crossed the bridge? All lit up? Didn't think anyone had to ask where this was, everybody knows the Cathedral.'

Eyot, thought Quinta. It might be a good idea. If they traced her to the bus station and found she'd booked for Scotland, then they wouldn't bother to search for her south of the border.

'I don't care about cathedrals,' she said. 'Can I get my luggage out?'

'Your ticket's for Edinburgh.' Grumbling faintly, the driver bent to open the luggage hold at the side of the coach.

'I'm not feeling very well. I'll go on in the morning.'

The other man glanced at her. 'You look poorly. Get yourself a good night's sleep somewhere. You can use that ticket tomorrow, no problem, I'll stamp it for you. There.'

She'd be all right, neat clothes, good luggage, not on drugs, no seedy boyfriend in tow.

'Expecting,' said the driver laconically, as Quinta walked slowly away, one shoulder humped up against the weight of her bag.

'You think so? Poor kid, doesn't look old enough.'

'You can always tell. I can, anyway; Margaret used to look like that early on. She'll be okay, that one. She's the sort who's got family, you can see. Ten to, Mick, on your way.'

Quinta blinked as she came out of the gloom of the bus station and into the light streaming from the floodlights around the Cathedral, which was visible above the rooftops. She set off towards the lights; there were always bed and breakfast places near tourist attractions. Her heels clattered on the cobbles of the narrow lane which seemed to run in the right direction.

School shoes, thought Quinta. Sensible shoes with reinforced heels, click-clack up and down the polished wooden floors.

The lane led to the Cathedral green. Quinta stopped and lowered her bag to the ground. Her eyes were drawn up to the soaring buttresses, the mass of the choir and the spire. The windows of the nave glowed eerily under the floodlights.

'Hello, God,' said Quinta. 'Remember me?'

Tears trickled down beside her nose, and she brushed them angrily away with the back of her hand.

'I don't think God's at home,' said a voice behind her. Quinta turned swiftly round. A tall, thin girl stood there, dark brown hair framing a bony but amiable face.

Quinta flushed. 'I was just being silly,' she said.

'I know,' said the girl. 'It gets you, that place, doesn't it? Smack in the solar plexus. You okay? You don't look it.'

Quinta pulled out a neat white handkerchief, name-taped in blue, capital letters, with surname followed by initials, not more than two, and also the girl's school number. She gave her nose a good blow, sniffed, and tried to pull herself together.

'I need a B & B,' she said. 'Not expensive,' she added quickly.

'They won't like you turning up at this time of night, by yourself, not the Eyot landladies,' said the girl. 'My name's Harriet, by the way.'

'I'm Quinta. Won't any of them not mind?'

'You could be lucky. But you can stay with me, if you don't mind a floor.'

Quinta turned her big round eyes full on Harriet. She hesitated for a moment, all the warnings of parents, teachers, elders, ringing in her ears.

'Thank you, I don't mind a floor at all.'

The voices vanished, she was beyond the reach of all those wise mentors now; she was on her own. Despite everything, the thought was cheering. She pulled at her bag, but Harriet took it from her.

'I'll carry it for a bit, you look all in. I'm much stronger than I look, I run a lot. Long distance, cross country, that kind of thing.'

Quinta followed her across the green, through an ancient arch and down another narrow, twisting street. Gradually the picturesque streets gave way to straighter lines of Victorian terraces. Harriet stopped by one, swung open a gate, and pushed Quinta in front of her.

'Don't make a noise. We don't want to wake Ma Hoodley up, she's the landlady, nosy old dink.'

They crept into a narrow hallway. Harriet inserted a key into the second door, which blocked off the stairs, and led the way up.

'In here. Mattress under the bed. I'll get some bedclothes for you.'

She was back in no time, pushed the foot of the mattress under the table, and slung a sheet over it.

'I'll do this, you don't look very competent at the moment. Bathroom's the door opposite. The other door is Jessica's room. Don't disturb her in the morning, she's a nurse, on nights, she needs her sleep. I'll be off early, I go to the library. I won't wake you; I'll be back about eleven.'

Ten minutes later, her aching back rested, Quinta shut her eyes, waiting for the nightly visitations of fear and panic to come stalking into her head. Two minutes later, for the first time in days, she was soundly asleep.

'Bye, Mum.'

'Hold on, Phoebe, your strap's loose.'

Quinta pulled the schoolbag strap through its buckle and bent down to kiss the wild red hair. 'You haven't brushed it,' she began, but Phoebe was off down the street.

Quinta looked out and waved to the man who was waiting for Phoebe. He returned the wave, and called to her: 'Shan't be back until tomorrow evening; you'll have to pick Phoebe up from school today.'

'Not from school,' Phoebe shouted. 'I'm going to Louise's; pick me up from Louise's house!'

Quinta nodded and waved again. She heard the phone ringing and went quickly back inside.

'Quinta? It's Simon. Is Alban there?'

'You've just missed him. He's going to London.'

'He said he was catching the eight thirty-nine. Why has he left so early?'

'He's taking Phoebe to school first.'

'Well, if he rings you . . .'

'He won't, he never does.'

'He might. If he does, tell him to ring me, will you? It's about the meeting. And, Quinta, if Alban's away, can I come tonight?'

'No, of course not. It's Tuesday, you can't come on a Tuesday.'

'But if Alban isn't going to be there?'

'It makes no difference.'

'I can just drop in for a few minutes . . . I could help Phoebe with her practice.'

'She doesn't need help with her practice, she's got to learn to do it on her own. No, Simon, the answer is still no.'

Quinta put the phone down, and stood in the hall for a moment. Then she shook herself and went through the inner door. She put her head round the door of Phoebe's room, winced, and shut it again. Coffee, she thought. Coffee, quick breakfast, then I can be in early, miss the traffic. And Phoebe going to Louise's meant no rush at the end of the day.

Good, Quinta said to herself as she clashed the dishes together in the sink. No Alban, either. Not that she minded her duty nights with him, but an extra evening off was a relief, she had to admit. A perfect gent, too, Alban; he never asked her to make up the nights she had off for one reason or another.

Altogether, thought Quinta, as she hunted under the sink for the washing-up liquid, altogether she had been very lucky to bump into Alban the way she had.

'Literally bumped into him, I expect,' practical Harriet had said, eyeing her very visible bump. Kind Harriet, who had found her work, held her hand through a tough labour and carried her through the tiredness and depression of the subsequent weeks. Kind Alban, who had employed her as a housekeeper when she was too pregnant to carry on as a waitress in the Garibaldi Cafe where he came to eat several times a week.

'I can't cook,' Quinta had said doubtfully. 'And I was never very good at domestic science at school.'

'Can't be worse than me,' said Alban. 'You have a merry face and a pleasing voice, and brains too, I wouldn't be surprised, when you aren't awash with hormones and blind with tiredness. I'll buy you a cookbook. Italian food, that's the thing. I love Italian food.'

He had remained unshocked when he found out how young she was; worse things can happen, he'd remarked cheerfully. He had waited until Quinta had grown up in all sorts of ways, and Phoebe was a tantrum-ridden three-year-old before inviting her into his bed.

Quinta had accepted. From gratitude. From a longing to be hugged. From a need to be comforted when she cried in the night. From physical desire: Alban was a vital man, with an amused smile and sensual hands. From friendship.

But not, as Alban quickly came to realize, from love or passion.

Why aren't I in love with him? Quinta asked herself as she briskly tackled the washing up. She liked the bubbles foaming in the sink; she always put in far too much washing-up liquid. It drove Alban into a frenzy.

'Such waste!'

'It's only soap. Look at the paper you waste, those big sheets of music manuscript paper, they cost a fortune. And you hurl them into the bin with just one note on the top of the page, quite unnecessary.'

'That's art,' grumbled Alban. 'Whereas the washing-up liquid, well, wanton waste makes wicked want.'

Quinta stacked the plates on the rack on the draining board, retrieved the towel from beneath Alban's large black cat and wiped her hands.

List, where was her list? Tuesday. It was Tuesday the first. Phoebe had woken her up chanting, 'White rabbits, white rabbits, white rabbits'; she firmly believed that if you did that on the first of the month, something exciting was bound to happen in the next thirty days. I hope not, thought Quinta. She wanted an organized and orderly life, much safer that way. No excitement, no corresponding horrors.

She looked at her list for Tuesday the first.

Phoebe – remember library book. Had she? Too late now, if she hadn't; she'd know when she got yet another note from Phoebe's teacher about the importance of the weekly library period . . .

Phoebe – tea with Louise. That was all right.

Alban, London. Yes.

Cat food. She could get that on the way home.

Van – see about squealing and clanking noises under the bonnet. No, not today, it could wait until tomorrow. She found a pencil and drew a line through that one.

Quite an empty day, really. An ordinary day.

An early day. Quinta arrived at work fifteen minutes before her usual time. She drove the van through the archway beside the shop and rummaged in her bag for the keys. She found the back door had been unlocked already, but it was still difficult to open. Hinges need oiling, thought Quinta, giving it an extra hard shove; put it on a list.

Quinta loved the smell that met her as she opened the door: varnish and wood and resin and polish and glue. You stopped noticing it almost immediately; Quinta breathed deeply to get her fix before her nose got used to it. She hung her tweedy jacket on the big hook beside Gustav's raincoat. It might be summer, but a chill June had followed on months of grey cold and wet; no question of going out without a coat or jacket.

Gustav's raincoat hung on the next hook; it had hung there for as long as she had worked for him. He never wore it. 'Likes to have it,' Sam had explained. 'Thinks it makes him into an English gent. Feels uncomfortable in it, of course, not his style at all, but he likes to know it's there. Cost a bomb, too.'

Quinta made her way along the unlit passage, carefully avoiding the hunks of wood which narrowed its width to about eighteen inches of clear space. Visitors were always amazed that the glowing instruments in the showroom upstairs could ever have started life as such unpromising pieces of grey and dirty-looking timber.

Sam was already there, pulling up the shop blinds and removing the leaflets which sat rather forlornly on the dark velvet display stands and tables in the window cabinets.

'Throw the lights, love,' he called to Quinta. 'I'm just giving this window a quick once-over; the dust from the outside! I can't tell you.'

'Same as yesterday in the window?' asked Quinta.

'No, Gustav left a message, he wants that new baroque cello from Germany in here. And I'm going to do an arrangement with the student violins over there, he's got someone from the *Gazette* wants a piccy; they're doing a feature about school music.'

'I'll leave you to it, then,' said Quinta. 'Coffee?'

'Naturally,' said Sam. 'Although I read in a mag last night at the hairdressers that coffee is death to the complexion, gives you dark rings under the eyes.'

'Life does that,' said Quinta cheerfully. 'Don't worry, Sam. your complexion's fine.'

'Should be, too, with the trouble I take. No sugar, I'm on a diet.'

Quinta brought Sam his coffee, picked up the pile of post which had just slid through the letter box, and went back upstairs. She put her coffee down on the workbench, yawned, stretched and idly turned the radio on. The nine o'clock news. Floods, plagues, famines; woe, thrice woe. Another day, thought Quinta, looking at her list. Replace a bridge, no. 4312, soundpost crack, estimate first; school cello, new pegs needed . . .

'. . . new Bishop of Eyot,' said the voice on the radio. 'The previous bishop was forced to resign after police allegations . . .'

Quinta yawned again, and twiddled the tuning knob. '. . . a new work by Harrison Birtwistle . . .' This time she reacted more quickly, and turned it off with a defiant click.

Sam's footsteps sounded on the stairs. 'Have you got a sixteenth violin up here? I'm sure we've got one, but I just can't lay my hands on it.'

'Over there,' said Quinta, wrapping her big white apron round herself. 'It lacked a string.'

'Busy day?' asked Sam, looking over her shoulder at her list.

'Not really,' said Quinta. 'Just the usual.'

'Time you stopped mending and started making,' said Sam, pausing in the doorway with the miniature violin in his hand. 'You're an artist, I can tell. And think how pleased Gustav would be.'

Quinta looked at him in astonishment. 'Oh, I don't think so,' she said. 'He employs me to do repairs and to rehair bows. He'd be horrified if I started making instruments.'

'Time someone did,' said Sam, shrugging his shoulders. 'He won't again, not with his arthritis. And there's that wood downstairs, going to waste. He employed you because you can make instruments, you've had all the training, lucky you. He loved your diploma piece, he told me so.'

'He's never said anything about it to me.'

'He wouldn't, would he? Not Gustav. I mean, if you're content to piddle around patching up other people's work, he's not going to stop you.'

'No, but he'd soon stop me if I started making a violin or a cello,' said Quinta. 'You know how high his standards are.'

'Your choice, duckie,' said Sam. 'No-one can force you. But

use it or lose it, that's what I say. If you don't make something soon, you'll find you've forgotten how.'

Quinta frowned. 'Very few people can make good instruments.'

'Yes, and if they all took your attitude, no-one would ever make one at all. It's being a woman, that's your trouble. You think little Phoebe's creation enough, but she'll grow up like lightning and off she'll go. While you'll still be here stringing fifty-pound violins. Oh well, your funeral, ducks; forget I spoke.'

'Sam,' began Quinta, but he had gone, with a cry of, 'Customer, I hear a customer.'

Quinta worked on diligently, her skilful fingers peacefully occupied, her mind much less peaceful. She enjoyed her work, and was good at it. She had been well trained, and had come with a glowing recommendation from the college. I'm lucky to have this job, she thought. Eyot was famous for its musical shops; musicians and dealers came from Europe and America to show and buy and sell, but once people came to work in the shops here, they stayed, and there were rarely any vacancies.

Gustav's shop was small, but very well thought of. The violins and cellos in the top showroom were all of the very finest, and worth a small fortune. And Gustav didn't turn away the routine repair work; he knew that as the small violinists and cellists grew, their ambitious parents would pay more and more for each instrument, moving on from factory-made Chinese to East European, to nineteenth-century German and French, and perhaps on to the serious five or six thousand pound ones. Then, if they eventually became professionals, they would buy even more valuable instruments; or as teachers, they would recommend Gustav's shop to students and parents . . .

Quinta went to the door and called down the stairs to Sam. He appeared a few minutes later.

'Anyone in the shop?' Quinta asked.

'No. It's always quiet at this time of the year, with Gustav away. How can I help?'

'I need to shift these clamps,' said Quinta. 'They're a bit awkward. Could you give me a hand?'

A smile flashed across Sam's dark face. He smoothed his hands down over his tight polo-necked shirt.

'Sure, great, Quinta. You know I love to use my muscles, makes all the time I spend working out in the gym worthwhile. Show me what you want done. Then I think it's time for another coffee.'

'Already?' said Quinta, surprised. The Cathedral clock chimed the half hour, and she looked at her watch. 'Goodness, you're right, it's half past eleven.'

'How time flies when you're hard at work,' said Sam.

More than 200 miles away in Oxford, others were not working so hard.

'Quick. Wake up, wake up!'

Lydia opened one eye, slowly, and closed it rapidly.

'It's half past eleven. I've come to say goodbye, I must rush, my train's at ten to twelve. I'll see you in London when you get back; lucky you, Angus to drive you home, then off to Greece, while it's slave, slave for me all summer. Oh, there's a note for you, from the devoted Angus, it was in your pigeonhole. Bye!'

The door slammed. Lydia plumped up her pillow behind her head. How quiet it was. Most of her year had already left, Finals over, just the last balls to enjoy, the farewell parties, promises to meet again, soon; the last cucumber sandwiches in Magdalen, the last punt . . .

Lydia yawned, and opened her eyes reluctantly. A stream of sunlight shone through the half-closed curtains on to the crumpled heap of last night's ball gown. Lydia slid her legs out from under the sheet and sat up, pushing the hair out of her eyes, yawning widely. She padded to the window, drew the curtains back, leant out to look over the lawns and the river and admire Magdalen Tower.

Lovely summer, she thought. No more essays, no more tutorials, no more exams, just blissful days in Greece, with Angus, no need to think about work until the autumn at the earliest.

She stretched, caught sight of the envelope left on the shelf. Funny old Angus, writing her notes when they had been together just a few hours before. Some arrangements for Greece that he wanted to make sure about, he was so fussy.

Lydia plonked herself down on her narrow college bed and opened the letter. Outside a bird burst into song, a hubbub of voices rose from a group rowing inexpertly and noisily along the Cherwell.

Lydia read the letter once, and sat, quite still, with it resting on her knee. Then she slowly reached out for her passport, ready on the chest of drawers.

Lydia Holbeck. Colouring fair, eyes grey, height 5'9".

A knock on the door. Lydia just sat, said nothing. The door opened and Mrs Ducat, Lydia's scout, clumped into the room.

'There you are, my duck, you should answer when I knock, though usually you do, I will admit, not leaving your manners at home like some of the young ladies I could mention. That Miss Byng, "I'll kill you, my duck," I told her, "if you do that again."'

The stream of words stopped for a few seconds as she looked at Lydia's still figure. 'You all right? Had a hard night, what you young ladies get up to, not like it was when I started here at the college, they were ladies then. I've come to tell you you're wanted on the phone, better get down there or they'll have rung off.'

Lydia was out of the room in a flash, leaving Mrs Ducat flattened against the doorpost, muttering balefully to herself about her young ladies.

'Hello? Angus?'

Silence. A clear, well-bred voice came down the line.

'I wish to speak to my granddaughter, Lydia Holbeck. Is there no-one there who can find her?'

Lydia slumped down into the hard chair that lived beside the phone box. She took a deep breath. 'I'm sorry, grandmama, I thought you were someone else. It's me, Lydia.'

'You sound exhausted. What have you been doing? And Angus, is this the young man your mother mentioned? A boyfriend?'

'No, not really, just a friend, grandmama. He was a friend, anyhow. It doesn't matter. Is everything all right? Nothing's happened to Mummy?'

'No, your mother is in France, as you know. That's why I'm ringing. I didn't like the thought of you being in the house in

London all by yourself while she's away, and then she told me you were going to Greece with a young man. Is this true?'

'No,' said Lydia wearily. 'It isn't true. I'm not going to Greece with anyone.' She didn't have the energy to defend her right to go to Greece with whoever she liked, that was a pointless skirmish at the moment.

'I'm very glad to hear it. Now, you must come up to me, at once, instead of going to London. The decorators are in, I gather, it would be most unsuitable for you to be there, and no doubt very inconvenient for them.'

'Eyot? Come up to Eyot?'

'Yes, what is the matter with you? You're very slow, Lydia. You are to come and stay with me. It's a long time since you were up here. I expect you are tired after exams and so on, you can relax and meet some nice young people, get back to normal after Oxford. Then we can talk about what you're going to do with yourself.'

'But, grandmama . . .'

'No buts. I'm looking forward to seeing you.'

Lydia looked at the earpiece, now buzzing at her. She put it back, resting her hand on it for a moment. She read the little cards pinned on to the soundproofing. 'Spire Cabs. Taxis Night and Day. Distance no object.'

She picked up the telephone again and dialled.

'Spire Cabs? Hello, I'd like a taxi to St Frideswyde's College please. In about half an hour. To go to the station. Yes, to the lodge, that's fine. Thank you, bye.'

An hour later, Mrs Ducat gave another perfunctory knock at Lydia's door and pushed it open. 'Well,' she said, her body quivering with indignation. 'Gone! And never so much as a goodbye, or a thank you.' Her beady little eyes flew about the room looking for a material thank-you if not a personal one. Ah, she knew Miss Holbeck wouldn't let her down. Not too bad, she thought, squinting into the envelope, not like that Miss Byng, who'd told her to use the tip to buy herself some sugar for her tongue. Sauce!

She glanced at the roped trunk in the centre of the room, she'd have to get Ted to come and fetch that down. She read the label. 'Lydia Holbeck, c/o Lady Wray, 4 The Cathedral Close, Eyot.'

'Posh,' she said to herself as she searched the drawers and cupboard for anything left behind. She was posh, that one, refined in her ways, even if she did have that young man to tea and lock the doors, as if everyone didn't know what they were up to. Yes, posh, there weren't many like that these days. 'Lazy, mind you,' she said to Mrs Riley as they met in the corridor. 'I never knew a student so idle, her idea of heaven was lying in a punt looking up into the sky, with someone else doing the punting and not having to say a word, that's what she told me.'

'She'll learn,' said Mrs Riley. 'Won't know what's hit her once she gets away from this place and has to live in the real world. They think life is all books and sex when they're at college here, it's a nasty shock when they find out how the other ninety-nine percent live.' Their feet thumped along the polished wooden corridor, dying away as they reached the scouts' pantry, time for a cuppa, dear.

'Look, there's Lydia!'

'Can't be. She's driving to London with Angus.'

'It's her double-bass, in a blue case, it must be Lydia. Yes, look, over there, on the other platform. Lydia!' She shouted and waved. 'Lydia! What are you doing, where are you going, where's Angus?'

Lydia looked vaguely up and down the platform, then saw the little group jumping up and down on the London side. She raised a hand briefly in acknowledgement, then dropped it round the neck of her double-bass again.

The London train, late, hurtled into the station and braked loudly. Staid citizens emerged, to be swamped by departing students cheerfully hurling their bags and rucksacks in before them. A head appeared from a window, and then another one beside it.

'Lydia, do tell, what's happened, what about Angus?'

Bother them, thought Lydia vaguely, Angus, Angus, I never want to hear his name again. She roused herself.

'Got to go north,' she shouted to them. 'My grandmother . . . telephone call, family problems.'

Her words were carried away by the sound of the train arriving at her platform; she hoped her friends had got the gist of what she was saying.

They settled themselves down as their train pulled out.

'What did Lydia say? Why is she at the station? Has she had a row with Angus?'

'Don't think so, they were very friendly at the ball last night, entwined, you might say.'

'Her gran's ill or something, she lives up in the north, doesn't she?'

'Yes, in a cathedral city. Poor Lydia if she doesn't make it to Greece after all, Angus will be fed up.'

'Perhaps her gran is dying, money, wills, you know.'

'Perhaps Angus has got other interests,' remarked a quiet dark girl installed in the corner of the compartment with a lurid magazine. 'Freddie said he saw him in London the other night, at a club, very heavily involved with an attractive girl. Not Lydia, this one had dark hair.'

'Poor Lydia, how awful,' said the chorus. 'No Greece, north of England, devoted swain deserting her, how dreadful.'

Unaware of the analysis of her affairs, Lydia padded along the platform to the guard's van. The guard was standing beside it on the platform, and he sprang into action to defend his territory.

'Sorry, miss, no room for that in there, too big to take on a train, have to send it luggage in advance.'

Lydia took no notice and hauled it up into the luggage van. She propped the instrument carefully against two big boxes and put a bag in front to protect it. Then she smiled her lovely leisurely smile at the guard. She held out her hand and dropped some money in his palm.

'It always travels with me,' she said. 'I get off at Eyot.'

'That's all right, then, miss,' said the guard. 'I'll keep an eye on it for you. Bit big to put under your chin, isn't it? Some fiddle, that.'

Lydia smiled again and walked down the train to find an empty compartment. She pulled a book out, sank into a corner seat, slipped her feet out of her shoes and swung them on to the seat opposite. The train started, the book rested on her knees and her eyes closed.

Tired as she was, she couldn't sleep. She gazed unseeing out of the window; fields, villages, towns slipped past. The train stopped, people got on and off, nobody disturbed her. Other passengers peered tentatively into the compartment, looking hopefully at the empty seats, but something about the tall girl wrapped in her thoughts put them off and they went away to find more congenial travelling companions.

After Birmingham the ticket collector arrived and pushed the door back. 'Tickets, please. All tickets, now.'

As though I had a sackful of them, thought Lydia, searching rather uselessly through her bag for her ticket.

'That's the one, miss,' said the collector, beaming with good-will as he bent to pick it up off the floor. 'And you've dropped a letter.'

'Thank you,' said Lydia, taking the letter as he departed whistling, slamming the door to as he went.

She turned the envelope over in her hands, looking at the familiar writing, Lydia Holbeck, St Frideswyde's College. His college crest on the flap of the envelope, inside, more of the neat writing, black ink, dear Lydia. No longer my darling, or Lydia dearest; no signing off, your adoring Angus, or love you always, A.

Just dear Lydia, and at the foot, Yours, Angus.

Through the haze of bewilderment a shaft of rage hit Lydia. Yours, Angus! How dare he!

She forced herself to read the letter again, phrases fixing themselves in her mind. 'At present, too great a commitment . . . with my demanding new job at the Foreign Office . . . the relationship perhaps too intense . . . a pause for reflection . . . no lessening of affection . . . not quite ready for a more binding tie . . .'

Drivel, Lydia said to herself. Why, it reads like a civil service memorandum, it isn't a letter from a human being at all. When they accepted him for the Foreign Office they did a transplant, replaced him with a non-human clone.

Then the flush of sense and anger faded into memories of his familiar face, hands, hair, body, being in bed with him, walking with arms wrapped round each other to the Perch for Sunday lunch, the easy, warm familiarity of morning coffee at Browns, the pub, his rooms, her room, 'What a poky place, they don't let you girls live in style, but there's a bed, that's something.' Unexpected meetings in the Bodleian, tea in country villages, parties, evenings on the river, toast in front of the fire in his rooms on winter afternoons, his friends, dinner at the Randolph with his parents, necking at the back of the cinema, too eager to get back to bed to stay for the end of the film . . .

Finished. Two and half years wiped out in a Yours, Angus.

Tears misted Lydia's eyes and she dashed them away with her fist, like a child refusing to give in to an excruciating graze or bruise, then, like a child, unable to hold her hurt back. Tears poured down her face.

The ticket collector came whistling back on his return journey. He popped his head into her compartment. 'Cheer up, may never happen. And if it has, not worth crying about, take my word for it, there's always someone better round the corner.'

He went on his heedless way, while Lydia sat and grew damper and more blotchy. Eyot, I don't want to go to Eyot, what is there to do in Eyot? I want to go to Greece, to the sun, abroad. She made instant plans, instantly abandoned; she would go to Egypt, take a job as a governess in Rome, pick grapes in France.

She had to admit to herself, even in the depths of her lachrymose state, that she would do none of these things, simply because it would all take so much trouble. Greece had been a wonderful idea, she had always wanted to go to Greece, and with Angus, bloody Angus, a classicist, he would tell her all about everything, best of all, he had organized it all. Leave it to me, he had said.

Looking back, she remembered his reluctance to give her the tickets, or any firm details. He had been planning this letter for some time, she realized. Too cowardly to have it out with her face to face, the last few weeks, maybe the whole term it had been a sham. She had taken for granted that she would see less of him before Finals, of course you had to work, and she herself had remained immured in her room.

Not, in her case, revising. Every morning she had risen, full of good resolutions; by half past nine every morning the pile of notes and files looked bigger and more trouble; by ten o'clock she was lounging happily in her armchair with her feet on the windowsill, eating an apple and reading yet another detective story.

Her friends were impressed. 'Lydia's working so hard, hours and hours, she'll get a First.'

And all the time, she had been sure that Angus really would be working hard, determined to get the degree which would assure his future as a diplomat.

'Bugger Angus,' Lydia said aloud, thoroughly alarming a brisk woman in a flowered suit who had been unwise enough to seek a place in Lydia's compartment. Her face darkened, she gave Lydia a disapproving look and strode off down the corridor.

Lydia gave a final sniff, pushed her thick brown and blonde hair behind her ears and deliberately tore the letter into little pieces. She hurled the bits out of the window, and they blew away into the distance as the train pulled into the curved Victorian elegance of Eyot station.

Lydia made her way to the luggage van and clambered down on to the platform with her double-bass. She hoisted her bag on to her shoulder, and nearly hit a passing woman with the large and unwieldy instrument.

'Sorry,' she said.

'I'll hold it while you hitch that bag on,' said a helpful voice. 'You don't want it to fall over. This isn't a very protective case for it, is it?'

'Thanks,' said Lydia. Then she put her bag abruptly down on the platform and looked properly at the owner of the voice. Round face, merry round eyes, flying coppery hair standing out from her head like a halo.

'I know you,' said Lydia slowly. 'You're Quinta!'

## 2

Quinta stood stock still on the platform, causing several efficient-looking people up for a conference to run into her with their hard briefcases. They muttered and shot dark glances at her before hurrying off to the Eyot Lodge for their first session on Marketing Today: Selling Cheese to Senior Citizens.

Quinta took no notice of them, but stood her ground, her face breaking into a wide smile.

'Lydia! Goodness, you're better looking than ever!'

'Mind the doors, stand back there,' shouted the guard.

'Let me take that,' said Quinta, grabbing the double-bass. 'This way. I've got a parcel to collect, and it was on the train, I saw it. We'll go to the parcels office.'

She hasn't changed at all, thought Lydia. The same smooth roundness about her, the same energy. How long was it, six, seven years, since she vanished from school, half way through a term? No explanations, tight-lipped teachers, never a letter or a word from her.

'What happened to you?' Lydia asked as they queued behind a dark, spiky woman who was signing for boxes of flowers and complaining about several dents and tears.

'When I left school?' Quinta moved up to the counter. 'It's a long story.'

The gloomy-looking man on duty saw off the woman with the flowers and turned his reluctant attention to Quinta.

'A package for Gustav Porlock, please. It was on the train from Oxford.'

'They haven't been processed yet, you'll have to wait.'

Quinta beamed at him. 'Oh, it's just there, I can see it, I must take it now or my boss will be terribly cross, probably sack me; he's a tyrant.'

The uniformed man shrugged his shoulders. 'Too bad, regulations, got to be processed.'

His colleague, as black and cheerful as his colleague was grey and mournful, joined him and winked at Quinta and Lydia. 'Give her the package, man, I'll do the papers in a minute. Just sign here.'

'Thank you very much,' said Quinta. 'Lydia, where are you going? I've got a van outside.'

'Is your boss a tyrant?' asked Lydia curiously as she followed Lydia out on to the forecourt.

'No, not at all,' said Quinta. 'And, even if he were, he's in America at the moment. Quick, there's a traffic warden peering at the van.'

Lydia followed at a more leisurely pace as Quinta reached the van just in time to remonstrate with the official, who was about to write a ticket.

'It's entirely their fault,' she said indignantly. 'Twenty minutes maximum stay, it says, and then the train's half an hour late. Come on, we can put the bass on the roof.'

'I can walk,' said Lydia. 'I'm going to the Close, it isn't far.'

'Anywhere's far with that thing under your arm. Are you expected?'

'Yes, well, sort of, it's my grandmother, but I didn't say which train.'

'Good, then come with me.'

'No, don't worry,' said Lydia. 'I can get a taxi, it's no trouble.'

'Expensive, they have a minimum charge,' said Quinta practically.

'It's not much,' said Lydia.

'I'd forgotten you were well off. You still are, I can tell,' said Quinta, taking no notice of Lydia's protests as she picked up the double-bass and lugged it to the van. 'We can have a natter on the way. I want to hear all about what you've been doing.'

'I'll put the bass up,' said Lydia. 'It's awkward.'

'Yes, it's not the instrument for little roundies like me,' said Quinta. 'Put your things in the back; not on that seat, though, that's where Phoebe sits.'

Quinta started the engine with a roar and the van lurched its way into a steady stream of traffic, the horn honking as it went.

'If you blow your horn very loudly, other people think they're in the wrong,' Quinta explained. 'So they hesitate, and you can nip in . . .' She accelerated with a roar under the nose of a large lorry, whose driver leant out of his cab and hurled abuse.

'There,' said Quinta, unmoved. 'The traffic's terrible at this time, people collecting children from school. I would be, too, but Phoebe's going home with a friend today.'

'Phoebe?'

'My daughter.'

'Are you married, then?' said Lydia. She was surprised; there was no reason why Quinta shouldn't be married, but she didn't look married, and she wasn't wearing a wedding ring.

Quinta laughed. Lydia remembered that laugh, it was so distinctive, and it had rung through the dreary corridors of their school. Disapproved of by the teachers, naturally, but Quinta had never been that bothered by the teachers.

'No, I'm not married.'

Quinta shot off the main road into a quieter area. She still drove in the same erratic way as before, but it was less alarming now there wasn't so much traffic. She drew up outside a neat little Georgian house and sounded the horn; a few minutes later the door opened and a smaller version of herself tumbled down the steps. 'Bye,' the child shouted enthusiastically as she headed for the van. 'Bye, Louise, bye Mrs Latimer.'

'Thanks, Maria,' Quinta called out of the window. 'See you tomorrow, five-ish.'

Phoebe clambered into the back of the van and sat herself down, peering forward to look Lydia over. 'What's that on the roof?' she demanded. 'Is it yours?'

'Phoebe, you should know what it is,' said Quinta, backing down the one-way street. 'It's a double-bass.'

'Is it yours?' Phoebe asked Lydia. 'Can I try it? I'd like to play a double-bass. I play the piano, I want to play something else, but Quinta won't let me. She says she can't afford it.'

'I can't,' said Quinta.

'My piano lessons don't cost anything, Simon won't let you pay.'

'No, and if he did, you wouldn't be able to play the piano either. Pipe down, where are your manners? This is Lydia, we were at school together.'

'Was she a friend?' asked Phoebe after she had politely held out a round little paw for Lydia to shake over the back of her seat.

'Of course,' said Quinta.

'Why of course? Most of the people I go to school with aren't friends. I hate them, especially that horrible Michaela. Louise is my only friend, and we loathe all the others, we don't want to stay at that school, it's ghastly, and Louise says her mum's going to take her away next year, send her to the Cathedral School. Can I go too, Quinta?'

'No,' said Quinta shortly. 'Don't go on about it, Phoebe, I can't afford it, and they don't give scholarships for girls, you know that.'

'Why does she call you Quinta?' asked Lydia.

'Sauciness, to start with,' said Quinta. 'To annoy me, Phoebe's like that. Then it became a habit, although she sometimes calls me mum. I don't mind, I don't think I'd like being called mummy. That's my mother, not me.'

She stopped under the archway which led into the Cathedral Close, her way blocked by a black and white striped barrier.

A man in a nondescript uniform came reluctantly out of his little glass hut at the side.

'Go away,' he said. 'No entry except on Cathedral business, tourist car-park round the back, and it's closed at this time of day.'

Quinta beamed at him. 'Open up, then, George,' she said. 'Don't pretend not to know who I am; even if you didn't recognize me, you know the van.'

She turned to Lydia. 'We're always in and out of here, we look after a lot of the school's instruments. He knows perfectly well who I am, but he's a disagreeable old sod, turn the milk sour. Look at him, Christianity welcomes you!'

George was resolute. 'Out of hours, you can't be on school business at this time of day, the music staff won't be there. In town up to no good, that lot.'

'No, not school business,' said Quinta. 'Close business. This is Miss Holbeck, Lady Wray's granddaughter come to stay. Better let us in quick or you'll get an earful tomorrow.'

Grumbling, but defeated, George opened the barrier and let them through.

'They're all afraid of your gran,' Quinta observed as they bumped slowly along on the cobbles. 'Doesn't stand any nonsense from anyone, formidable character.'

'You know her?' Lydia was surprised.

'Everyone knows Lady Wray,' said Phoebe, pausing momentarily from the entertaining task of pulling horrible faces at George out of the back of the van. 'To look at, not to speak to. She's very grand.'

'Phoebe, sit down this minute,' said Quinta. 'Phoebe's right, your gran's a big cheese here in Eyot.'

'Big cheese, big tomato, big sausage,' Phoebe chanted.

'That is rude and silly,' said Quinta as she braked violently outside a fine late seventeenth-century house. She dived into the bag which she had squashed behind the seat, and took out a neat notebook. 'This is my phone number,' she said, scribbling. She tore the page off. 'If a man called Alban answers, you haven't got the wrong number; it's his house.'

She swung down from the driver's seat. 'You take the double-bass, Lydia, and I'll carry the other things. Phoebe, go ahead and ring the doorbell – quietly!'

'When are you going to get married?'

Lydia, deep in a sumptuously upholstered and wonderfully relaxing sofa, was so startled that she swallowed her drink in one gulp.

'I don't like to see you drinking like that,' said her grandmother. 'Pull yourself together, child.'

Lydia was speechless with surprise and the effects of swallowing whole the piece of lemon in her drink. She stared at her grandmother, who was sitting opposite her on a firm, armless chair.

How does she keep her back so straight, thought Lydia. And why?

'You're twenty-two,' Lady Wray went on remorselessly.

'You've finished at university, no harm in that, although you've missed the best opportunity you'll ever have to find a good husband, so many men there, and despite the no-hopers they let in these days from ordinary schools, plenty of young men with the right background. What about this Angus?'

All Lydia's cat-like ease had vanished. 'He was just a friend,' she muttered. 'Nothing serious. You wouldn't have liked him, he went to a grammar school.'

'Which grammar school? What was he reading? What is his career going to be?'

'Greats. Latin, Greek, philosophy, you know. He's been accepted for the Foreign Office.'

Lady Wray's face brightened. 'The Foreign Office? Well, there's no better career for an able young man, and although it's a pity about the grammar school, that won't hold him back in his profession, not these days. Where does he live?'

'Grandmama, forget it, please. We were friends, went out a bit together, that's all.'

'You can invite him to stay, I very much enjoy having young people in the house.'

Lydia realized that if she let this slide, usually much the easiest course, it would just mean more effort and trouble later.

'No, grandmama,' she said with unusual firmness. 'I'm sorry to disappoint you, but I am not going to invite Angus here, let alone marry him. He's gone to Greece for three months – with a girlfriend,' she invented wildly. Probably exactly what he had done, thought Lydia glumly, and she should have been there as well, on the ferry to the islands instead of sitting in the chilly formality of her grandmother's drawing room wondering if it was going to be fish again for supper.

It was.

'I eat a lot of fish,' said Lady Wray. 'I find it suits my digestion; at my age, you have to be careful what you eat. Don't push your food around your plate like that, Lydia, you had beautiful manners when you were at school. I can see Oxford hasn't improved you.'

She touched her mouth with her napkin, and nodded to Lydia to take the plates away and bring the strawberry mousse.

'And don't slouch like that,' she said irritated. 'You look like a soft toy which has lost its stuffing, stand up straight. I know you're tall, but you don't improve matters by moving about in this indolent way.'

Lydia spooned the mousse into her mouth, Slops, she thought. Weeks of slops and grandmama nagging me.

'Don't stay, then,' said Quinta cheerfully, when Lydia rang her up. 'Go home, buy a bike and cycle round the coal mines of the north, canoe up the Amazon. No need for you to stay, you've got plenty of lovely money. Goodness, I wouldn't put up with fish and criticism.'

'It's not as easy as you think.' said Lydia gloomily. 'Look, I must escape this evening; I can, because grandmama's got some cronies coming in. Can we meet and have something to eat? I'm dying for proper food. My treat, of course.'

At the other end of the phone, Quinta leant against the arch into the kitchen as she reached for her list.

'I hardly ever go out in the evenings,' she explained. 'Because of Phoebe. I can't afford a babysitter often, and besides . . .' she paused. 'Actually, Phoebe's very difficult to babysit, sets out to make the babysitter's life a misery, and succeeds, so you see . . .'

Lydia had been about to offer to pay for a babysitter; clearly that wasn't the answer. 'What about this Alban, can't he keep an eye on Phoebe?'

Quinta laughed. 'No, it's not fair, they argue, and Phoebe always makes him angry. Then she doesn't sleep, because she's all wound up. I know it sounds silly, wait until you have children, especially if any of them are like Phoebe. A friend takes her for the night sometimes; Phoebe doesn't muck about with Pauline, no-one does, but I have to arrange it a long way in advance. Sorry, Lydia, because it would be lovely to see you.'

'I'll come round then,' said Lydia. 'But I need meat, I'm starved of meat. I'll bring food, steaks . . . Will Phoebe eat a steak . . .? No? Never mind, we can do some chips, she'll eat those, I suppose? I always loved chips when I was little. Half past seven, is that all right? What's the address?'

Quinta gave her directions.

'Sounds complicated,' said Lydia, 'but I expect I'll find you. What about your Alban? Shall I bring food for him?'

'Not really my Alban,' said Quinta. 'But in any case I think he's going to be out, and when he gets back he'll dive straight into his studio. That's his working time; he's an owl, works until the early hours, then crashes out until midday.'

Lydia approved. She was finding it very hard to get up for breakfast at 8.30; the first morning she had slept through her grandmother's commanding summons to the breakfast table and wished she hadn't. Less trouble to heave herself out of bed, even though she could do with another hour or two's sleep.

'I don't know how you managed at Oxford,' her grandmother had said disapprovingly. 'Presumably you had to go to lectures and so forth. I know when your mother was at university she worked extremely long hours.'

'You do with sciences,' agreed Lydia. 'That's why I changed subjects, from physics to history. With physics you had to spend hours in the lab, exhausting. I didn't go to many history lectures, very boring, most lecturers; quicker and easier just to read their books. They've all written books. And tutorials were never early, not mine, anyhow.'

Lady Wray was shocked. 'It's your father, you must have inherited this indolent disposition from your father; my family are all very hard-working. It is never right to do something because it's easier. Where is the challenge, where is your pride in yourself?'

Lydia's pleasant smile stayed, her mind went walkabout. The words, like the words of her mother, her headmistress, her tutor, washed over her.

'You will never make anything of your life, Lydia, if you don't learn to apply yourself.' Her grandmother looked at her sharply. 'I don't believe you've heard a word of what I've been saying!'

'Oh, but I have, grandmama,' said Lydia politely. 'You're quite right, I should apply myself.'

Her grandmother didn't have a very believing look on her face, so Lydia changed the subject.

'I'll be out this evening, I'm going to have dinner with Quinta.'

'Who is Quinta?' asked her grandmother suspiciously. 'I didn't think you knew anyone here.'

'Oh, an old friend from school, I bumped into her at the station.'

'She was at Grisewood with you? Is she married?'

Lydia thought for a moment. If she said no, and then grandmama found out about Phoebe, she would be deeply disapproving. If she said yes, then grandmama would expect a dutiful husband to appear, the kind girls from Grisewood usually married.

'Her husband's out east,' she said, improvising rapidly.

'Why didn't she go with him?' Lady Wray disapproved of young husbands being abroad without their wives; she knew what that led to. 'Is he naval?'

'Naval?' Lydia was momentarily puzzled. She pulled at the braiding on one of her grandmother's stiff cushions.

'Stop fiddling, child. Is this Quinta's husband in the navy? You do seem very inattentive these days, Lydia, pull yourself together.'

'No, no, he's not in the navy. Quinta isn't with him because, oh, because of her daughter. She's got a little girl, she can't take the heat. And the insects, there are a lot of insects out there. And snakes, very dangerous.' She looked at her grandmother, who didn't seem convinced.

'Rabies,' she added. 'Quinta and, er, Claudius, didn't want to risk it.'

Lady Wray shook her head. 'I spent several years in the east when my father was posted to India, it did me no harm, no harm at all. Too much fussing about children these days, it gives them a sense of self-importance, a big mistake. Claudius, did you say? What an extraordinary name. Where was he at school?'

'I'm not sure, Rugby, I think.'

'Now that is interesting,' said Lady Wray. 'A lot of my friend Sybil's family were at Rugby, perhaps she knows this Claudius.'

'No, it wasn't Rugby, um, let me think. No, it was that school the spy went to, I can't remember the name.'

Lydia was beginning to feel trapped, she'd have to remember all these fictional details and brief Quinta if she ever met her grandmother. Much better not, though; Lydia had a feeling they wouldn't get on.

'Spy? Which spy?'

'Um, I can't remember his name, but he was at this school in Norfolk. The one Claudius went to.'

To Lydia's relief, Lady Wray lost interest when she mentioned Norfolk; there were no great schools in Norfolk.

Living in the last century, thought Lydia, obsessed with good schools; goodness, she should have seen the dire products of the best schools she'd met at Oxford. That was one thing she was sure about, if she ever got married and had children, they weren't going to go to schools like that.

## 3

Quinta felt slightly alarmed at the thought of an unplanned evening. Since Alban was eating out, she had intended to have a quick supper of chicken soup. It was her evening for reading this month's *Strad* magazine, and Phoebe's new knickers were due for name-taping.

'Go on, live a little!' chided Alban, as he dived into the fridge for some cheese. 'Who wants to dine off chicken soup? Food for old ladies and invalids.'

'I thought you were going to eat out,' said Quinta. 'If you eat all the cheese, there won't be any more until I do the shopping on Friday.'

'It's going to be bitty food, after quite a lot of not very good wine, you know the kind of thing. Best to stock up now, then I won't topple over. Don't know why I'm going, boring lot of people, and I've had a lousy day. If I don't get this score finished soon, they'll boot me off the job, and then we'll all be homeless.'

Phoebe got up from the table and stretched. 'Pooh!' she said. 'You're always saying we'll be homeless, and we never are. It's your fault; you want notes on the paper, you should get it in your head first, and then just write it down. That's what real composers do.'

Alban looked crossly at her. 'Been to the Oxfam shop again, have you?'

Phoebe was strangely dressed in a skirt that appeared to have been made out of an old rug, set off by thick yellow tights and a faded velvet smock.

'This skirt is very smart. It comes from Louise's dressing-up box, and I like it.'

Alban inspected the messy exercise book on the table. 'If that's your homework, you're going to be in trouble.'

'I'm not. And we aren't given homework, this is just finishing work I was doing in class.'

Quinta sighed. 'Maths, I suppose.'

'Could be,' agreed Phoebe.

'Why didn't you finish it in class, like everybody else?'

'Because it's so boring.'

'Looks pretty basic to me,' said Alban disapprovingly. 'Don't they teach them anything these days.'

'Times have changed, Alban,' said Quinta. 'It's all relevant now, not like it was in your day.'

'Doesn't look relevant to me. Anyway, she's got it all wrong. She's supposed to have sorted these into groups and look, she's put the rabbits in with the bears.'

'Why not?' said Phoebe, wrenching the book from his grasp. 'As anyone can see, those rabbits and bears have the same looks on their faces. They're instrinting animals. All the others are boring.'

'Interesting,' said Quinta and Alban together. 'Go and run a bath, Phoebe,' Quinta said firmly. 'And no arguments, please; it's Thursday, you always have a bath on Thursdays.'

'I haven't had any supper.'

'You're going to have it after your bath tonight; I've got a friend coming, and she's bringing some food.'

'Is it that double-bass lady?'

'It's Lydia, yes.'

'Good. I liked her. So, just to oblige, I will go and have a bath.'

'Who is this Lydia?' said Alban suspiciously. 'I've never met any Lydia, have I? Is she a parent?'

'No, she's only just come to Eyot. She's staying with her grandmother, who is Lady Wray. She was at my school, I haven't seen her for years, she was at the station and I ran into her.'

Alban shook his head. 'Dangerous, letting people from your past into your life.'

'Oh, go off to your do,' said Quinta in exasperation. 'She's a friend, people do have friends. And what do you think Pauline is, if she isn't a friend from my past?'

'Pauline, sadly,' said Alban, 'is all too present. Just be careful, that's all. And you're going to have to do something about Phoebe's education, that maths is a joke.'

'There's nothing I can do. She reads a lot, so she must be learning something. They give her this baby maths because it seems to be all she can manage.'

Alban looked at the book again and let out a snort of laughter.

'Instrinting faces, she's right, too. Tell you what, Quinta, if you don't get her a proper education, she'll still be sorting bears and rabbits when she's eighteen.'

Alban poured himself a pint mug of milk and drank it down in one go. 'That's to line the stomach,' he said, picking up his huge tweed coat and cramming a disreputable black felt hat on his head. 'One of these days, summer will deign to appear, and we won't have to dress as though it's November.'

He stretched out a hand and caressed Quinta's shoulder. 'Enjoy your evening, I will mine because it's Thursday, thank goodness. Kiss me, mmm, I'll see you later.'

Lydia walked across the third bridge. Where was she, this must be wrong; Quinta had never mentioned all these bridges when she had given her the directions.

'I don't remember Eyot at all,' Lydia had told her grandmother. 'I'm bound to get lost. I'd better take a map.'

'You don't need a map,' said her grandmother briskly. 'If your friend lives where you say she does, then it really is very simple. Just remember that the centre of Eyot, here, where the Cathedral is, is on an island in the river. Over on the east bank is the more modern part of the town. The castle, which is now the university, is there, also the station, where you arrived.' She paused, and gestured towards the window. 'That way, on the west bank, is the Bishop's Palace and the old town, that's where your friend lives, in Fulke Place.'

Lydia's face revealed that she was none the wiser. Pride kept her from confessing that she had never been quite clear about where east and west were.

'Go across the Close, past the south side of the Cathedral, that's the side with the big statue, cross the bridge, go along the street on the other side until you come to . . .'

Her words echoed in Lydia's ears as she looked across the dimly lit, cobbled square. A minute church stood on one side, and its tinkling bell rang out the hour, followed almost immediately by the big, bossy booms of the Cathedral clock.

I wonder which one is right, Lydia said to herself. A lamp came on unexpectedly in the gloom of an overcast evening, and illuminated the name of one of the narrow streets which led off the square. Ah, this was it, Fulke Place. Number 15, the Manor House. How could this be a manor house, thought Lydia, looking at an impeccable eighteenth-century frontage, exactly matched by the other houses in the street. She rang the big brass bell, and a few moments later heard a succession of thuds and squeaks from within.

The handsome panelled front door opened suddenly, and there was Quinta.

'Hi,' she said. 'Come in.'

Lydia expected a fine hallway, black and white chequered floor, a turned staircase. What she got was another door, only a few feet further in. It was uncompromisingly old; it looked heavy and serious. Quinta shut the front door and pushed hard at the second wooden door.

'How peculiar,' began Lydia, and then stopped in amazement as she saw the stone-flagged passage which led via an arch into a cloistered courtyard. Light spilled on to it from what seemed to be dozens of little mullioned windows. Above the arches, on two sides, ran a wooden gallery supported with stout barleysugar columns.

'Good gracious,' was all she could say.

Quinta grinned. 'I didn't warn you; it's so surprising you need to come on it unawares, don't you? The house is Elizabethan, but they wanted to look smart in the eighteenth century, keep up with the times, so they put a façade on. They probably didn't have enough money to do the job properly, which was fortunate.'

She led the way along the cloisters and opened another heavily hinged door. 'In here, mind your head.'

Rubbing her head where she had caught it on the lintel,

Lydia blinked and looked around her. It was a charming room, long and low, lit by a series of lamps with heavily tasselled lampshades. Beneath the row of windows which looked out on to the courtyard were three unmatching sofas covered in a fuchsia print on a dark cream background. Fat, light and dark pink cushions, thick with braiding and yet more tassels, were strewn over them.

Phoebe was sitting on one of the sofas with books scattered around her. She stared ferociously at Lydia, as though checking to make sure she was the right person.

'Did you bring your double-bass?' she asked at last.

'No,' said Lydia, shifting under the child's scrutiny. 'No, it's a bit big, I don't carry it around with me very often . . .'

'Do you like cats?' went on Phoebe.

Lydia looked across to where she was pointing. On one of the other sofas, a large black cat and an even bigger tabby turned tawny, indifferent eyes towards her. 'Yes' she said. 'I do like cats. Are these your cats? They're very big.'

'They're huge,' said Phoebe with pride. 'Actually, they're Alban's cats, but they prefer being in our part of the house, because we feed them here. What's in that bag?' she added, fixing her glance on the brown carrier in Lydia's hand.

'Oh, it's food,' said Lydia.

Quinta, who had vanished, reappeared through the arch at the end of the room.

'The kitchen's here, Lydia. Phoebe, get on with your book, leave Lydia alone.'

She took the bag from Lydia. 'Ignore her, she's at a difficult age,' she said in a whisper.

'I'm not,' said Phoebe from the other room.

'Ears like a rabbit,' said Quinta. 'Look, I've got some chicken soup . . .'

'No,' said Lydia. 'There's steak in there, I told you I would get some. Not chicken soup, nothing runny or slushy, that's what my grandmother eats all the time. If I stay up here for long, my teeth will all fall out through lack of use.'

She sank into a pew which was drawn up to the kitchen table. 'Must sit down, this is an exhausting city, it seems you have to walk everywhere.'

'It's the easiest way to get around, at least in the centre,' Quinta agreed. 'I suppose your grandmother could have brought you. No, she's got guests, hasn't she?'

'Mmm,' said Lydia. 'Grim-looking lot, come to play bridge.'

'One of them will be Sybil Stixwould,' said Quinta. 'Bound to be, thick as thieves, those two.'

'Sybil what?' said Lydia.

'Stixwould. She's a widow, her husband was Dean here about a thousand years ago. She's a neighbour of your gran's, has a lovely house in the Close. Far too big for her, but she won't give it up. She teaches the flute at the school; she played in a London orchestra before she married into the clergy and then became Mrs Dean. Now she has a finger in all the pies: the Close, the Cathedral, the school. Must be in her sixties, but full of beans. A big, soft-looking woman, but appearances are deceptive. You want to watch it with her, she's a real toughie.'

'Don't suppose I'll have much to do with her,' said Lydia hopefully.

Quinta unwrapped the parcel of meat which Lydia had dumped on the table.

'Lydia, there's far too much here; goodness, fillet steak, it must have cost a fortune.'

'Vulgar to talk about money, that's what my grandmama says.' She yawned widely. 'Sorry, it's the fresh air. I'll perk up when I've got a good chunk of that inside me.' She shot a look at Quinta from beneath droopy eyelids. 'And, if you don't mind me mentioning it, you look as though you could do with a bit of good red meat yourself.'

'I eat very well,' said Quinta. 'The chicken soup is only because Alban's out, and I can't be bothered to cook for myself. When Alban's here, we eat properly, he's very greedy.'

'What's he like?' said Lydia with interest. 'Fat?'

'Not at all, he's one of those lean and lanky men who never puts on weight however much he eats. Lucky him. He says he burns it all off being creative; he must do, because he rarely takes any exercise.'

'Sounds like a man after my own heart,' said Lydia appreciatively. 'Creative? What does he do? Why are you living here? I mean, do you live with him?'

'Not exactly,' said Quinta, busying herself at the sink. 'I'm a kind of housekeeper, but we're friends as well.' She gave a quick look towards where Phoebe was sitting.

'Ah,' said Lydia, as she turned her head to look through the arch. 'Is he . . . Phoebe's?'

'No, no,' said Quinta. 'I look after the house and cooking and so on, and in return we have a part of the house at a peppercorn rent. It's a big house, I'll show you the rest of it later.'

'Does he pay you, as well?'

Lydia always liked to know exactly how people lived. Her laziness didn't extend to her friends and acquaintances; other people's lives seemed so much more interesting than hers.

'No. I have a job, I like to get out, and I need a proper salary, children are expensive.'

'She makes violins,' Phoebe called from the other room.

'I mend violins,' corrected Quinta.

'Yes, but you can make them, Sam says so, and Alban says too, and I know anyway, because you made the violin that hangs in the workshop.'

Lydia's eyebrows rose. 'Violins! How surprising. How on earth did you get into that?'

'I went to college,' said Quinta. She unhooked a heavy cast iron pan which hung in a line of pans suspended on heavy hooks from a beam. 'Are these chips? This is a wonderfully idle way to cook. And look, all kinds of exotic veggies, I know where these came from.'

'I don't want any veggies,' Phoebe said, appearing in the archway. 'I'll have some of those chips, though, and fishfingers. Three. Mind they're crispy.'

'Go away,' said Quinta. 'You were asking about the violins. I trained, when Phoebe was little.'

'I remember, you always were good at art and woodwork, and you played the violin, too, didn't you.'

Quinta nodded as she rummaged in the freezer for Phoebe's fishfingers.

'I'll do Phoebe's supper first, if you don't mind,' she said, arranging the fishfingers on the grill and licking the breadcrumbs off her fingers.

'Do you still play?' Lydia felt in the bottom of the carrier bag. 'Look, I got these.'

'Olives,' said Quinta. 'Huge black olives. Wonderful. No, I used to play the viola a bit, but I don't really have the time for it nowadays.'

'She played with Alban when I was smaller and not such a nuisance,' said the ubiquitous Phoebe. 'He makes fun of her, tells all sorts of terrible jokes. Do you know what's wrong with a mini going over a cliff with two viola players in it?'

'Phoebe!' said Quinta crossly.

'No,' said Lydia. 'You tell me.'

'Room for two more viola players in the back.' Phoebe collapsed in giggles at her own joke.

Lydia laughed. 'Is Alban a musician? You said he was creative.'

'He's a composer. Quite a distinguished one.'

Lydia's mouth dropped open. 'Alban! You don't mean to say he's Alban Praetorius!'

Quinta nodded. 'You've heard of him, then.'

'Definitely. Terrific film music – he won an Oscar, didn't he? And distinguished concert hall work as well, oh, very high-powered. I'd have expected him to live in London, though, not up here.'

'His family comes from Eyot,' said Quinta. 'He has a flat in London as well. He works better here, though, or that's what he says.'

'Open that wine,' said Lydia. 'I need a glass. Grandmama says I drink too much if I have so much as a sip when I'm with her.'

'Here's the corkscrew,' said Quinta. 'Phoebe, your supper's on the table, you can read while you're eating, just this once. There's cold milk in the fridge.'

'I bet it isn't really cold,' said Phoebe, carrying an armful of cat and her book. She arranged the cat carefully beside her on the pew. 'Then I suppose I have to go to bed, while you two yak; you'll yak for hours, I know. What's for pudding?'

'You can have a banana.'

Phoebe demolished her plate of food with astonishing rapidity. Lydia watched her with amusement as Quinta poured out two glasses of wine and then pulled out more pans and dishes for the various goodies which Lydia had brought.

'I've finished,' announced Phoebe, sliding along the pew.

'Then go to bed,' said Quinta. 'You can read for half an hour.'

'Hug,' said Phoebe, wrapping herself around Quinta.

'Off,' said Quinta. 'I'll come and tuck you up in half an hour.'

Lydia watched appreciatively. 'Lovely, a huggy daughter like that.'

'She's often not very huggy,' said Quinta, collapsing into another sofa. 'More like an alligator or a porcupine.'

'How old is she?'

'Eight.' Quinta took another gulp of her wine and closed her eyes.

Lydia straightened herself. 'Eight! But how old are you, Quinta?'

'Twenty-six.'

Lydia stared at her. 'You aren't, you can't be. I'm twenty-two, you were in the year above me at school.'

'True,' said Quinta. 'However, here in Eyot, I'm twenty-six.'

Lydia frowned. 'That means you had Phoebe when you were fifteen.'

'Just.'

'Quinta, wake up.'

'I'm not asleep, just relaxing.'

'How on earth, at that school, did you get pregnant at fifteen?'

'I didn't.'

'You just said you did.'

'I got pregnant when I was fourteen.' Quinta opened an eye and looked at Lydia. 'Shocked?'

'No, it happens. What I want to know is how, at that school, you could possibly manage it. And why.'

'I fell in love, desperately and totally. He was willing, I was too naïve to think about any precautions. If I'd thought about it for more than ten seconds, I suppose I would have told myself that he would see to that. And of course, at that age, I didn't think to ask him. Not until it was too late.'

'So, one single fling, and you get pregnant. It does seem terribly unfair.'

'Who said anything about one fling? It went on for quite some time . . . well, a few weekends. I lied about cousins and so on wanting to take me out; I don't know why they believed me at school, because no-one from my family ever took me out.'

Quinta paused, and sighed. 'I'd have gone on for much longer, I didn't want to stop doing anything so delightful, and he was obviously enjoying himself, too.'

Lydia got up from the sofa and padded towards the kitchen. 'Time to get those steaks on, do you like yours rare?' she called to Quinta.

'Yes, but not too bloody.'

'I'll give yours a bit longer than mine, then. I like it dripping,' added Lydia carnivorously. She appeared in the doorway. 'Why did it stop?'

'Circumstances,' said Quinta. 'And then, of course, I started feeling ill.'

Waking up in the morning feeling very peculiar, waiting on the hard little grey chair outside sister's office, asking for medicine because she'd been sick, yes, very sick, sister, yes, I have cleared it up . . .

The doctor, middle-aged, grim and disapproving. Then the housemother, her form teacher and, finally, the head. Quinta was sure she had leukaemia, since nobody thought to tell her what was wrong. The headmistress began with trained sympathy; lulled, Quinta had trusted her with the truth.

A gardener's boy, an errant sixth-former from the nearby boys' public school, that, Quinta realized from eight years on, the head could have coped with. The truth, she couldn't.

She had been furious with Quinta, called her a liar, a slut, an attention seeking little monster. Then, afraid that it might just be true, all the blame came flying back on to Quinta. She must have seduced him, led him on, had doubtless done it before, the man could be ruined by what Quinta had done to him, a distinguished man, with a family . . .

'What?' said Lydia, fascinated, standing with the salt in one hand and the pepper in the other. She waved the large wooden pepper-pot about dramatically. 'Your fault? How did she work out that one?'

'He, Phoebe's putative father, was a good man. I was a bad girl. End of story.'

'What happened then?'

'My parents arrived, they all went into a huddle. Clearly, they decided, I was lying, I was making this dreadful accusation in order to protect some spotty youth.'

'What was this man doing while all this was going on?'

'He knew I was pregnant, he'd known for a while. He was very wily. He told them he'd noticed I had been looking unwell, had been going to mention it, because as a married man with children of his own . . .'

'Ah!' exclaimed Lydia. 'So he was married. Did you know that?

'No, that was another horrible shock. It made it worse, of course. He was giving a series of lectures at Cuthbert College; you remember those visiting lectures, they used to take us over in a gaggle.'

Lydia nodded.

'So his wife wasn't with him. I never asked.'

'What did he do, when you said he was the father?'

'He was concerned, adult, responsible. Quite understood how a young girl would come up with a fantastic story to protect her boyfriend. They all cooed over him. He had moral scruples, personally, about abortion . . . However, if my parents felt that in the circumstances . . .'

Furious hissing came from the kitchen as Lydia slopped wine liberally over the steaks in the pan.

'Careful,' said Quinta. 'Don't set anything on fire.'

'I know exactly what I'm doing,' said Lydia, roused to a most unusual state of indignation. 'How could he do that?'

Quinta laughed. 'You know exactly how he could do that, Lydia. He had to find a way out of the nasty little mess without sullying his own spotless reputation.'

'How old was he?'

Quinta hesitated. 'Forty-three,' she said.

Lydia dropped the dish she was holding, and it shattered as it hit the floor.

Quinta leapt to her feet. 'Don't worry, it's not a special dish or anything,' she said, seizing a dustbin and brush.

'Bugger,' said Lydia, crouching down to retrieve a piece which had gone under the table. 'Sorry about that, Quinta, but you startled me. Thirty years older than you were, and you under-age, and he couldn't even use a condom!'

Quinta tipped the remains into the bin and retreated to her sofa in the other room.

'I did finally ask him about condoms – although to tell you the truth, I didn't actually know what a condom was. But some of the girls at school were more knowledgeable, and they had been talking about them, so . . . He said that making love with a condom was like eating a Mars bar with the wrapper on.'

Lydia came through the arch, stared at Quinta and then let out a peal of laughter, jeopardizing the pan she still had in her hand. Quinta seized the pan; then she, too, began to laugh.

They didn't hear Alban coming in; he found them, sitting side by side on the floor, still laughing.

'What the hell . . .' His eye fell on the steaks. 'Those will be ruined if you let then get cold . . . And why are you sitting on the floor with the pan anyway? Here, give it to me.'

He swept up the pan, and looked down at the two girls. 'You must be Lydia, how do you do? I'm Alban Praetorius. Quinta, do get up. May I share this exquisite joke?'

'Mars bar,' was all Quinta could manage to say.

Alban raised one of his bushy eyebrows. 'I don't get the point, sorry, Quinta.'

'No, I don't suppose you do, Alban,' said Quinta, pulling herself together. 'I don't suppose you do.'

Quinta struggled to her feet. Alban looked at her suspiciously. 'I've never seen you laughing like that.'

'No, I haven't laughed like that for a very long time.'

'Not for about eight and a half years, I should think,' said Lydia, getting up and brushing her skirt down. She gave Alban a mocking look. 'Don't you like laughter? Quinta used to laugh a lot. When she was younger, at school.'

'She laughs a lot here,' said Alban, rather stiffly. He looked at Lydia with a cold eye. 'Not in quite such an abandoned way, however.'

Lydia looked back at him, appraisingly. Goodness, she thought. Lucky Quinta!

Alban raised his eyebrows, and nodded down at the pan in his hand. 'You were going to have something to eat, I suppose? Before you got carried away by this joke you are so unwilling to share.'

'Yes,' said Lydia. 'Steaks, as you can see. Give me that back, and I'll finish them off. Why don't you have some too?' There's plenty in the fridge.'

Alban investigated the bag of meat which Lydia had put into the fridge. 'It's leaking; better get a cloth. There's a lot here.'

'I'm not very good on quantities,' said Lydia, 'but I find steak usually goes, one way or the other.'

'Mmm, good, I just had two or three horrible little pastry things there, and Simon's coming, too, he's just gone for a pee.'

'Simon?' said Quinta. 'Was he at the meeting?'

'Naturally, since it was to do with the organ restoration appeal.'

'Simon is the Cathedral organist,' Quinta explained to Lydia. 'Alban's brother.'

'Better put on some more steaks, then,' said Lydia practically. 'There's more wine in the bag, Alban, why don't you open some?'

'How old are you?' said Alban, looking at her disapprovingly.

'Twenty-two, why?' said Lydia.

'Just wondered.'

'Don't be churlish, Alban,' said Quinta. 'I don't have so many friends that I can afford to have you scare them all away.'

'I've never managed to scare Pauline away, more's the pity,' said Alban.

'Who is this Pauline?' asked Lydia.

'A friend of sorts,' said Quinta. 'She means well.'

'Oh dear.'

'We met when Phoebe was a toddler, Pauline's got a boy exactly the same age, and they were at playgroup together. Pauline felt sorry for me, single mum, all that. She gives me a lot of good advice; she thinks of me as one of her many charities. She's married to a solicitor, and is very active in Eyot affairs.'

'She sounds ghastly,' said Lydia.

'She is,' said Alban.

'Here, take this cloth, Alban, open the wine, and go and let Simon in,' said Quinta. 'I can hear him struggling with the catch on the door, it's stuck again. I must put oil on my list.'

She pushed him gently out of her way, and he shot Lydia a fierce look.

'Lady Wray's granddaughter, you said? Yes, that figures. Of course Lady Wray is a Mountjoy; dangerous, the whole pack of them.'

'Nonsense,' said Lydia, laughing.

Simon was silent as he escorted Lydia across the square. 'Quinta's right, best to see you home, nowhere's safe these days, although I expect you can look after yourself.'

'I'm always glad of company,' said Lydia politely. She stole a quick look at him. Why was he so glum?

'You must know Quinta very well.'

'I wouldn't say that, we lost touch when she left school.'

'Do you think Alban's in love with her?'

Lydia eyed him again. 'I really couldn't say. I thought theirs was a business arrangement.'

He let out a crack of mirthless laughter. 'Business arrangement, yes, that's exactly what it is. Only the business arrangement includes spending the night with him twice a week, Tuesdays and Thursdays.'

'Today's Thursday,' said Lydia helpfully.

Simon sighed. 'I don't want to go home quite yet,' he said. 'Let's call in at Horatio's, that's a wine bar along here . . . What about your grandmother? Will she be expecting you at any particular time?'

'I have a key,' said Lydia primly. 'What about you, do you live in the Close?'

Simon grimaced. 'Yes, of course. Organist's house, one of the finest in the Close. The canons would like to get me out of there, too good for a lowly musician, but they can't.'

'Why not?'

'Because it's got two bloody organs in it, one downstairs, one upstairs, tools of the trade. It would cost a fortune to get them moved anywhere else, and then, where would they fit? Canon Holigost, who's a mean-minded evangelical, argues that we could sell them, modern church music should be more up-to-date and less organ-centred; put the organist in a tiny house, give him a tambourine . . .'

'Do you need two organs?' asked Lydia.

'No, of course not, it's nothing to do with me, they were there when I came. My wife hates them, too; says other men don't bring their work home, why should I? She doesn't mind the money my pupils pay, though. I teach them at home, couldn't have them squawking and booming out in the Cathedral, they'd put the tourists off. I make them pay through the nose. I'm regarded as one of the finest organists in Europe, can you believe that?'

'I'm sure you are,' said Lydia. What on earth was the matter with the man? He was obviously suffering from some major grievance, was he keen on Quinta, too?

'Keen on her?' Simon's voice rose, startling an amiable-looking elderly man with glasses who was walking home from his Rotary meeting.

'Oh, yes,' he went on bitterly. 'You could say I'm keen on her. You could say I was desperately in love with her. You could say what you like, she won't have anything to do with me, not in the way I want. And she's sleeping with my brother!'

I hope he isn't going to burst into tears, thought Lydia.

'I'm not drunk, you know; just fed up. And I don't want to go back home to my wife and children, so let's just go and calm down in that wine bar, shall we? We can talk some more about Quinta.'

He pushed open a small dark door; and they were suddenly in the dark.

'Careful,' said Simon. 'There's a flight of stairs.'

A beam of light shone out from the darkness below, revealing the stairs. Lydia made her way down sideways, to be greeted by a round, olive-skinned little man, perspiring and immensely cheerful, who was standing at the foot of the stairs.

'Mr Simon, good, good. Come in, come in, no-one here tonight, only friends. Sit here at the bar, who is this nice young lady?'

As he hustled them towards the wide wooden bar that ran along one side of the cellar his eyes slid over Lydia.

'A friend. A whatsit of wine, Horatio, please, and a big orange juice, lots of ice.'

Lydia had wondered if she would have to carry Simon home to his wife and children, but to her surprise he only drank a single glass of wine.

'You finish the rest, I'll stick to the orange juice. If I have any more wine, I'll be bad-tempered in the morning, and the boys hate that.'

'Boys?' said Lydia. 'Are your children all boys?'

Simon looked at her, puzzled for a moment. 'My children? Oh, not them, they just have to put up with me. No, no, the choristers, the Cathedral boys.'

'Of course,' said Lydia. 'How stupid of me.'

'Not really,' said Simon. 'One forgets, bound up in the Cathedral world, how small it is, how far removed from reality, and how unimportant it seems to everyone leading a normal life outside it.'

'I wouldn't say that,' said Lydia. 'Perhaps people don't think about it very much, but the Cathedral matters to them, I'm sure. Here in Eyot, and outside as well. Not in the same way as you do, of course, it's your job. After all, look at the millions of people who visit cathedrals and like listening to the music.'

'Oh yes? And when did you last go to a cathedral service?'

'At the weekend,' said Lydia smugly.

'Yes, because Lady W took you, you can't stay with her and not go off to the Cathedral on Sunday. And before that? Come on, let's have the truth.'

'A year ago,' said Lydia. 'All right, I confess, I never go near cathedrals normally. I went to a friend's wedding in Christ Church . . . at Oxford. It was sweet.'

'Sweet!'

'Christ Church Cathedral, I mean. It's tiny . . . but of course, you must know all the cathedrals.' Lydia frowned. 'The service wasn't sweet, it was awful, all chummy, and sounded like someone reading from a post office leaflet. Dire hymns, too; I bet that marriage doesn't last.'

'There you are, then.' Simon's gloom descended again. 'That's what young people think. And here am I, forty-five, I've spent my life in cathedrals, and what for?'

'Getting maudlin, Simon?'

What a lovely voice, thought Lydia. Velvety. She turned on her stool to see who had spoken and found herself looking into mocking dark eyes.

'Hello, Titus,' said Simon. 'Back from Germany? Come and join us.'

'Thanks, Simon, but I'm with a friend. Some more of this, please, Horatio.'

Curious, Lydia watched Titus go back to the table. A girl-friend? She must be at least fifteen years older than him, he looked as though he was in his early thirties at the most. The woman, welcoming him back to his table with a daz-zling smile must be much older. Exotic, elegant, yes, but not young.

Simon followed the line of her gaze. He raised his eyebrows

slightly. 'Titus has got another one, he does collect the most amazing women.'

'Is that his aunt? A friend of his mother's?'

'No, definitely not. Titus goes for older women. Finds it less hassle, or just finds them sexier. I don't know. He seems remarkably happy, unlike the rest of us.'

'Is he something to do with the Cathedral?'

'In a way. He sings there sometimes, as a lay clerk. One of the men in the choir,' he added, seeing Lydia didn't know what he was talking about. 'He's a bass, and a good one. Apart from that, he's at the university.'

'A lecturer?'

'No, I don't think so, he works with some bigwig professor in an arcane field; very high-powered.'

He didn't find me attractive, thought Lydia. Not at all, he hardly noticed me, and nor does Simon, I can tell. Simon is obviously obsessed with Quinta, so is Alban. Yet Quinta isn't a beauty; well-rounded, unglamorous, no ostentatious come-on . . . so what was it? Her liveliness, Lydia supposed, her vivid face, her quick definite movements . . .

Lydia wished Angus hadn't dropped her, that she was still with him, a couple, in the centre of things. Not an onlooker, an outsider.

Not that she wanted any of these men to be interested in her, she didn't. I don't understand men at all, she thought glumly.

'You feel ill at ease, yes?' Horatio's sharp eyes were on her. 'Don't worry about these people, they live in a world of their own. You're new here in Eyot?'

Lydia nodded.

'Then, not to worry. Soon, you make new friends, meet people your own age. Young people, with straightforward, uncomplicated lives.'

Lydia smiled back at him, impossible not to, when he was so full of good humour.

'Sorry,' said Simon. 'I'm not very good company. Let's go.'

They passed Titus's table; he raised a friendly hand to them, then, as they reached the door, called out to Simon.

'Any news about the new Bishop?'

Simon stopped, surprised. 'Yes, it was announced days ago,

haven't you . . . oh, no, you've been abroad, I forgot. Lennox-Smith, he's coming from Cambridge, do you know him?'

A strange expression came over Titus's handsome face. Not exactly surprise, thought Lydia; he is surprised, but he's pleased, too.

'Oh, I know him all right,' said Titus, his face lighting up with a generous smile. 'A . . .' He hesitated. 'An interesting man, very able, so they say. I know his family, too.'

'You can fill us all in, then.'

Titus turned back to his companion; Lydia obediently followed Simon out into the dark stairway.

'Goodnight, Mr Simon, goodnight, pretty lady, come again, come soon.'

'Nice old bugger, Horatio,' said Simon. 'Never tells on me, or on anyone else, and he could tell a few things, don't doubt it. Oh, my god, talking of telling, quick, pretend to look in this shop window, oh, hell.'

'Mr Praetorius,' said a booming woman's voice. 'You're out late, I thought the meeting was going to finish about nine, I know Evie was expecting you home.'

Cornered, Simon turned and smiled unconvincingly. 'Good evening, Marjorie. Is it safe for you to be out alone at this time?'

'I'm just taking the dog for a walk.'

Simon hadn't noticed that Marjorie was attached, via what looked like a fishing reel, to a wandering basset hound.

What a repulsive dog, thought Lydia, looking at its red-rimmed and watering eyes. It sniffed round a lamppost and then cocked its leg. Lydia watched the steady stream heading for Simon's shoes and gave him a friendly shove. 'Mind out.'

Marjorie looked her up and down disapprovingly. Hoyden, she said to herself. Probably after poor Mr Praetorius.

Simon looked down. 'Thank you, Lydia, I hadn't noticed. Marjorie, this is Lydia, Lady Wray's granddaughter. Lydia, Mrs Jessop, a pillar of our Cathedral society.'

Marjorie looked at Lydia with a new interest. 'I heard dear Lady Wray had a young member of her family staying with her. She is so good with young people.'

'I'm just making sure Lydia gets back to the Close safely,' said

Simon. 'Since I'm going that way myself. I live there,' he added helpfully.

'I know,' said Marjorie, puzzled. Even stranger than usual, of course musical people were different. She turned back towards her house. She would give Evie a quick ring to say Simon was on his way home, she might be worried about him.

Two figures stalked across the vast stone floors of the Cathedral. Despite it being the end of June, the grey skies outside meant that little light penetrated the world-famous stained glass windows. Later on, the Cathedral would be illuminated for the tourists; at this time of the morning it was a place of vaulted shadows. A verger emerged from the choir, wished the two women a hushed good morning, and drifted into a side-chapel. Footsteps echoed in the crossing as they emerged from the mediaeval gloom of the nave, skirted Queen Ethelburga's tomb, and headed purposefully towards the small door set in beside the entrance to the Chapter House. The wooden door opened with a creak and banged shut behind them.

'And was she worried about him?' asked Daphne, sniffing as she seized a brick of oasis and plunged a knife into it.

'Cross, I'd say.' Marjorie cut decisively into a hapless stem and gave it a good shake. 'Wonderful colour these have, plenty of focus. Where's Wyn? She's late this morning.'

'No, I'm not,' said Wyn, coming into the flower room – creak, bang – bearing a large green bucket. 'I was here first, so I started at once. Who's cross?'

'You should wait for us, dear,' said Marjorie. 'Best to work as a team, you know that.'

'Evie Praetorius,' said Daphne. She switched on the kettle and reached into her bag for the bottle of milk she had brought with her. 'Simon was out late last night, Marjorie says. Marjorie bumped into him, he was with a young woman. A very young woman!'

'Yes, but nothing in it, Daphne, I told you. He was in a very bad mood, not good company for her or anyone else, I'd say. It was Lady W's granddaughter, Wyn, the one who's just finished at Oxford.'

'Her mother is Lady Wray's second daughter, the clever one who's a doctor,' said Daphne helpfully.

'Did she marry another doctor? This girl's mother, I mean?' asked Wyn.

Marjorie and Daphne stared at her. 'No, why?'

'I just wondered. Women doctors tend to marry other doctors, the only men they meet, I suppose, with the terribly long hours they work. Except for patients, of course, and they're ill.'

'Presumably they get better, if the doctor's any good.'

'Yes, but rather unpleasant, don't you think, to marry someone you met when they had a disease, or were on the operating table . . .'

'It didn't arise, in this case,' said Marjorie. 'Mr Holbeck, that's the son-in-law, was an architect.'

'Is an architect,' corrected Daphne. 'He's still alive.'

'Yes, and living abroad,' said Marjorie. 'He ran away with the cook,' she explained to Wyn. 'You wouldn't know about it, it was before you came to Eyot. He was a very lackadaisical man. I wonder if his daughter takes after him or after the mother.'

'Mrs Gridlock, who does for Lady W, says she's very idle,' said Daphne, pouring water into three cups of instant coffee granules. She put the kettle down and drew a little bottle out of her bag. 'Drops,' she said. 'A new remedy, to stop my nose running.'

'It's to be hoped it works,' said Marjorie. 'Sniffing is so bad for you, dear.'

Creak. The door opened, and Canon Feverfew, the youngest and nosiest of the canons, peered round the door. 'Good morning, ladies.'

'Come in,' said Daphne. 'Have a cup of coffee, we're just making some.'

'Ah,' said Canon Feverfew, coming into the room and closing the door carefully behind him. 'Thank you, thank you, I would indeed like some coffee. Especially if you happen to have any of those delicious ginger biscuits . . .'

He munched vigorously. 'I just popped in to ask if you'd had any preliminary thoughts about the flowers for the enthronement of the new Bishop. The Dean happened to mention it yesterday.'

'Yes, we're having a meeting next week, to arrange a co-ordinating committee,' said Marjorie. 'I shall be chairwoman as usual, I expect.'

'Good, good. I told the Dean I was sure you ladies would have everything in hand.' He helped himself to another biscuit. 'May I? Mmm. Any news?'

'Lady Wray has got a granddaughter come to stay. She's just finished at Oxford,' reported Marjorie.

'Ah, but what you ladies may not know is that Mrs Stixwould's grandson is coming to Eyot for the summer, too. He's got some work on up here, she says.'

The three women let out long contented sighs.

'Adam,' said Marjorie. 'Of course. Let me see, how old is he . . .'

'Twenty-eight,' said Daphne.

'Just right,' said Marjorie.

'I thought you'd be interested,' said Canon Feverfew as he rose to his feet and dusted the crumbs from his black cassock. 'Well, I must be about my tasks, a busy time this is for us, a busy time.'

Marjorie and Daphne gave sighs, of pure, interested delight as they gathered buckets and stands and armfuls of greenery. Wyn followed them out of the flower room. 'Sybil Stixwould's grandson,' she said. 'Wasn't he the one . . . Well, wasn't there a little problem when he was at Eton . . .? I mean . . .'

Marjorie stopped abruptly. 'It's not very nice to mention these things, Wyn, you should know that. It was just gossip, and he's older now, all that's behind him. Besides, I don't believe half of what they say goes on at these public schools, discipline can't be that loose, not when parents are spending all that money.'

Marjorie set up her metal ladder with a click. 'I'll green up,' she said authoritatively.

She and Daphne worked steadily, Marjorie giving commands and Daphne obediently passing up armfuls of greenery and then the great longy lilies set off by roses and trailing alchemilla mollis, with its tiny, fluffy flowers.

'Canon Feverfew will like this,' said Daphne, stepping back with her head on one side to admire the balance. 'Lovely,

Marjorie, only don't overdo it, we must allow space for the butterflies.'

'I think I know all about space for the butterflies,' said Marjorie majestically. 'Come along, Daphne, hand me some more of that, and then you can begin to clear up. Tidy as we go, that's our motto, isn't it? Then we'll go and see what Wyn's been doing, before we start on the altar flowers.'

Wyn hummed to herself as she carried her bucket towards the choir gates. Her designs were quite unlike the stiff formality of Marjorie's towering masterpiece. 'A wild, woodland piece,' said Canon Feverfew as he came past. 'So natural, so refreshing. And what beautiful roses.'

'Yes,' said Wyn. 'They're from my garden. Buff beauty.' She gave a snort of laughter. 'Better in a bed than up against the wall.'

'What?' said Canon Feverfew.

Wyn turned an innocent eye on him. 'The roses,' she explained. 'Buff beauty. It's a trailing rose, you see.'

'I see, I see,' said Canon Feverfew, and went on his way, shaking his head.

Marjorie surveyed the arrangement in a regal manner.

'Coming along quite nicely,' she said. 'But not too wild, Wyn, dear. Remember we are on holy ground; I don't feel that unrestrained Nature has any place in a cathedral.'

Wyn added another branch of trailing greenery.

'Doesn't Mr Praetorius's brother live near St Kentigern's Church?'

'A strange man,' said Marjorie disapprovingly. 'Although very distinguished in his field, I understand. Yes, he lives near there; it used to be Lucy Praetorius's house before she went to live abroad.'

'And doesn't he have a lodger, well, that's what they call her?'

'Yes,' said Daphne, with a sniff. 'The one with the funny name. Quinta. Very young, much younger than Alban Praetorius.'

'She is very young, yes,' said Wyn. 'I'm told that Mr Praetorius – our Mr Praetorius – goes there a lot.' She paused. 'Very devoted, for a brother.'

Marjorie and Daphne both took deep, satisfied breaths.

'Evie's out a lot at the moment,' said Marjorie. 'Spiritual Development Circles, I believe. Women's Bible classes, too, so I hear. It was near St Kentigern's that I met our Mr Praetorius last night.'

'Mmm,' said Daphne with satisfaction.

'But he was with Lady Wray's granddaughter,' Wyn pointed out.

'Mmm,' said Daphne again.

'I expect we'll hear more about this,' said Marjorie. 'Now, come along, girls, half the morning's gone, what are we thinking of!'

## 5

The old-fashioned Victorian bell clanged as Lydia came into the shop.

Quinta looked up from the counter, where she was lolling over prints of violins in an old book. 'Hello, Lydia, I thought you said you never got up early.'

'I don't if I can help it, but grandmama has her own ideas about lying in bed. Up to seven o'clock, it's healthful, from seven to half past with a cup of tea – in the finest china and, I must admit, a treat – is allowable; after that the bed becomes an unseemly, untidy, unwholesome place.' She yawned. 'And then Mrs Gridlock comes in, her beady eyes everywhere. I think she's a spy. No, I don't think I'll ever get used to getting up early. My ma's exactly the same, up at the crack of dawn, full of life, ugh.'

Quinta grinned. 'Wait until you have children. They all keep early hours, and they long for you to share them.'

'Delightful as Phoebe is, I have to say the thought of children fills me with horror. I'm going to be an aunt.'

'Oh?' said Quinta, interested. 'I didn't know you had any brothers or sisters.'

'I don't. I speak figuratively.'

'I'm an aunt,' said Quinta. 'But it isn't very irksome. Most of my nieces and nephews are grown up, or live a long way away.'

'You're the youngest, aren't you?'

'By a long way,' said Quinta. 'Number five, the afterthought. My parents had two boys, two girls: the perfect family. Then, seven years later, I came along. A mistake, as my mother never tired of pointing out. She tried to get rid of me, actually, before I was born. Only it didn't work.'

Lydia was shocked. 'How do you know?'

'She told me, one day when she found me more of a nuisance than usual.'

'I hardly remember them,' said Lydia, frowning. 'I must have seen them at school . . . '

'Not necessarily. They usually arranged for some other parent to bring me and take me back at the beginning and end of term. They never came for exeats or anything like that. I believe they were devoted parents to my brothers and sisters; they probably felt they'd done all that by the time I came along.'

'How horrible!' said Lydia, thinking of the effort her mother had made, in a busy life, to make the long journey to the school for weekends, school plays, matches. And her father, arriving unexpectedly always, and carrying her off to sumptuous meals and lazy afternoons by the river. The sun always seemed to shine when her father was around, thought Lydia. Poor Quinta, the sun hadn't done much shining on her. Certainly not where her parents were concerned.

'Did they come to speech day ever?'

'Yes, they felt obliged to come to that, put on a good show and so forth.'

'Was your father very stiff? Army type? I'm sure I saw them, once.'

'Yes, and my mother looked as though she'd grown on an embassy lawn. Big, hideous hats. A very cold woman.'

Quinta spoke without emotion; it seemed a lifetime away.

'I had an aunt, I went there for half term sometimes. Out of a sense of duty, I think, because she never knew what to do with me. She died when I was ten, though, so that was that, unless a friend invited me. My parents weren't very keen on that, they felt they might have to ask the friend back in the holidays, which would have been a bore.'

'Do you ever see them?' asked Lydia.

Strange, Quinta didn't sound at all bitter; it was as though she was talking about someone else, not about her own family at all. It was the way you might talk about a comparative stranger, with momentary interest but no involvement.

'No, I haven't seen them since I came here. They traced me in the end, don't know why they bothered, actually. The only one who cared about me was my eldest brother George. He was all right, in his way. He was going through a messy divorce when I found I was expecting Phoebe, otherwise he might have helped. Or not, as the case might be. Anyway, it didn't arise. They found me two days after my sixteenth birthday; that was very lucky.'

'Why?'

'They couldn't make me go back. At sixteen, the social services and all that lot lose interest in you. You're grown up, your parents can throw you out, you're on your own. I can't think what my parents might have tried to do if they'd found me sooner. Have me put away in a home, I shouldn't be surprised.'

Lydia shook her head. 'They say that if your parents didn't love you, you can't love your own children. You look as though you love Phoebe all right.'

'I do,' said Quinta fiercely. 'I give her all the love I never had. She may not have a father around, but she's not going to miss out on love the way I did.'

'Don't your parents mind, having a granddaughter they never see?'

'In a way I think they do. George's wife got custody of their children after the divorce, and she won't let them near my parents. My other brother never married, he was always a bit strange. One of my sisters took off for Canada after university and refused to have anything to do with my parents; so although she's married and has children, it isn't much use to them. My other sister has no children; she and her husband don't think it's right to bring children into this terrible world.'

'So your parents would like to see Phoebe after all.'

'They'd like to take her over. They've offered to pay for her education. As long as it's at a boarding schoool they've chosen, and she spends the holidays with them.'

'Not a good idea,' said Lydia gravely.

'No,' said Quinta, equally gravely. Then she laughed. 'They live on another planet as far as I'm concerned, so I don't let it cast any shadows.'

She pushed a stray red curl off her face and raised her hands in a query.

'So, why are you here?'

'D string,' said Lydia.

'Ah, business. For your bass?'

'Yes.'

'Is it full size or three-quarter?'

'Full size.'

'Hmm . . .' Quinta bent behind the counter and pulled out one drawer after another. 'There should be some here, no, that's oboe wipes and bassoon mops.'

'Over there?' said Lydia helpfully, pointing to a different rack of drawers marked with stringy names.

'Of course,' said Quinta. 'Sorry, Lydia, I don't usually work in the shop, but Sam's popped out to collect a parcel.'

''Sam? Young? Tall? Big? Hunky, by any chance?'

Quinta shook her head. 'You said you'd had an unhappy love affair and were off men. Anyway, no, Sam's young, but he's a lot shorter than you, and very slender. Fit, though.'

Lydia lost interest. 'Must be tall, when you're my height you feel uncomfortable with small men.'

'I don't know,' said Quinta. 'Lots of small men are dynamic. Powerful, you might say.'

'Exactly. Very unrestful,' said Lydia.

'In any case,' said Quinta, as she opened another drawer, 'Sam isn't interested in women.'

Lydia leaned over the counter and looked at the bundles of square envelopes in the drawer. She pointed. 'There you are, Pirastro. That's the one. How much?'

'Don't hurry me,' said Quinta. 'We take our time here, none of your vulgar rush.' She pulled a desk calculator towards her. 'Plus VAT . . .'

'I'll give you a cheque,' said Lydia. 'And I'll have some rosin as well.'

'You are a nuisance, I'll have to do a new bill,' said Quinta. 'Here you are. Which one do you use?'

Lydia bent over the little boxes of green and amber-coloured rosin. 'Like some apothecary's cure-all,' she remarked. 'I met someone from the university last night on my way home with Simon. Called Titus. Striking-looking, do you know him?'

Quinta shook her head. 'I know hardly anyone in Eyot.'

'That's true,' said Sam, closing the door neatly behind him. 'You've made a mess of my string drawers, Quinta, it isn't safe to leave you alone in here.'

'Sorry, Sam. Lydia, this is Sam.'

His big brown eyes looked gravely at Lydia. 'Are you a friend of Quinta's?'

'Yes,' said Lydia, pouncing at last on the rosin she wanted. 'This one, Quinta, please.'

'I'll do it,' said Sam. 'You go and be crafty upstairs, Quinta. Give your friend a cup of coffee. Make a change, you having some company.'

'Sam's very sociable,' Quinta explained as she plugged in the coffee machine in the workshop. 'Don't sit there, Lydia, there's glue on it.'

Lydia removed herself from the workbench and shifted to the safety of a stool.

'You've lived here for eight years, you must know everybody, have masses of friends. You always had a lot of friends at school.'

'True,' said Quinta, 'but times have changed. With a small child, you can't get out much. I did, to college, but it was hard juggling everything. I was too tired and had too little spare time to make friends. I still don't have much time to myself, what with the job, and looking after the house, and Phoebe, of course. I know quite a few parents at her school, but they think I'm strange.'

'Alban must have friends round, entertain.'

'Not often. He has a flat in London, that's where he goes out on the toot and sees his friends. He comes to Eyot to work; very antisocial, strumming away at three in the morning.'

'I thought he was in bed with you at three o'clock in the morning.' Lydia gave Quinta a quick sideways look.

'Sometimes. He starts off in bed, and then he gets up again and goes off to work.'

'Simon doesn't like your going to bed with Alban.'

'It's none of Simon's business,' said Quinta furiously. 'He's just jealous of Alban, jealous of his music and his house, and me, because he thinks of me as being another one of Alban's possessions. All ridiculous, probably goes back to who had the porridge bowl with rabbits on it when they were children. Simon's as successful as Alban in his own way. He's got a nice family, respect of the community – and he doesn't sully his art as Alban does.'

'Sully?'

'Film music, TV, that kind of thing. Commercial. That's where the money is. Nearly all serious composers do that kind of work nowadays, but Simon likes to think of it as a betrayal of art. Of course, Simon could do it too, and probably very well but he thinks it's beneath him. And he's too lazy; you get like that after years in the Church.'

'So why is he jealous of Alban's music?'

'Simon writes church music. What did that humorous history of music call them: the serried ranks of solemn, second-rate hymn and anthem composers . . .? Simon's afraid he's one of those. Whereas Alban has his music performed all over the world, he's a big international name.'

'Very big,' said Lydia vaguely, her eyes scanning the workshop.

'What are you looking for?' asked Quinta.

'Something to eat, I'm starving. Have you got any biscuits?'

'I have, hidden in the cupboard over there.'

'Why are they hidden?' said Lydia, retrieving the tin. 'Is Sam a biscuit thief?' She prised off the lid and looked inside. 'Chocolate digestives, oh, good.'

'No, I am not a biscuit thief,' said Sam, putting his head round the door. 'Quinta, Sylvester Tate rang, he has a problem with his spike, can we fix it? He'll be in later on this morning, at eleven.'

'Okay,' said Quinta. 'I'll clear a space. Literally,' she added for Lydia's benefit. 'Sylvester's a big man, and he likes to watch the repairs, looks after his cello as if it's a baby.'

'*The* Sylvester Tate?' asked Lydia.

'The,' said Quinta.

'He lives in a village near here,' put in Sam. 'With Gabriel Jay, the violinist.' He helped himself to a black coffee. 'While I'm here,' he said, removing the tin from Quinta's reach.

'Sam is concerned about my figure,' said Quinta, laughing. 'Lost cause, Sam, you know that.'

'Your friend here, look how slim and fit she is!'

'Yes, and if I starved and ran a marathon every week, I still wouldn't look like that, I'm not the type. Besides, Lydia isn't fit. She was born like that.'

'True,' said Lydia. 'I dare say that when I'm old I'll be unmuscled and totally weak, a modern Ivar the Boneless. Still, playing the double-bass is good exercise, not to mention lugging it around.'

'Your string and rosin are downstairs on the counter,' said Sam. 'Did you pay?'

'No,' said Lydia, 'I'll give you a cheque on my way out.'

Quinta dipped a brush in a dark, evil-smelling tin and picked up a small violin. She dabbed it expertly, and then held it up to look at it.

'Goodness, the size of it,' said Lydia. 'Midget violin. Whoever plays that?'

'It's a child's violin,' said Quinta. 'Not the smallest, by a long way. They start incredibly young, Suzuki classes, you know, when they're hardly out of their push-chairs.'

'Heavens,' said Lydia. 'Do they want to?'

'No, but it keeps their mothers occupied.'

'Does Phoebe learn the violin? Oh, no, she told me, she plays the piano.'

'She can play another instrument when she's older. If I can afford it. If she wants to. With a teacher, by herself; the whole point of Suzuki training is that the mother works with the child. It wasn't designed for children like Phoebe, she'd wrap the instrument round my ears at the first bars of "Twinkle, Twinkle, Little Star".'

'Sounds grim,' said Lydia. 'Clearly, Phoebe's a sensible child.' She picked up her mug and took it to the sink. 'Have you finished?'

'No, not yet,' said Quinta. 'I like it when it's cooled down. Don't bother about washing it up.'

'Each for each is what we teach,' said Lydia idly. 'Quinta, this place is full of lists.'

'Mmm,' said Quinta. 'Schedules, lists of work coming in, things to be ordered, the usual.'

'Library, cat food, M & S for knickers,' Lydia read out.

'Monday, Alban London; Phoebe 4.15 at gym; piano 6.30; ring Maria. That doesn't sound like work to me. And what about this one, Hedgehogs, badgers, foxes . . .'

Quinta grinned. 'That one's something to do with a project of Phoebe's, I think.'

'Do you live by lists?' Lydia was amazed.

'Yes,' said Quinta. 'I'm basically very disorganized. If I don't plan everything, and time it, then I never get it all done.'

'Do you plan menus?'

'Yes, and what Phoebe's going to wear each day, and what Alban's timetable is, and a rota for cleaning the rooms in the house, and my work here of course . . . if I do it, it's on a list.'

Lydia was concerned. 'I don't think a psychologist would think that's healthy, Quinta. Where's the spontaneity?'

'There isn't any,' said Quinta cheerfully. 'I haven't got time for spontaneity. I hate the unexpected, and I've found that by keeping lists, the unexpected never happens. All probabilities or possibilities are on a list somewhere.'

Sam's voice floated up the stairs. 'Can you help with a customer, Quinta?'

'Coming,' said Quinta, removing her large work apron.

'I must pay and go,' said Lydia. 'I have a list, too, this morning; shopping for my grandmama. Only the ordinaries, of course, she wouldn't trust me with anything that needs choice.'

Quinta came forward into the shop, a questioning expression on her face. The man standing in the shop turned round.

'Hello,' said Lydia, following in Quinta's wake. 'It's Titus. The one I met last night that I told you about, Quinta,' she said in explanation.

He frowned. 'Oh, yes, you were with Simon Praetorius, weren't you?'

'Yes,' said Lydia. 'You were with an older woman,' she added; rude, but he was rude too.

Surprisingly, he smiled. 'I was.'

'Can I help you?' said Quinta again. I can see why Lydia called him striking, she thought.

Quinta usually felt herself safe from men, she didn't mind whether they found her attractive or not; she wasn't interested in them, and any interest they showed in her she found tiresome. It worried Sam dreadfully. 'You're so young, Quinta, so attractive, men pant for you; it isn't natural, this life you're leading. Where's the fun?'

'Oh, I quite enjoy life in my own way,' said Quinta. 'I have plenty to occupy me, I have Alban for male company, what more could anyone want?'

'Passion, plenty of uninhibited sex,' Sam said firmly. 'It's like marble, your life. You need to let go, lose control, let lust and zest for life sweep you off your feet.'

'Yes?' said Quinta. 'And who looks after Phoebe while I'm being swept off my feet?'

'Phoebe, that's all you think about. It's not so good for her either; you're cramping her space. She needs to see you enjoying life more, you're setting her a bad example.'

'And who do I start enjoying life more with?' said Quinta, beginning to get cross.

'Someone nearer your own age,' said Sam. 'Find some virile young man with a beautiful body. Alban's no good to you, crotchets in his head when he's making love, and then when he's finished it's off to his other, more interesting rhythms. It's no way to live, Quinta. Sex is too important!'

Laughing, Quinta had to admit that Sam had a very good idea of what Alban was like, although he had missed the sentimentality which always preceded his love-making. He was a romantic soul, but never for very long, and certainly not when in a post-coital mood, then all he wanted to do was get back to his score. I'm a vessel for his creativity, thought Quinta. How depressing.

How young, thought Titus. But an interesting face, and one that would grow more interesting with age. 'Music for the Cathedral,' he said. 'For Simon Praetorius.'

What an amazing voice, thought Quinta. And what charm. And, she thought before she could stop herself, I bet he's got a beautiful body. Sam's influence, she told herself severely.

'Sheet music? It's not really my area,' she said politely. 'Sam?'

'I know that,' said Sam. 'But you've been down here this morning, nothing is in its place. The parcel of music was on the counter, ready for collection.'

'Oh, that one,' said Quinta. 'I wondered what it was, it didn't say anything on it. It's on that chair over there.'

Lydia finished writing her cheque and handed it with her card to Sam. 'For these,' she said, pointing out her purchases. 'Titus sings in the Cathedral,' she told Quinta as she slid past her. 'And you're a scientist at the university too, aren't you? I think that's what Simon said.'

'I am,' he said, signing an invoice. 'Chaos,' he added.

'What?' said Quinta.

'That's my field. Chaos theory.'

'Then you won't get on with Quinta,' said Lydia. 'Her life is a long battle against chaos, isn't it, Quinta?'

'I suppose so,' said Quinta. 'Chaos,' she added thoughtfully. 'Isn't that poetry, rather than science? You know, Milton. Hell:

> where eldest Night
> And Chaos, Ancestors of Nature, hold
> Eternal Anarchy . . .'

Titus raised his eyebrows. 'Poetry? Perish the thought. No, it's a big theory, I'd try and explain it to you if I had time, but I'm in a hurry. Thank you.'

Quinta flattened herself against the counter to let him past; an alarming man, she thought.

Lydia had different views. 'Hmm,' she said. 'Patronizing. He shouldn't be allowed to get away with that!'

'Too old for you,' said Sam. 'Not as old as Alban,' and he glanced meaningfully at Quinta, 'but still too old.'

'And he only likes older women,' said Lydia. 'It's a challenge, don't you agree?'

Sylvester rolled into the shop on the dot of eleven.

'Punctual as always,' said Sam, running to open the door for him.

'Hello, Sam,' said Sylvester. 'You look revoltingly healthy. If you spent as much time improving your mind as you do your body, you'd achieve amazing things.'

'My body has more potential, I'm not an artist like you. Shall I carry the cello upstairs for you? Quinta's in the workshop.'

'No, I can manage. I've hauled this thing up worse staircases than this one, I can tell you.'

Quinta gave him a wide and happy smile; she was very fond of Sylvester.

'Well, young Quinta, what are we going to do about this spike?' Sylvester opened the case and took out his cello. He held it balanced on the workbench with a single huge hand, while Quinta peered at the spike.

'This is loose, I'll try tightening it, but I think it needs replacing.'

'It's very annoying,' complained Sylvester. 'The cello's been with Scroll and Bridges for a new spike, can't think what they were doing with it.'

'Sloppy work,' said Quinta gravely. 'You can't trust these London firms these days.'

Sylvester roared. 'Like to get your hands on a really good cello for a change?'

'No,' said Quinta with dignity. 'I mean yes, of course, but we handle a lot of very good cellos here, you know that.'

'Yes, you've got a nice-looking baroque cello in the window.'

'Not your period, though, is it?'

'Oh, we all have to be authentic these days, it's the coming thing. Don't hold with it myself, not to the extent that the purists do, tuning down half a tone, no spike, all that kind of thing. They're fanatical, like all converts, get carried away with the gimmickry and forget the music, most of them.'

He squeezed his considerable bulk between the bench and the sink. 'What's this hanging on the wall here? I like this.'

Quinta looked up. 'Oh, that's my diploma piece, from college.'

'I like the carved head, did you copy it from an eighteenth-century violin?'

'The design is my own, I like strange faces.'

'You surprise me. An orderly girl like you shouldn't have any room in your life for weird things.'

Sylvester gave his booming laugh and then shuddered as he came face to face with the tiny violin which Quinta had hung on the rack.

'I bet that sounds ghastly, cats on the prowl would have nothing on that.'

'You wouldn't buy one of those for its tone, no,' said Quinta, without looking up. Sylvester watched in momentary silence as she worked with swift skill.

'Why don't you make instruments?' Sylvester asked. 'That's what you trained for.'

'Don't you start,' said Quinta. 'Sam was nagging at me a few days ago. No time, for one thing, and who would buy anything I made?'

'If it's good, lots of people,' said Sylvester practically. 'What a ridiculous way to think. If everybody had that attitude, no-one would ever make anything. If you were a man, now, those kind of thoughts would never cross your mind, you'd just get on with it.'

'If I were a man, I probably wouldn't be bringing up a daughter single-handed.'

'What's that got to do with it?' demanded Sylvester.

'Time,' said Quinta. 'And dedication, and energy. All the things you need to make something, whether you're a craftsman or an artist.'

'Phoebe will grow up, and you'll still be attaching strings to microscopic violins. Then what?'

'Then perhaps I'll do something about it.'

Sylvester snorted with disbelief. 'Nonsense. Anyway, no point telling young people what to do with their lives, you have to make your own mistakes and learn the hard way, just like the rest of us. Now, there's a concert at Midwinter Church on Saturday evening, I'm playing, with some others. I've brought two tickets, for you and Phoebe. A present, from me, there's nothing to pay.'

Quinta was touched. 'Sylvester, that's really kind of you, but . . .'

'But you won't be able to come,' Sylvester finished for her. 'No, you never can, but this time I'm insisting. I certainly won't let you do any work on my cellos if you never come to hear me play. There!'

Quinta gave him one of her most enchanting smiles, her eyes creasing up to little sparkling slits as she laughed at him.

'Blackmail.'

'Exactly. It's a supper concert, lots of lovely food, Lily's catering so it will be first-rate. Chance for you to meet some people, let your hair down. And it's in a good cause, proceeds to the Cathedral Organ Appeal. Got to pull together for the musical life of the community and so on, though personally I can't stand organ music. You need to be a plumber to play those things, not a musician.'

'There,' said Quinta, giving the spike a final twist. 'Ask Scroll and Bridges for a refund next time you take it in, they've got no business doing such a lousy job.'

Sylvester tested the spike and gave a grunt of satisfaction. 'Good. Tell Gustav to send the bill. So I'll see you on Saturday?' He plonked the tickets down on the bench.

Quinta shook her head. 'No, Sylvester, I know it's a good cause, but since I'm not paying for the tickets, I'm hardly contributing . . .'

'I shall lose my temper in a minute,' said Sylvester. 'And that's very bad for a man of my size. Think of other people for a change.'

'What other people?' said Quinta, squatting on her heels to fasten the last catch on the cello case.

'It would please me, for a start. Then, your Phoebe would enjoy it. And other people would enjoy your company, bring a bit of joy and zest into their lives.'

'Phoebe would probably behave abominably.'

'So? If you can't behave badly when you're eight, when can you? No, don't look alarmed, I don't suppose for a moment that Phoebe will misbehave, does she usually when she goes to concerts?'

Silence.

'You look shifty,' said Sylvester. 'You don't mean to say that you've never taken her to a concert.'

'Well, it's not exactly . . . No, all right, I haven't.' Quinta was beginning to feel very defensive. She hadn't wanted to push Phoebe into music, she saw enough mothers dragging their uninterested offspring to this and that cultural event. They came and talked about it in loud voices in the shop: 'Of course, Daniel's been going to concerts with us since he was two, I know he's a wonderfully musical child, so it's different for him, but all children can benefit from a musical experience . . .'

Besides, she found taking Phoebe anywhere exhausting. It was bad when Phoebe expressed her dislike of whatever was on offer; almost worse waiting for her to do so.

Sylvester was looming over her. 'Well, that is disgraceful. Simon Praetorius tells me she's a musical child, get off your bum, Quinta, get out of the house. With or without Phoebe, it's time you woke up and took your place in the sun.'

With which he departed. The room looked diminished when he had gone, it always did.

'Personality, that's what it is,' said Sam as they sat on the bench in the yard with their sandwiches. A watery sun struggled to break through the clouds. Quinta felt very depressed.

'Cheer up,' said Sam. 'Something's brewing, I can tell, something's going to happen to liven us all up. Good thing, we need shaking up, getting seedy all of us here.'

Quinta smiled and ran a hand through her thick curls. 'Oh, and just what is going to happen? Why shouldn't life be exactly the same in a year's time, both of us sitting here, the weather bad; nothing will have changed except we'll both be a year older.'

'No, it's all going to change,' said Sam decidedly. 'Trust me, I can feel it in my water.'

6

The rain lashed against the windscreen. The inefficient wipers squeaked disconsolately as Quinta craned her neck to find a patch of clear glass. The road, sky and surrounding countryside were uniformly grey.

Phoebe grumbled in the back of the van. 'I hate England. Why do we live where it rains more than it does anything else? Why can't we emigrate? I want to live somewhere warm, where the sun always shines.'

Don't we all, thought Quinta gloomily. Why was she out on this horrible evening? It might be summer, but it felt and looked like March; she'd known this concert was going to be a bad idea.

The concert-goers squelched their way along the path into the church between the gravestones. 'Remarkably good turn-out, considering,' said Sylvester cheerfully, as he peered round the vestry curtain.

'All those rubber boots and old macs will smell as they dry,' said Gabriel disapprovingly.

'Ha,' said Sylvester. 'Too much high life, that's your trouble; great concert halls of the world, everyone in smart clothes, do you good to get back to basics. This is where we started, remember that.'

Gabriel did remember. Recitals in cold churches, in badly-lit village halls, in schools. He remembered the long train journeys, often arriving in distant places, at small, deserted stations, then walking to the concert venue. Him with his fiddle, Sylvester with his cello in one huge hand and a stool in the other . . . he had learned to take his own stool after a memorable concert at Weston-super-Mare, when the chair had collapsed under the cellist, and the pianist had also collapsed – in laughter. 'Very undignified,' Sylvester had said.

They had learned a lot in those lean times. Brilliant, gifted students, both of them, cosseted and given awards and appreciated; it had come as a rude shock. It had taught them to woo audiences, to ignore their surroundings, to welcome their listeners, however few; and to please them.

Gabriel smiled at Sylvester, his grey eyes full of humour. 'It was a long time ago, Syl, we are grown-ups now, and still we have to play in cold, wet places.'

'Listen, Gabriel, when we die and go to heaven, they'll put us artists on a damp cloud, you can be sure of that. The fat cats and the critics will get the soft pink fluffy ones, and first go at the nectar, just you wait and see.'

'Quiet, now, I need to be quiet,' said Gabriel. 'Put your jacket on, I hope you remembered a vest, you mustn't get a chill.'

Despite Quinta's forebodings, Phoebe behaved beautifully. She snuggled down in the pew, her feet tucked up beside her, the hawkish gaze which so alarmed her teachers directed intently on the musicians. She applauded rapturously at the end, gave a great sigh and tumbled down into the aisle. 'Food,' she said. 'There's supposed to be food.'

'Not for us,' said Quinta, who had no intention of staying. 'We'll just say thank you to Sylvester, and then it's home to bed for you.'

Phoebe stopped abruptly, sending two old ladies richocheting back into their seats. 'Why? Why can't we stay? Why can't we ever do what other people do? Look, there's Pauline and Gavin; if Gavin can stay, why can't I?'

Simon pounced on her from behind. 'Did you enjoy that, Phoebe?'

Phoebe nodded vehemently. 'Yes, and I would enjoy it more if I could stay for the food, but she won't let me, oh no, we have to go!'

Simon turned to Quinta and urged her to stay, it would be rude to go, he said. Quinta disagreed, Pheobe needed her sleep and besides, she didn't know anyone there.

'We do, we do,' said Phoebe. 'Here's Simon, we know him.

And we know Sylvester, and there's Pauline and Gavin, and,' she added, suddenly catching sight of him, 'there's Alban.'

Alban, hearing his name, turned round. His very expressive eyebrows rose, and, ignoring the protests of the body of people moving towards the church doors, he pushed his way back to where Quinta stood, looking cross and worried.

'What are you doing here?' he asked abruptly. 'You didn't tell me you were coming.'

'I didn't know you were going to be here, if it comes to that,' retorted Quinta.

'I don't have to keep you informed of my every move.'

'And nor do I,' said Quinta.

'Besides, you knew I'd be out, you wrote it on one of your bloody lists.'

'Yes, and I also wrote on the list that Phoebe and I were going out.'

'Well, you'd better go now, take Phoebe back, it's far too late for her to be up.'

'No,' said Quinta furiously. 'Come on, Phoebe, let's go and find this food.' She flashed a wide smile at Simon. 'We'll see you there, Simon.'

Phoebe took her by the hand and dragged her out of the church at top speed, before she could change her mind.

'I've never seen you cross with Alban like that before,' she said as she hauled Quinta across the road. 'Quick, or we'll get very wet, and those people who went out ahead of us will eat up all the best food.'

No, I've never snapped at Alban like that, not ever, thought Quinta as she trudged damply up the drive to Midwinter Hall. Others were driving there, and showers of water flew over her feet and legs from the puddles at the side of the drive.

'Why were you cross with Alban?' Phoebe asked, as they followed a stream of people into the hall. 'Look, a chessboard,' she said with delight, gazing at the black and white chequered floor. People turned round to look at her, and smile at her remark. Phoebe gave them a dark look. 'Nothing to stare at,' she said under her breath.

'It's a good thing,' she went on, returning relentlessly to the thought uppermost in her mind, as she always did. 'Alban walks all over you, that's what Gavin says, and although he usually talks rubbish, I think he's right.'

Quinta flushed. 'You shouldn't discuss me with Gavin,' she said.

'Why not? He tells me things about his mother, far worse than anything I can say about you. I can't say much about you, because you really lead a very boring life,' said Phoebe.

With this final devastating remark, she relinquished her grasp on Quinta's hand and tunnelled her way towards the food.

'Lovely food, Lily.'

Lily accepted Marjorie's congratulations with a quick smile, and looked around for Daphne and Wyn. There they were, cooing at Sylvester, their eyes still raking the room so as not to miss anything. Lily caught Titus's arm as he went by.

'Rescue Sylvester,' she hissed.

'What? Oh, I see, yes, Lily, I will. Do you want me to set the good ladies on to anyone else?'

Lily glanced over to the other side of the room. 'Yes, tell them Sybil Stixwould has something she wants to ask them, they'll be over there in a flash.'

Titus raised an ironic eyebrow, and went obediently on his mission. Lily watched as Daphne and Wyn, now joined by Marjorie, headed for the other side of the room. Titus reappeared at her elbow.

'Done,' he said. 'Any more commands?'

Lily looked at him approvingly, she liked his humorous mouth and his unassailable good nature. Also, he liked women, and that was unusual enough in a man to make him interesting. She told him so, and he laughed.

'It's true, women are much better company than men, not just for the obvious, but for conversation, for a varied view of life, for intelligence. Men are so set in their ways.'

'Still,' went on Lily, 'if what I hear is true, you only like some women; you don't find the conversation of young women, or even women near your own age so interesting.'

'No,' said Titus. 'They aren't interesting at all. They haven't lived, they're too shiny and squeaky clean. I like my women by candlelight, glowing with the patina of age.'

'Get on with you,' said Lily. 'So who is your latest antique? Foreign, so I hear.'

'I don't understand how you know so much, marooned out here in Midwinter,' complained Titus. 'Yes, she is foreign, Austrian, and unfortunately only here on a brief visit; I brought her to Eyot to show her the sights, and now she has to go back to her husband.'

'Then you'll have to find yourself someone new,' said Lily. 'I'll keep an eye open for you. Tell Sylvester, he loves to help.'

Titus laughed. 'Concentrate your mind on the younger ones, Lily. I'm sure Lady Wray is on the lookout for someone suitable for that gangly granddaughter who's staying with her.'

Lily protested at that, Lydia was quite lovely, she said, besides having a lot of character. But Titus said she was too unripe for his taste, she wouldn't be interesting for another twenty years at least.

'Why not?' said a voice at his elbow.

Titus, surprised, looked down. 'Who's this?' he said.

'I'm Phoebe.'

'Quinta's daughter,' said Lily. 'I'm glad you persuaded your mother to stay, Phoebe, she doesn't get out nearly enough.'

'No, we never go anywhere that's fun, except on holiday and museums and things at weekends, and that's not people. I like going where there are people. So why isn't Lydia interesting?' she persisted, fixing her gaze on Titus. 'I think she's very interesting. She's a friend of my mother's. She plays the double-bass.'

'That's something,' admitted Titus. 'I just think people get more and more interesting as they get older.'

'That makes me not interesting at all,' said Phoebe. 'I think that's a silly idea. This is Gavin. He's a pain.'

Gavin, an earnest child about two years older than Phoebe, blushed uncomfortably. 'Phoebe, you don't have to make nasty remarks about me.'

'Why not? You're always criticizing everyone else.'

Lily cackled. 'You tell him, Phoebe.'

Titus intervened, sorry for the boy. 'I know Gavin. You're one of the choristers, aren't you?'

'Yes, sir,' said Gavin. 'You sometimes stand in for one of the lay clerks, don't you? You're a bass.'

'That's right,' said Titus. 'I shall be doing it full time this year, because one of the men is going to America until after Easter.'

'No work for a grown man,' said Lily disapprovingly. 'Dressing up in those robes and prancing about with candles and I don't know what.'

Titus roared. 'You're a dreadful old pagan, Lily, better get the Bishop to do a bell, book and candle job on you.'

Phoebe's eyes widened. 'You mean, she's possessed of an evil spirit, like it says in the Bible about pigs?' She gazed at Lily with admiration.

'Now see what ridiculous ideas you're putting into the child's head,' said Lily. 'Phoebe, and you too, Gavin, come over here, there's a plate of sausage rolls I made for you.'

'Did I hear you talking about the Bishop?' said Simon, materializing at Titus's elbow. He caught sight of Gavin. 'Oy, what are you doing here at this hour? You'll be exhausted tomorrow, yawning all over the choir stalls. Get that mother of yours to take you home.'

'He's all right,' said Phoebe, her mouth full of sausage roll. 'Yummy pastry, this, you should try one, Simon. Gavin doesn't need much sleep, that's what Pauline says. She says it's because he's so intelligent. I like lots of sleep, so I must be very stupid.' She lunged forward and dealt Gavin a swift blow. 'You've had two more than me, Gavin, those are mine, don't be so greedy.'

'A choir debit tomorrow if you yawn in the service, don't say I haven't warned you,' said Simon. He led Titus away. 'Now, let's have the low-down on the new Bishop. Sybil and Wilhelmina are in raptures about him; according to them, he's a true Christian, yet with a good knowledge of the world, kind, gets on with high and low alike, devout, prayerful . . .' He paused and took a good gulp of his wine. 'Such a paragon, it can't be true, and even if it's half true he sounds ghastly.'

'Charismatic,' said Titus laconically. 'So people see in him what they most admire in any man. He's very clever, articulate, and not a man you can know well.'

'How come he's been given a bishopric? He doesn't sound the type.'

Titus shrugged. 'You'd know more about that than I do, I know nothing about the arcane workings of the Church. I thought the really able ones became deans, not bishops, but on the other hand Lennox does look exactly as you would expect a bishop to look. He'll be magnificent in a mitre. Anyway, you'll see for yourself fairly soon. Isn't it all going to happen quite quickly?'

'Mmm, yes,' said Simon. 'He was due to take a sabbatical year from his college, so he's available right away.'

'Does it make any difference to you? Does he have much say in Cathedral affairs?'

'Not on a day-to-day basis, no. The Dean runs the Cathedral, with the Chapter. The Precentor looks after choir matters, as you know. I'm a bit concerned, though, this man was on that recent commission on Church music, got one or two strange ideas . . .' His voice tailed off.

'Tambourines and so forth?' said Titus. 'He didn't used to think like that, not when I knew him, but I would imagine he'd take on any views that he felt were modish and likely to attract attention. Actually, I suspect he's virtually tone-deaf. His wife is the musical one. I'm surprised if he's gone happy-clappy in his musical tastes, though, I would have thought she'd have put a stop to that.'

A posse of women had crept up on them, and Titus jumped as Lady Wray's crystal tones rang in his ear.

'Wife?' she said. 'Are you discussing the new Bishop?'

'No,' said Titus with great presence of mind. 'We're talking about *Here and Now*, the New Zealand soap on TV. Do you watch it, Lady Wray? Simon and I are great fans.'

Lady Wray gave him a disapproving look, and Sybil Stixwould said, 'Rubbish,' in forthright tones.

'You were discussing the new Bishop and his wife. Don't deny it, Simon, you never could lie, look at your face. He was just the same when he was a little boy,' she said disparagingly to Marjorie. 'Like your eldest, some children just look shifty when they tell untruths. Simon's never grown out of it.'

'That must be a handicap in your work in the Cathedral,' said Lady Wray unexpectedly. 'Now, Titus, you know the Bishop and his family well.'

'Knew; I haven't seen any of them for several years. I saw quite a lot of them in Cambridge, but then I went to the States, and then I came here, so we've rather lost touch.'

'I don't suppose he has changed very much,' said Sybil

Stixwould. 'Tell us about him. We are so impressed by what we've heard, but a man's view may be different. He has children, I believe; is he good with young people?'

Titus hesitated, and chose his words carefully. 'Yes, he has children, three older ones, and I heard that they had had another child, after I had gone to America.'

'Four children. So he is a good father?'

'I believe so, there were no tales of bruises, runnings away, visits to the child psychologist . . . Of course, how can one know what goes on in any family?'

'This is not a matter for levity, Titus,' said Lady Wray.

'No, but how can I possibly say? He takes a great interest in young people as far as I remember, always been keen on education, sits as governor on the boards of several schools, very enthusiastic about moral crusades among the young, that kind of thing.'

The women beamed. 'Excellent,' said Sybil Stixwould. 'And his wife, a good church woman?'

Titus looked wildly about him for inspiration. 'Faustina? Yes, I'm sure, an admirable woman, as a wife and mother . . .'

'Faustina?' The women tried the name out. An unusual name; not what you would call a churchy name . . . An unEnglish name.

'Faustina?' repeated Sybil Stixwould. 'An unsuitable name for a bishop's wife, I would have said.'

'People call her Tina,' Titus said helpfully.

They relaxed. Tina. Tina was a small name, an unassertive name. Tina was all right; a little frivolous, but all right.

'Look,' said Titus, 'please excuse me, I have to go in a minute, and I must just have a word with Gabriel . . .'

He fled.

'Rather an abrupt man,' said Marjorie disapprovingly.

'Unmarried,' said Wyn.

They turned on her. 'What has that got to do with it?'

Win went red. 'Nothing, of course, I'm sorry, I spoke without thinking. I just remembered, he is an unmarried man. It has no relevance.'

Titus gratefully seized another glass from the table and went to lurk out of sight. He wanted to laugh. Naturally the Bishop's wife was a good churchwoman, she had to be, but he had suddenly had a vision of Fausty, as he called her, laughing and swapping bawdy stories with the Aspasia Professor of Greek at one of his livelier University parties.

Quinta thought Titus looked better when he laughed; she liked people to laugh. He saw her watching him; a merry face, he thought. Quinta looked as though she smiled a lot. Praiseworthy, for if half of what he had heard was true, she didn't have much to smile about.

'Are you enjoying this?' he said, waving a hand around the crowded room.

'I suppose so,' said Quinta. She fingered the stem of her glass rather nervously, feeling suddenly shy with Titus, who seemed so at ease. Lucky man, to be so sure of himself. 'I'm a bit out of practice, I don't get out such a lot.'

'Waste of time, don't know why Sylvester does this kind of thing,' complained Alban, abandoning a tall, thin, blonde woman who had been talking admiringly to him. 'Where did I leave my mac? Foul evening, bloody weather.' He looked around as though his coat was suddenly going to appear from nowhere. 'That's the difference between a performer and the creative artist, I don't have time for all this kind of thing.'

Quinta stared at him in astonishment. 'I don't believe a word of it, Alban; from what your mother says, you lead a riotous life in London.'

'Not at all, just some gatherings connected with my work. If you do film and television work, you have to mix a bit. But I don't enjoy it.'

Titus winked at Quinta, who looked startled for a moment, and then smiled back at him.

'Anyway, I'm going now, I've got work to do. Quinta, you must get Phoebe home, it's disgraceful her being here at all, and she certainly should be in bed.'

Quinta glared at him as he threaded his way out of the room. Titus looked amused.

'Is he always like that?'

'No,' said Quinta. 'But then, I don't usually see him in company of this sort.'

'You live with him, don't you? Hadn't you better catch him up, or are you going to walk home?'

'I live in his house,' said Quinta with dignity, 'but I don't exactly live with him, I mean, we're not really a couple . . .'

'I don't mean to pry,' said Titus quickly. 'I can give you a lift home if you like.'

'No, I've got transport, thanks,' said Quinta. 'He's right, I must take Phoebe home, she'll be getting above herself. I can't see her . . .'

She looked slightly anxiously around. 'You're tall, can you see her?'

'Over there, with Lady Wray's granddaughter,' said Titus. 'Quite a character, isn't she?'

'Phoebe, or Lydia?' said Quinta.

'Your daughter. I hardly know Lydia.'

'She's an old friend,' said Quinta vaguely. 'Excuse me, I think I'd better go and collect Phoebe.' She gave him a quick, uncertain smile and headed towards Lydia.

Titus watched her go, surprising himself by thinking what a good figure she had; how he hated thin girls, no use at all for a bottom man like him. That was one of the best things about women, proper, grown-up women; they had voluptuous bodies, something to get hold off. Not hard, skinny thighs and bones that made you feel you were likely to be suddenly spiked in unexpected places. His thoughts drifted off to happy memories of warm, generous curves, and dark inviting places.

Quinta bore down on Phoebe, who was holding court to an admiring circle. Sylvester beamed at Quinta. 'Amazing girl, this Phoebe, the things she comes out with.'

'Hm,' said Quinta. 'Come on, Phoebe, time to go.'

'Hello, Quinta,' said Lydia. 'I haven't had a chance to talk to you. Can you give me a lift if you're going?'

Sylvester protested that it was bad enough Quinta going off so early, as though she had to sign in at some girls' boarding house; there was no need for Lydia to go as well. Lydia explained.

'My grandmother keeps on introducing me to people, young men, all ghastly, I wish she didn't think I was hanging out for a husband.'

'Husband?' said Sylvester with interest. 'Who worries about husbands these days? Girls of your age should have a good time, look around, try things out, you don't need a husband yet.'

'Exactly, but you try telling her that.'

Sylvester eyed her appreciatively. 'You must have a boyfriend tucked away somewhere, Lydia, I don't believe you haven't. In Oxford?'

Lydia shook her head ruefully. 'Don't ask, no, there's no-one, and that's the way it's going to stay.'

Phoebe gave Quinta a quick prod. 'I think Pauline is looking for you. I wasn't very nice to Gavin, and I think she perhaps wants to say something to you about it.'

Quinta looked round, alarmed. 'Phoebe, you wretch, I don't know why you have to wind Gavin up all the time. Come on, quick, we must go.'

'Gavin's a pillock,' said Phoebe, and surprised herself and Sylvester by giving a big hug to as much of the cellist as she could get hold of. 'That Beethoven was lovely,' she breathed into his ear. 'It made me feel funny inside.'

Sylvester was delighted. 'Listen, make Quinta bring you out here, in your holidays, or at a weekend, or Lily can fetch you. Then I'll play all kinds of music for you.'

Phoebe gave him her most charming smile, and then nipped smartly away behind Quinta and Lydia, who were making a rapid getaway.

'It's all right,' said Lydia. 'If that dark woman with the firm expression is your friend, she's been buttonholed by a man in a dog collar.'

'Canon Feverfew,' said Phoebe knowledgeably. 'He'll keep her yakking for hours, he never stops talking.'

They were soaking by the time they reached the van, and Phoebe plumped herself down indignantly in her seat in the back. 'Why couldn't we take the van up to the house?' she demanded.

'Because it's very difficult to get it into reverse just at the moment,' said Quinta. 'I don't have to turn it round here, I can just drive round the village memorial and then I'm pointing it in the right direction.'

'It needs mending so that it can go backwards,' observed

Phoebe. 'Why didn't you take it to the garage? It was on a list.'

'I know,' said Quinta. 'My lists haven't been very reliable recently, I'll take it in on Monday.'

'Is the list reliable, rather than you?' asked Lydia with interest. And then, 'Help, mind out, oh, careful, Quinta!'

Quinta had swerved wildly to avoid a huge puddle in the middle of the road, which she suspected of being a deep pothole. The van lurched as she straightened it, and then there was a squeak and two bangs under the bonnet. The engine spluttered and died.

The windscreen wipers squealed backwards and forwards as the three of them sat in the motionless car.

'We've broken down,' said Phoebe helpfully. 'In the rain.'

Lydia looked at Quinta. 'Don't say it,' she advised. 'Child in the back.'

'Is she about to say something really strong?' said Phoebe.

'No,' said Quinta. 'I've said it all in my head.'

'I'd better find a phone,' said Lydia. 'Are you a member of the RAC, AA, anything like that?'

'No,' said Quinta. 'I'd ring the garage, but the nearest phone is miles away, and I expect it's out of order, it usually is.'

'How far are we from a village?'

'Too far to walk in this rain. We're about three miles from Midwinter, and Gossiby's the same distance that way. No, we'll have to sit and wait for someone to come past. Then we can ask them to phone.'

'It'll most likely be someone from the concert supper,' said Phoebe prophetically. 'I hope it isn't Pauline and Gavin.'

It wasn't. 'Such luck, it's that Titus,' said Quinta. She opened her door and slid down on to the road.

Titus stuck his head out of his window. 'Trouble?'

'It went bang,' said Quinta.

'Want me to have a look?' said Titus. He got out and yanked up the bonnet. 'Your alternator belt has gone by the look of it. Was it loose?'

'I don't know,' said Quinta, peering gloomily at the engine. 'Is that the one you can tie up with a stocking?'

'Supposedly.' He glanced down at her legs. Very nice legs, he thought. 'You aren't wearing stockings or tights, are you?'

'No,' said Quinta. 'But I'm getting very wet, and so are you.' She looked over towards Titus's rather elegant car. 'Can we come with you? Are you going to Eyot?'

Titus shook his head. 'No, I was going to see someone, but it can wait.'

'Are you sure?' said Quinta doubtfully. 'I hate to be a nuisance.'

'I don't,' said Lydia briskly, leaning out of the van window. 'Come on, Phoebe, we're getting a lift.'

'Wish we had a car like this,' said Phoebe, settling herself down into the back seat with a sigh of pleasure. 'It goes, I bet it goes always, and it's quiet.'

'Shut up, Phoebe,' said Quinta, laughing despite herself.

'To the Manor House?' inquired Titus.

'Please,' said Phoebe. 'Oh, Lydia, the Close would be better for you, wouldn't it?'

'No,' said Lydia firmly. 'I'm going to keep out of grandmother's way for as long as I can. I'll come with you if that's all right.'

'I don't know if Alban will be back,' said Quinta doubtfully.

'He left before us,' said Phoebe. 'He wasn't in a very good mood, I don't think.'

'In that case,' began Quinta.

'Tough,' said Lydia. 'He was jolly rude to you this evening, Quinta, he doesn't like you going out anywhere, does he? What a dog in the manger, typical. It's all right for him to spend half his time in London making whoopee, but you're not supposed to follow suit.'

Phoebe flared up in Alban's defence. 'He likes us to be there, he hates coming back to an empty house, he always says that.'

'Time he grew up,' said Lydia briskly. 'Doesn't want to come back to an empty house, indeed, at his age! I'm definitely inviting myself, Quinta; I daresay he'd like to have a nice quarrel with you if he's in that kind of mood.'

'Oh, dear, do you think so?' said Quinta. She hated rows and arguments; they brought back memories of her childhood and her endlessly feuding parents. They had argued mostly about her: why is she so difficult, so unlike her sisters; why can't you control her; she must get her temper from *your* side of the family . . .

Alban was indeed already there, pacing up and down the cloisters.

'You're back at last,' he said angrily. And then, as he saw Titus and Lydia following Quinta in, 'What are they doing here?'

Lydia took one look at his furious face, and burst out laughing. Alban glared at her. He's thwarted, thought Lydia. And jealous. Obviously, Quinta wasn't supposed to go off and make merry on her own. Lucky Quinta, arousing that much passion in a man like Alban. Then, looking at Quinta's pale, taut face Lydia felt a surge of anger; it was unforgivable to bully her.

A thought sparked in her mind: if Alban were her lover, she wouldn't let him behave like that. The thought was followed by the realization that she found Alban very attractive and the simultaneous realization that even if things were difficult between him and Quinta, this was one relationship there could be no interfering with. Quinta depended on Alban in a way Lydia never would, but then, she, Lydia, had plenty of money, no child and didn't have to depend on anyone.

She took charge. 'Titus very kindly gave us a lift, because that old van of Quinta's, which is a disgrace, broke down.'

'Couldn't you fix it?' said Alban ungraciously to Quinta.

'Not in the pouring rain, she couldn't,' said Lydia. 'Look, we're all sopping wet. How about offering us a drink? And it wouldn't be a bad idea to light a fire. This summer is a joke.'

'You are astonishingly bossy for one so young,' said Alban furiously.

'No, I'm not,' said Lydia with spirit. 'It's just that, although indolent, I am not a doormat, and nor is Quinta. And I don't like men with commanding ways.'

'Commanding? Me?' Alban was genuinely surprised.

'Aggressive,' went on Lydia.

Alban snorted. 'Not at all,' he said. 'I get annoyed, sometimes, that's all.'

'Yes, whenever you don't get your own way,' said Lydia.

Alban gave her a sceptical look. 'And you, no doubt, never like to get your own way.'

'I usually do get my own way,' said Lydia. 'But I do so with grace and tact.'

'I'll have to take your word for it,' said Alban. 'Meanwhile, I've got work to do.'

He shot a last, angry look in Quinta's direction, and strode away towards his study.

'Appalling manners,' said Lydia.

'I can't think what's got into him,' said Quinta, worried. 'He's not usually as bad as this.'

'Jealousy,' said Titus in a neutral voice. 'No, I pass no judgements, and I certainly don't want to know anything about your situation, but that's what's eating him. Makes sound men do very stupid things, and behave very oddly.'

'That's how Simon looks when he sees you with Alban,' put in Phoebe brightly.

They looked at her in silence. Titus's mouth twitched. 'All very complicated,' he said. 'Well, thank you for the offer of a drink and a fire on Alban's behalf, Lydia, but I won't take you up on it. I'm late already.'

'An assignation?' suggested Quinta.

'Exactly,' he said.

## 7

It was flower day at the Cathedral again, and Marjorie, Daphne and Wyn were taking a break from their labours. It had been a hard-working morning: this Sunday coming, the fourteenth of July, the Cathedral celebrated the day of its founder and benefactor, Guillebert the Half-hearted.

He would have been surprised to find himself remembered with all the panoply of modern Christian liturgy and music, since his life had been far from exemplary. Most of his youth had been spent in the unremitting pursuit of young boys, a habit he only dropped when tempted to offer his hand to the daughter of a local earl, who was as pious as she was rich. He had founded the original church at Eyot in order to curry favour with her; had married her and then promptly expired. A monkish chronicler of the time remarked severely that Guillebert's unfortunate demise was brought about by the exhalations of holiness from his wife's body, the like of which he had never known before.

The three ladies knew nothing of this insalubrious history, and in fact the official guidebook made little mention of it. The Church has never been fussy about where its gifts come from, and Eyot was no exception. To Marjorie, Daphne and Wyn, Guillebert meant only the third tomb along the north choir aisle, where they always had problems with the flowers because of the strong blues in the stained glass window opposite.

They sat in the meagre sun on a bench outside the Cathedral, each with a cup of coffee and a homemade biscuit, watching the world go by with quick, inquisitive interest.

A roar broke the peace as Simon Praetorius shot round the edge of the green on his Harley Davidson and screeched to a halt outside the organist's house. He opened the gate with one hand, and pushed the bike inside.

'He must be very hot in that helmet and all those black clothes,' said Marjorie.

'Leathers,' said Wyn.

The other two looked at her. Wyn did say the most extraordinary things.

'That's what they call those clothes they wear. The black jacket and trousers and so on. They're made of leather.'

'I don't think it's very suitable, the organist wearing black leather,' said Daphne at last.

'He doesn't wear them in the Cathedral,' said Wyn helpfully. 'I mean, he doesn't have them on under his robes. At least, I don't think so.'

'I don't think it's very nice to think about what they have on under their robes,' said Marjorie severely. 'It's hardly for us to know.'

Wyn took another bite of her biscuit. 'There's Canon Feverfew, going across to the school.'

Daphne gave a sniff and looked at her watch. 'Confirmation class. There are five going to be confirmed this time.'

They drank some more of their coffee. 'The Dean's in London today,' offered Daphne. 'I saw him on his way to the station, and then I bumped into Mrs Jonquil, and she mentioned he was going to London, to a meeting.'

'He's a very busy man,' said Marjorie. 'And he'll have extra work with the new Bishop coming.'

They sighed with pleasurable anticipation. There would be plenty to notice and talk about with a new bishop. Of course, the Palace wasn't exactly in the Close, it lay across the river on the other side of the Cathedral, but they had friends inside the Palace, it was easy enough to keep up with the news.

'There goes Lydia Holbeck,' said Wyn.

They all sat up.

'She's got Lady Wray's Pug,' said Daphne. 'There's no point in carrying him if she's supposed to be taking him for a walk.'

They watched her walk with long, easy strides across the grass. 'Can't she read the notices?' whispered Daphne, scandalized.

'She's going to the vet,' said Marjorie suddenly. 'To the surgery in St Polycarp Street.'

'David Jabbe and Fergus Tayle,' said Wyn. 'Does Lady Wray go to them? I thought she went to old Mr Drenche.'

'Yes, but he's retired,' said Marjorie. 'Don't you remember, it was in the paper, he's gone to live in the West Indies.'

'Shows why they charge such a lot,' said Wyn. 'I do believe you're right, though. I hope Pug isn't ill.'

'No, it's his yearly injection,' said Marjorie. 'I heard Lady Wray mention it to the chemist the other day, saying that it was due. The notice about vaccinations reminded her, she said.'

'Has Sybil Stixwould's grandson arrived yet?' asked Daphne.

'Yes,' said Wyn. 'I was talking to Mrs Gridlock yesterday, and she mentioned that he had arrived.'

'Come along,' said Marjorie briskly. 'There's the Angelus ringing. Twelve o'clock; we haven't time to sit and gossip all day here, plenty to do. Shake those crumbs over there, Wyn, and then the birds can have them.'

Lydia sat in the surgery with Pug on her lap, listening to his snuffly breathing. A line of people sat along the wall opposite, looking very much like their animals. At least Pug isn't mine, thought Lydia, at least I don't look like a pug. Nor do I breathe stertorously.

A langorous, fair assistant wandered out. 'Anyone for injections?' she asked in an uninterested voice.

'Yes,' said Lydia, getting up.

The assistant cast a contemptuous eye over Lydia and Pug and went to the desk. She ran an excessively long fingernail, painted in bright pink, down the names. 'Lady Wrag's dog?'

'Lady Wray's dog, yes.'

'Room 9.' She gave a quick flick of her head towards a glass door. Lydia hitched Pug more firmly under one arm and went to find Room 9.

Unfortunately, the dim assistant had already sent an animal to Room 9. A large, fierce black cat, who took one look at Pug, hissed, screeched, arched its back and spat furiously before launching itself at the hapless dog. The cat's owner was there, too, and he rose from his chair with cries of alarm and horror to drag his cat away.

Pug retreated, furious, behind Lydia's back.

'I am so sorry,' the man began.

Goodness, thought Lydia, as she found him towering over her. What an enormous man. Like a Viking.

He was exactly like a Viking, immense, fair and with clear, cold blue eyes. Lydia, despite herself, was impressed. He had a handsome turn of phrase, too, as he apologized profusely, soothing his cat with a huge stroking hand.

'I'll take Pug away,' said Lydia. 'We can wait in the other room.'

The big man was looking at Pug with a faintly puzzled expression on his face. 'I'm sure I know that dog. There aren't many pugs about these days. Isn't it Lady Wray's dog?'

'Yes,' said Lydia. 'Do you know her? She's my grandmother.'

The man laughed; a deep, reassuring laugh. 'Ah, then you're Lydia. How do you do? I'm Adam Stixwould. My grandmother and yours are great cronies.'

Lydia stared at him. She had been so cross when her grandmother had gone on about Sybil's grandson who was coming to Eyot, how well they would get on together, what a fortunate thing. Lydia had, of course, taken an immediate dislike to the unknown grandson; certainly, she had never expected anything like this.

The door flew open and a dark, busy woman, wearing peculiar clogs and wrapped in a large white coat, came in.

'Take that cat out,' she said without preamble. 'It shouldn't be in here. Take it into Room 8, and I'll see to it in a minute. Now, this one's come for its jab, let me see . . .'

Adam gave Lydia a wink and sidled out of the room. 'I'll see you again,' he said. 'Bound to.'

I do hope so, thought Lydia as she walked back to the Close. An interesting man, she could do with a new interest. Not a word from Angus, not that she had expected one. Then of course, there was Alban, who was extremely interesting, but clearly marked 'Off bounds', and 'No trespassing'.

'I know they say all's fair in love and war,' she confided to Pug who looked up at her with dark, bulging eyes, 'but it isn't always so. You can't go smashing up people's lives just for your own gratification. Besides, who's to say he'd look twice at me? I'm probably not his type.'

She deposited Pug in his basket in the kitchen, and wandered upstairs to the sitting room. 'What do you do all day?' Quinta had asked her. 'I don't know,' said Lydia. 'This and that, think, read, potter about . . . you know.'

Quinta didn't know. Her own life had hardly a spare half hour in it, she couldn't imagine the hours of empty leisure which Lydia seemed to be able to pass so pleasantly. In fact, Lydia was beginning to be very bored. It had been agreeable for a while to do nothing, but she felt that life would be better with more purpose. Her grandmother had some ideas, ranging from doing a secretarial course to taking up flower-arranging. Strange, thought Lydia, when her daughter is a doctor, a professional woman, that she should have such old-fashioned ideas about what I could do.

Lydia's mother wrote her brisk letters, suggesting job possibilities, vocational guidance.

'I tried that,' Lydia wrote back. 'Hopeless, they seemed surprised by my answers, suggested I take up bee-keeping or taxidermy, hardly very practical.'

Lydia picked up the *Times* from the table in front of the sofa and idly started to read it. How dull the letters were, she thought. Who wrote to papers, why did people think their views or observations could be of interest to the rest of the world? But perhaps it was good to have convictions, and to feel sure that other people shared them.

Lydia turned to the obituary page, but before she started to read about the life of Tatiana Oblomov, a Russian ballerina who had danced with Diaghalev, her eye was caught by the Court page. Angus Limerick. Angus! A marriage is announced . . . Angus . . . to Selina Chatham, only daughter of . . .

The words blurred on the page; Lydia felt sick. She sat completely still, the paper in her hand, unable to take in what she had read. She knew Selina Chatham. Jamie, Angus's best friend, had taken her to a ball the previous summer. A small, dark girl, with a vivid little face. Charm, lots of charm, and not much else. She and Angus had laughed about it together, why did Jamie always go for nitwits?

She didn't mind, she had got over the whole Angus business, so why did she feel as though someone had dug a knife into her? She got up slowly, laying the paper neatly down on the table. She had to face it, at the back of her mind was the hope – no, the belief – that things weren't really over between her and Angus. After a breathing space, a time apart, he would come back into her life, they would get together again.

Clearly not, Lydia said to herself.

The door creaked, and as though she was in a dream, Lydia turned to look at it. The handle twitched, the door opened slightly, and Mrs Gridlock stomped into the room.

'Oh, I am sorry, I didn't think there was anyone in here. I know Lady Wray's gone out. I've come to do the room out, for the dinner party tonight.' She looked hopefully at Lydia. 'Of course, if it's inconvenient.'

Lydia looked at her with wide, unfocused eyes. 'No, I'm just going out.'

I wonder if she takes drugs, Mrs Gridlock said to herself as she went out to fetch her trug of dusters, polishes and sprays. What a strange look on her face. On the other hand, her voice is quite clear. Was she ill?

Lydia drifted out of the room, with a nod towards Mrs Gridlock. Mrs Gridlock unfolded the newspaper which was tucked under her arm, and placed it neatly on the floor before putting the bucket down. Her eyes flickered round the room, as though the spindly chairs and tables held some clue to Lydia's strange behaviour. She saw *The Times* lying on the sofa where Lydia had been sitting, and she sidled over to have a closer look, one eye on the door in case Lydia should come back.

The Court page, nothing there to alarm anyone. No scandalous headlines; it seemed a very dull paper. Deaths. Had Lydia lost someone? Engagements? She shook her head. She would ask Wyn when she came to do the flowers. Wyn would know if anything in the paper could have upset Lydia like that.

With a movement which was surprisingly neat and quick for so large a woman, Mrs Gridlock swept the paper up and tucked it into the top of her cross-over apron.

\*     \*     \*

'It came to me in a flash,' said Wyn triumphantly as she helped Daphne clear up in the flower room over in the Cathedral. 'One of the young men, well, I suppose it's a young man, because people generally get engaged young rather than older, though of course you do see these announcements that Mrs Somebody has married Mr Thing; probably a divorcee, although perhaps a widow; if I were divorced, I shouldn't announce another marriage in the paper.'

'What about this young man?' demanded Marjorie. 'Which young man?'

'One of the men was Angus, Angus Limerick. Now, I happen to have overheard Lady Wray mention an Angus to Sybil Stixwould. They were talking about Lydia, whether she was involved with any young man, and the name Angus was mentioned.'

'Jilted,' said Daphne, rummaging in her handbag for a hankie before Marjorie commented on her dripping nose. She gave a surreptitious sniff. 'No wonder she was upset. If he was her boyfriend, what a shock to read about his engagement to someone else in the paper, no warning.'

'I think she did have a boyfriend at Oxford, but they weren't seeing each other any more,' said Marjorie. 'So why would it be such a shock?'

'Because Lydia didn't really think it was over,' said Wyn with certainty. 'They had quarrelled, perhaps, but they do that, young people, and then before you know where you are, they're back together again.'

The other two thought it over as they disposed of some foul-smelling pieces of oasis. 'Dreadfully sloppy, these Cathedral School parents,' said Daphne, sniffing again. 'It's a good thing they only do the flowers once a year.'

'Where did Lydia go?' said Marjorie. 'When she left Mrs Gridlock.'

'To her room, to have a good cry?' asked Daphne, hopefully.

Wyn shook her head. 'I went to see, I thought she might like a cup of tea. But there wasn't a sound from her room, and then I heard the front door click, you know the way it does. I looked out of the window, and she was walking towards the old town. Very thoughtful, she didn't look happy at all.'

'Well,' said Marjorie. 'It's all very interesting. I wonder where she was going.'

Lydia herself didn't have any idea where she was going. She just wanted to walk, to think. She felt jolted rather than jilted; the announcement had given her a shock, and had made her realize she had been floating in limbo, attached to an old life which no longer existed. She couldn't idle from day to day for ever; it was time for some new life.

New interests, she said to herself. I must do things, not just exist, from day to day. Why even grandmama, old as the hills, she must be sixty-seven now, does more with her time than I do.

'Do you always talk to yourself?' said a sardonic voice. 'Or may anyone join in the conversation?'

'Hello, Alban,' said Lydia. 'Don't you talk to yourself? Or perhaps you hum, being a composer.'

'Never,' said Alban. 'I hear it all privately, inside my head. There's enough aural pollution without my adding to it.'

'You sound very cross,' said Lydia calmly. She still felt quite numb.

'That's the kind of pointless comment that women make.' He frowned. 'You don't seem your normal forceful self. Lady Wray been at you?'

Lydia shook her head. 'No, just some news that was unexpected, it's made me a bit thoughtful.'

'Something to do with a man, I expect,' said Alban perceptively. 'Usually is, at your age. I hope you're not going to pour your heart out to Quinta, I don't want her made all gloomy. *Are* you going to see Quinta?' he added suspiciously.

Lydia had had no intention of going to see Quinta, but a spirit of mischief rose in her as she glanced at Alban's dark, brooding face.

'Yes, I am, actually. Since today is what passes for a fine day this miserable summer, I thought I would invite her out to have a sandwich by the river.'

'She won't come,' said Alban quickly, falling into step beside Lydia. 'She doesn't take lunch hours, she saves up the time for Phoebe's holidays, when she needs to take extra time off.'

'Perhaps she'll take a little while off for once,' said Lydia. 'I can give her a hand with Phoebe this summer, I haven't got anything else to do. When does term end?'

'Quinta doesn't like being helped,' said Alban.

'She won't mind my helping,' said Lydia, just to annoy. 'We're old friends. Where are you going?'

'To Gustav's shop,' said Alban. 'I asked Quinta to bring me back some manuscript paper from the shop last night, and she forgot. I can't think what's got into her, she's always been so organized. It's going out, meeting people, it's quite wrong for her.'

Lydia was indignant. 'How can it be wrong for her? She's young, only, well, however old she is, I forget; there's got to be more to her life than work and Phoebe and house-keeping.'

'Seems a busy enough life to me,' said Alban. 'It satisfies most women. She's not alone, she has me for company, I don't see where the problem is.'

'You have other friends, you go to London, meet people.'

'That's different.'

'Hmm,' said Lydia. Was he always as unreasonable as this, she wondered, or was he just in a bad mood? Perhaps his work wasn't going too well, she thought charitably, although more likely he was just plain unreasonable and honestly thought Quinta should be satisfied with what she, Lydia, thought must be a very dull life. He wouldn't get away with all this if I lived with him, she said to herself. Not for a moment. Quinta's far too indulgent with him.

Quinta laughed at Alban for being so cross about the paper. 'I'm sorry, I must have written it on the wrong list,' she said cheerfully.

'It's most inconvenient,' said Alban crossly. 'I've had to interrupt my work to come here to fetch it.'

'Unless you've been working at a Handelian speed, you had enough to last you for several more days,' said Quinta.

'That's hardly the point,' said Alban.

Lydia had had enough of Alban's complaints.

'Quinta,' she said, changing the subject without apology, 'did you make this violin, this one with the lovely scroll? Look, Alban, a wicked little face on it.'

'I know,' said Alban, without looking at it. 'Now, look, Quinta . . .'

Lydia went on remorselessly. 'Did you, Quinta?'

Quinta nodded. Alban was starting to make her feel uncomfortable; he was being so difficult just recently, not the easy companion she was used to. Phoebe had noticed it, too.

'He wants you to stay at home, like his mother did until his father died. She took off quickly then, though, didn't she?' she had said, wise beyond her years.

Quinta had told her not to be silly and rude, but the thought alarmed her. His mother, perhaps she could ring his mother and have a chat with her. Lucy Praetorius had always been so kind to her.

She jerked her attention back to what Lydia was saying '. . . with a funny scroll like this one; only not perhaps a human face.'

'What?' said Quinta.

'Listen, Quinta,' said Lydia patiently. 'This is work for you. Could you make me a double-bass, or perhaps a bass viol, with a decorative scroll?'

Alban snorted. 'No, she couldn't. She won't make any instruments, she hasn't got time for one thing, and she's forgotten how, for another. She only does repairs.'

Quinta flared into a startling temper, the quick rage that went with her red hair and which she kept so carefully under control.

Her voice was cold and high as she glared at Alban. 'How would you feel if someone said to you, oh no, you couldn't write a symphony, you hadn't got time, and you'd forgotten how?'

That was hitting below the belt. Alban had been talking about a symphony for some considerable time. His standing and success as a composer made it a reasonable plan, he would be able to get it performed; but it had never come off, it remained an idea.

He flushed. 'Thank you, Quinta. If you think the cases are the same, there's no point in saying anything. I won't be in tonight, I'm going to London. I don't know when I'll be back.'

Quinta looked conscience-stricken as he went out, shutting the door behind him with deliberate care.

'It's Thursday, too,' she said to herself. 'Damn.'

'Do you look forward to your Thursdays?' asked Lydia. 'And your Tuesdays, of course.'

Quinta sighed. No, she didn't, not really. 'Not much,' she said rather dismally.

'Angus, my ex, has just got engaged,' said Lydia casually, her finger tracing the foxy features of the face on the violin scroll.

'And you mind,' said Quinta, looking with sympathy at Lydia's expressionless face.

'I find I do,' said Lydia. 'I wouldn't have expected to. We were together some time.'

'How did you split up?' asked Quinta. And then, when she heard about the Yours, Angus letter, she wrinkled her nose contemptuously. 'You don't think so now, but you're better off without him.'

'Easy to say.'

'Were you in love with him?'

'I thought I was. I found him very attractive, he had a vigorous mind as well as vigorous everything else. Big willie, he had a very big willie. He was known for it, probably used to wave it around at those ghastly boat evenings. Probably shared it with all sorts of other people. This girl he's got engaged to, he must have been seeing her for some time. What a skunk.'

'That's better,' said Quinta.

'Don't you mind?' Lydia asked curiously. 'Not having a proper, oh, love life, sex life, whatever you want to call it? I mean, if you don't really mind whether you go to bed with Alban or not, it's obviously not a grand passion.'

'No, not a grand passion,' said Quinta. 'Perhaps they don't happen very often.'

'Was it a grand passion with Quinta's father?'

Quinta looked out of the window, across the roofs to the spires and towers of the Cathedral. Oh, yes, that was different. That had been overwhelming, all-devouring. Love? Passion? Lust? Obsession? All of that. For her, at least. For him? Quinta couldn't believe it could have been less for him.

'Men of that age can fall in love with young girls,' said Lydia doubtfully. 'But a relationship like that is, well, different, isn't it? Secret, unlawful, unapproved by society at the very least.' She cast her mind over the much older men she knew. 'I wouldn't have wanted to go to bed with any of them when I was fourteen. I had a crush on the art master, mind you. But he was twenty-seven, it's a bit different. And, of course, it never came to anything. Did he go for young girls generally? Or were you a one-off?'

Lydia was opening up a Pandora's box, thought Quinta with alarm. She didn't want to analyse it, look at it in those terms. It was the one perfect love, and, she felt sure, the only one she would ever have. Lydia would soon get over Angus, find a new boyfriend, marry in due course . . . All quite normal. Whereas Quinta would never have that. She felt affection, great affection, for Alban. Love, of the most intense kind, for Phoebe. And that was her lot.

'His wife was quite a bit younger than he was,' she said in a neutral voice. 'I didn't know about her at the time, but I overheard some people talking about him. They envied him, I think.'

'What a bum,' said Lydia. 'I hope he pays for it in the end.'

'Oh, no,' said Quinta quickly. 'I was so angry with him at first . . . bewildered, I suppose. But I can understand the way he behaved, and I would hate anything bad to happen to him. He's the kind of person who was bound to be very successful.'

'What was he? What was his profession, job? Was he a teacher?'

'He was in the Church.'

Lydia stared at Quinta in astonishment. 'You can't be serious? Honestly, the hypocrisy . . .'

'Being ordained doesn't stop you falling desperately in love,' said Quinta.

'No, but it should help you to be able to tie a knot in your willie to keep it away from young girls!'

She wouldn't understand, thought Quinta ruefully. She would have had to have known him to understand.

'Have you ever seen him since?' asked Lydia. 'What was he called?'

'A very ordinary name,' said Quinta. 'Jon. It didn't seem ordinary to me, though.'

'Men,' said Lydia.

'Where?' said Sam hopefully, as he came into the workshop.

'Alban Praetorius went off in a very nasty temper. You'd better be careful, Quinta, don't want to bite the hand that feeds you.'

'Shut up, Sam.'

'I was just thinking how loathsome men are,' said Lydia to Sam.

'Not all men, some of us are super,' said Sam. 'Now what have you been saying to get Quinta upset? It takes a lot to take the merriment out of her face, and just look at her. Cheer up, ducks, it'll all be the same in a hundred years.'

Lydia felt guilty. Misery was infectious; she had brought her own gloomy thoughts and feelings here, and made Quinta depressed as well.

'I want Quinta to make me a double-bass,' she said to Sam. 'What do you think?'

'Marvellous,' said Sam instantly. 'Exactly what she needs, a new purpose in life. Wonderful, a double-bass, Quinta, aren't you pleased?' He turned to Lydia. 'Have you discussed money? You mustn't expect her to do it on the cheap for you, just because you're a friend.'

'Don't be silly,' said Quinta, embarrassed. 'Of course I won't charge Lydia anything more than the cost of materials – if I do it at all; I'm not sure that I can.'

'Ten minutes ago you were telling Alban you could,' said Lydia.

Quinta grinned, looking more like her usual self. She dragged a hand through her curls. 'That was to annoy him, I was so cross.'

'You'll have to do it if you told Alban you were going to,' said Sam. 'Otherwise he'll despise you, and trample all over you more than he does already.'

'He doesn't trample,' said Quinta indignantly. 'He's normally the kindest, nicest man, and I'm extremely fond of him, and I can't think what's got into him.'

'I'll arrange it all,' said Sam. 'On a proper commercial basis, Quinta. Lydia, where are you getting the money from? Are you taking out a bank loan? Has a premium bond come up? Or are you planning to sell your present instrument?'

Lydia laughed. 'No, I like the bass I've got now. But I want a baroque one, I want to play more old music. And I want a beautiful one, with a decorative scroll.'

'A face?' said Sam.

Lydia looked thoughtful.

'No,' said Quinta. 'Not a human face, anyhow. It's too big, it would be a grotesque, and I don't think that would be right for Lydia. If you're serious, Lydia, I'll do some drawings.'

'Right,' said Lydia. 'And I'll fix up the money side with Sam. There's no problem, Sam, I know how much good basses cost, and I've got the money.'

Sam raised his eyebrows. 'Lucky old you!'

Quinta protested again, but the other two overruled her. 'If you can use some of the wood here, then I'll come to an arrangement with Gustav,' said Sam. 'I know how much he paid for it all, so I won't let him charge anything extortionate. Then you'll pay him a commission, of course, because you'll use his workshop, and do some of it in his time.'

'Oh, dear,' said Quinta. 'It's all very complicated. The holidays are coming up, and I don't know if . . .'

'The summer is always quiet in the shop on the workshop side,' Sam pointed out. 'And I don't suppose Lydia's in any hurry.'

'Of course not,' said Lydia. 'A beautiful fingerboard, too, Quinta; no, I'm not in any hurry, but I long to have it.'

'You'll need a bow, as well,' said Sam. His beautiful face and graceful ways hid a very sharp business mind, as Gustav knew and appreciated.

'I couldn't make a bow,' said Quinta. 'I'm not an archetier.'

'We can arrange for you to try several baroque bows when the time comes,' said Sam.

'Yes,' said Lydia. And then, 'Quinta, why are you giggling?' It was so infectious that she and Sam both started to laugh, too, without knowing why.

'It was looking across at the Cathedral gave me the idea,' said Quinta. 'Look.'

She passed over the scrap of paper that she had been drawing on; there was a pattern for a scroll, with a bishop's head, complete with mitre. Only a few lines, but she had brought the face to life, the face of a worldly, glinty bishop.

'That's a gem,' said Sam, laughing harder than ever. 'Who is it? The new Bishop?'

'I have no idea who the new Bishop is,' said Quinta. 'This is just out of my head, a type of a bishop.' She took the paper back and held it at arm's length to look at it. 'He's good, isn't he? Perhaps I should give it to Harry, down at the stoneyard, to carve in stone so that he can loom over the congregation. But it won't do for you, Lydia, you couldn't play good music with that peering over your shoulder.'

'No,' agreed Lydia. 'He's neither baroque nor jazzy. Keep it, though, Quinta, it's too good to throw away.'

'I'll pin him on the board,' said Quinta. 'Next to my lists.'

# 8

'Aren't you going to change?'

Lydia looked down at herself, puzzled. 'Is there a stain on my shirt or something?'

'We have people coming to dinner tonight,' said Lady Wray. 'Really, Lydia, you are so vague; surely you remember.'

Lydia didn't. What an appalling way to spend the evening, she thought, as she obediently got to her feet. Grandmama's cronies, all at least ninety, all full of interrogation marks, all asking me what I'm going to do with my life. I wish I knew, she said to the mirror, as she pulled a dress over her head.

Whatever it is, it's going to be something that means I can wear outrageous clothes without upsetting anyone, she decided. All her clothes were dull. Suitable. She would go out tomorrow and buy some new clothes: flamboyant, wild clothes. The sort of clothes, she thought grimly, which would worry Angus. The sort of clothes that an ambassador's wife could never wear. For he's sure to end up at the top of the pile, he'll work his way up to the top of the mole hill, and sit there, sleek and pompous and complacent, until he retires.

Tears prickled at the back of her eyes, but she ignored them. She sighed, looked longingly at her bed, how wonderful to spend the evening lolling, not to have to talk to anyone, not to have to eat slops and make polite conversation.

Lydia had maligned her grandmother. The food and the company were much better than she had expected. Her grandmother had put aside her fishy ways; when men were present, especially young men, the food must be more substantial. And the guests included Sylvester, whom Lydia had taken a great liking to, and Adam Stixwould.

'My grandson tells me he's met you,' said Sybil Stixwould, her sharp eyes running over them. 'At the vet's.'

'Yes,' said Lydia. And then, to Adam: 'Is your cat all right?'

'The cat is fine. It's always the same when I bring him here, he has to reassert his territorial rights, so of course he gets into terrible fights with neighbouring cats.'

'I don't know why you've brought him,' said his grandmother. 'You'll be away a lot; who is going to look after him?'

'I'll find someone,' said Adam. 'Let me get you a drink, Lady Wray has put me in charge.'

'Thank you,' said Lydia.

'If you're giving her a gin,' came Lady Wray's authoritative voice, 'make it very weak, lots of tonic. It isn't a suitable drink for a young girl.'

Adam gave Lydia a questioning look, and winked at her. He busied himself with the drinks tray, standing in Lady Wray's way so that she couldn't see the refreshingly strong drink he poured for Lydia.

'Thank you,' said Lydia.

'You've just come down from Oxford, haven't you?' said Adam. 'Had an abstemious three years there, I expect.'

Lydia laughed and Sylvester raised an eyebrow at her. 'Which college were you at?' he inquired.

'St Frideswyde's.'

'Did you come across Cleo Byng?'

'Yes, her room was just along from mine. She wasn't reading history, and was out a good deal, so I didn't get to know her very well.'

Sylvester roared. 'I bet she was out a lot, wild as they come, Cleo. Good thing it's all single-sex colleges at Oxford and Cambridge, none of this mixed halls of residence business that they're starting at the new universities, is there?'

'No, unfortunately.'

'It's not unfortunate at all,' said Sybil Stixwould sharply. 'It's quite inappropriate, young men and women at such a very susceptible age living at close quarters.'

'Yes, but the men's colleges are much classier than the women's colleges, which are all like boarding schools.'

'Which men's college would you like to have gone to?' asked Adam.

'Christ Church,' said Lydia.

Her grandmother tut-tutted. 'That won't happen in my life-time, thank goodness,' she said. 'I don't know why you chose to go to Oxford anyway, Lydia, the Mountjoys have always gone to Cambridge.'

'Good reason for going somewhere else, I would have thought,' said Adam, bestowing a cool smile on Lady Wray. 'Christ Church was my college; I think it would be improved by having women in residence. They'd have to smarten up the bathrooms and lavatories for a start; dire, most of them.'

Sybil Stixwould frowned at the turn the conversation was taking. Lavatories in the drawing room, what was Adam think-ing of?

'Adam was a don at Christ Church,' she explained to the assembled company, lest anyone should take him for a very overgrown undergraduate. 'But now he's at Cambridge.'

'I'm sorry I never met you,' said Lydia frankly. 'You're fairly noticeable, aren't you, and I had a lot of friends at the House. I don't remember ever seeing you there.'

'I spend a lot of time away,' said Adam. 'In Italy.'

'Is that your field?' asked Lydia. 'Italian? History of art?'

'No,' said Adam. 'I'm an archaeologist. Roman trade is my particular field.'

'That's why Adam is here now,' said Sybil Stixwould. 'He's involved in a dig near here.'

'Fascinating,' said Lady Wray. 'You must tell us all about it at dinner, Adam.'

Adam followed Sylvester into the dining room. 'Should I tell Lady Wray that I know a lot about Roman latrines as well?'

Sylvester beamed at him. This big, cold-looking young man had a sense of humour after all. 'Better not,' he said. 'Remember hints for dinner parties, no teeth, death, feet or religion. I think you could add latrines.'

'Mmm,' said Adam. 'Mention pigs, then, and we can listen

to my grandmother talking about the trouble her best sow had with her most recent litter.'

Lydia giggled.

'Not pigs, if you please,' said Sylvester. 'I'm very tolerant, but Sybil's pigs are too much.'

'That leaves sex and the weather,' said Adam, waiting to push Lydia's chair in.

'Grace,' she hissed.

Canon Feverfew gave a placatory smile and quickly chanted a grace. The chairs scraped back as they sat down.

'They won't talk about religion,' Lydia whispered into Sylvester's ear, 'but I bet they'll discuss the new Bishop.'

'Roman loos are much more interesting,' said Adam on her other side.

'Anything is more interesting than a bishop,' added Sylvester, who was notoriously anti-episcopal. 'Glum lot. I went to the House of Lords the other day, oh dear, they were dreary. Give me a good dean any day. I meet quite a lot of deans in my line of business, quite sound, many of them.'

Lydia talked of this and that to Adam, he was very easy to get on with. Wonder what he'd be like in bed, she found herself thinking as she ate the last few mouthfuls of a very good iced pudding.

'You eat your pudding lasciviously, Lydia,' said Sylvester. 'What are you thinking about, or shouldn't one ask?'

Lydia blushed, and she felt Canon Feverfew's eye resting on her as he tore his attention away for a moment from the pudding.

'I think there should be a fund for hungry clergy,' said Lydia, changing the subject. 'Look at him, that must be his third helping.'

'Sssh, he'll hear you,' said Adam. 'And don't change the subject, Sylvester and I both want to know about your lascivious thoughts.'

'Iced pudding lust,' said Lydia briefly. 'That's all.'

Adam gave her a quizzical look, but said nothing more. Sylvester laughed as he wiped his napkin generously across his mouth. 'She's right, that was excellent, Lily will be so annoyed when she hears about it.'

'Why?' said Lydia. 'Is she a jealous cook?'

'No, she's a very good cook, no need to be jealous of anyone else's cooking. But she watches my figure, tries to keep me in trim.' Sylvester looked down happily at his large girth. 'Good thing, really. This is quite slim for me, believe it or not. I don't know what size I'd be if Lily didn't keep an eye on me.'

As they settled down to coffee in the sitting room, Sybil Stixwould drew Sylvester away to talk music, and left Lydia with Adam.

'Tell me about this dig,' said Lydia.

'Are you really interested?' he asked. 'Or are you simply showing a polite interest in what I do in order to please me, as well-bred girls are taught to do?'

'I'm too lazy to bother with talking about things that don't interest me,' said Lydia. 'Where are you going to dig? Do you realize that it's rained all summer, and all your helpers will get trench-foot in the mud?'

He pulled a face. 'Yes, if it goes on like this it's going to be hard work. That's why we're doing the dig, in fact; it's an emergency excavation. It's on the coast, there's a lot of erosion, and with the weather this summer there's a danger the whole site may slip into the sea. That's why I'm here, I'm the only one free, most archaeologists are booked up for the summer years in advance. My archaeology is more of a desk job, so my professor asked me to come and take charge up here. He knows I've got a house in Eyot, so it isn't much of a problem for me.'

'Have you got a house?' said Lydia. 'Where?'

'Jasmine Terrace, just off St Polycarp Street.'

'Right in the centre; what a pity you don't live in it much.'

'No, I usually rent it out, but the students who've had it this year have left. I'll find new tenants in the autumn. Where do you live? In London?'

'My mother does, although she's abroad at the moment, and the decorators are in. That's why I'm staying with my grandmother. She doesn't approve of me being in the house in London on my own with all those strong young men coming and going.'

'Are you enjoying Eyot?'

Lydia thought for a moment before she answered. 'It's very

restful, after Oxford. And I've met an old friend from my schooldays.'

'Do you work?'

Lydia shook her head. 'No, I'll have to in the autumn, but I'm on holiday at the moment.'

'What did you read?'

'History,' said Lydia.

'Modern or ancient?'

'Ancient.'

'Why don't you come and give a hand on the dig, then?' said Adam.

Lydia sat up abruptly. 'Do you mean it?'

'Why not? We need volunteers. I can't pay you, but . . .'

'I don't need money,' said Lydia. 'But it would be something to do.'

And I'd get to see a lot of you, she thought to herself. 'Are you going to be there most of the time, or will you be flying backwards and forwards to Cambridge?'

'No, I shan't go back to Cambridge until just before the end of the vac.'

Good, thought Lydia. 'Where are your volunteers staying? In Eyot, and going out every day?'

'No, it's too far. I've fixed up some rooms near by and there's a youth hostel we can use for some people.'

'You don't want to stay in a youth hostel,' said Sylvester as he joined them again. 'Ghastly places. People snore all night, like being back at boarding school.'

'Have you ever stayed in one?' Lydia asked curiously. She couldn't visualize this large, urbane, distinguished cellist in a youth hostel.

'Of course I have, of course I have. When I was at school, and when I was a student. How I loathed it. Spartan surroundings, and invariably very strange people in charge, who would throw you out in the morning whatever the weather. And in the north, they're worse – damp, you know. Fatal for musicians.'

Lady Wray had been listening. 'Youth hostel? What are you planning, Lydia?'

Lydia explained. Adam didn't say a word, he simply sat, with his long legs stretched out in front of him, gazing into the middle distance.

Lady Wray was torn. She wanted Lydia to get on with Adam, and clearly, this would mean their spending a lot of time together. At the same time, she would rather have Lydia here, under her eye.

'We can arrange a c⸱ for you, perhaps, Lydia,' she said. 'Then you can stay here and drive over every day.'

'I can't drive,' said Lydia. 'At least, I can drive, but I haven't got a licence.'

Sybil Stixwould was shocked. 'My dear, you don't mean you've lost your licence? At your age?'

'No, I never had one. I know how to drive, but I couldn't have a car in Oxford, and if I had one in London for the vacs, what would I have done with it in term time?' She smiled at Adam. 'It won't matter, will it?'

'No, there'll be plenty of people who can drive.'

'That's all right, then. I'll stay in the youth hostel, or rooms, grandmama. It won't do me any harm, and you can have your house to yourself again.'

'I like having you here,' said her grandmother.

Lydia felt ungrateful, but she wasn't going to give in, it would be a relief to be away for a while. Creature comforts were all very well, but it was hard having to be on her best behaviour all the time.

Canon Feverfew helped himself to another chocolate and came over to engage Adam in earnest conversation about Roman Britain. He taught some junior classics classes at the Cathedral School, and prided himself on his knowledge of local history. Adam regarded Roman Britain as a bleak outpost of the Roman Empire, interesting for its tin and lead trade, but not for its tribes, walls or local uprisings. He listened politely, watching Lydia and Sylvester out of the corner of his eye; she seemed a very restful person, with her sleepy eyes and languid body. He glanced across at Lady Wray; surprising that so vigorous and determined a woman should have such a granddaughter.

Wiser Sylvester also appreciated the calm and restfulness of Lydia's aura, but he had noticed the far from weak mouth and chin. He would be prepared to bet that she would prove to be every bit as formidable as her grandmother in her own way.

They were talking about Quinta. 'Yes, a baroque bass with a decorated fingerboard, and, best of all, a decorative scroll – like the one on the violin in her workshop; have you seen it?'

'Yes, of course,' said Sylvester. 'Are you having a face on your bass?'

'Probably not. Quinta's working on some ideas. She drew a lovely bishop's head.'

Sylvester looked alarmed. 'Not a good idea, very bad joss to have a bishop leering at you. Go for something more pleasant, a little devil, perhaps, or a fine woman's head.'

'Like on the prow of an old ship, you mean?' said Lydia with interest.

'A goddess,' said Adam, who had managed to escape from Canon Feverfew's clutches. 'Diana the huntress would be a good one.'

'You need something more solid for a bass,' said Lydia. She had been compared to Diana before, and certainly she had the long-limbed, clean-cut look of so many representations of the goddess. The men who admired her for those looks, though, were usually disconcerted to find that she was not in the least sporty, and much enjoyed the pleasures of the flesh.

Sylvester expressed his delight at the news of her new double-bass, loudly and vigorously, drawing the attention of the others.

'Excellent thing for Quinta. I sense an artist there, she will probably be much happier if she begins to make beautiful instruments. I hope you are going to pay her a proper price for it; never impose on friends.'

'Of course not,' said Lydia indignantly. 'Why does everyone ask that? Do I have a dishonest face? Do I look like a person who would cheat on her friends?'

Sylvester gave his deep, rumbling laugh, and Adam thought that she looked even more attractive with the slight flush which her indignation had brought to her face.

'I don't approve of the double-bass,' said Lady Wray. 'I don't know why you play it, Lydia, it's an unsuitable instrument for a young girl to play, most unfeminine and highly impractical. Why did you choose it?'

'It chose me,' said Lydia. 'The cello was such hard work, so the director of music at school suggested I try the double-bass. I like it, it has such a lovely deep sound. And no effort at all to get into orchestras, they're always desperate for double-basses.'

'More laziness,' said Lady Wray disapprovingly.

'Do tell,' said Wyn eagerly. 'Who was there?'

Marjorie snipped busily, reducing the abundant greenery to a seemly shape. 'I don't know why things grow so wild,' she said. 'I spend a lot of time trimming and pruning in my garden, but just take your eyes or secateurs off it for a day, and it burgeons in a very unruly way.'

'Like in the jungle,' suggested Wyn.

'My garden is not like a jungle.' Marjorie was affronted.

'No, no, I'm sure Wyn didn't mean that,' said Daphne hastily. It was so important for them to work together harmoniously, to work as a team. There was no denying Wyn did often annoy Marjorie, you never quite knew what she was going to come out with.

Wyn hadn't noticed Marjorie's huffy remark. Her mind was thousands of miles away, and long ago, when she had been a little girl standing in an Indian garden drenched in sunlight after the weeks of monsoon, looking at the plants which had all burst their neat beds and spread with rampant energy upwards and outwards and all over the place. 'I am sure,' her mother had said, 'that if you planted an umbrella at the end of May, you would have an umbrella tree by August.'

'I never heard of an umbrella tree,' said Marjorie sharply. 'An umbrella plant, yes, of course, but there's no such thing as an umbrella tree.'

'No,' said Wyn, 'except in the imagination.'

Marjorie snorted. 'You shouldn't be thinking about the imagination at your age, Wyn. You should have grown out of all that kind of thing by now.'

Daphne intervened again. 'You said you bumped into Mrs Gridlock this morning.'

Marjorie relented, she was longing to impart her items of gossip; really, you just had to take Wyn as you found her. Basically she was sound, there was no question of that.

'Yes, I was walking Petal, my basset, you know, and Mrs Gridlock was taking her granddaughter to school. She's a dear little girl. Well, we knew Lady Wray was having some friends for dinner last night. Sylvester Tate, Canon Feverfew . . .'

'Sybil Stixwould?' asked Daphne eagerly.

Marjorie ignored the interruption '. . . her granddaughter, naturally, and, not only Sybil Stixwould, but her grandson Adam, as well.'

The three of them turned this over in their minds. 'It's the first time they've met,' went on Marjorie.

Wyn gave a little cough. 'No,' she said.

The other two stared at her.

'What do you mean, no?' said Marjorie.

'It wasn't the first time they've met.' Wyn lowered her voice and glanced around the vast emptiness of the Cathedral as though scores of people were listening. At half past eight in the morning, the only eavesdroppers were the statues of the kings of England on the choir screen, and they weren't all that interested.

'They met at the vet's. When Lydia took Lady Wray's Pug.'

Marjorie breathed out heavily, and Daphne gave a satisfied sniff. 'Quite romantic, meeting at the vet's.'

'Don't be silly,' said Marjorie. 'You haven't got an animal, you never go to the vet, what do you imagine it's like there? How do you know this, Wyn?'

'My sources are good,' said Wyn mysteriously. 'One of the assistants there, I fear not altogether a very nice girl, is going out with my neighbour's nephew. She told my neighbour that there had been a really funny mix-up at work, that the other assistant had sent a young woman with a pug dog into a consultation room where there was a young man with a cat. The cat and dog fought, and there was, she said, ever such a to-do.'

'How do you know it was Adam Stixwould?'

'The girl told my neighbour that the man with the cat was ever such a lovely man, really fanciable . . .'

Marjorie and Daphne winced.

'. . . very tall, fair, with piercing blue eyes that looked right through you.'

'Adam Stixwould has a big black cat,' said Marjorie thought-fully. 'I've heard his grandmother complain about it, she thinks it a strange pet for a man like Adam.'

'A dog would be more suitable,' said Daphne. 'More manly, somehow.'

'Perhaps he finds a cat more convenient,' said Wyn, who liked cats. 'Easier to leave if he's out and about a lot. Dogs can be rather a tie.'

'I think we can take it that they did meet, then,' said Marjorie, summing up the meeting. 'I wonder if they introduced them-selves, or if they were surprised to meet again at Lady Wray's.'

'I wonder how they got on?' said Daphne.

'We could pump Canon Feverfew,' said Wyn.

Marjorie and Daphne turned disapproving eyes on her. 'Pump?' said Marjorie. 'I hope our interest in our fellow beings, and our wishes for their happiness, aren't to be considered in that light.'

'No, of course not,' said Wyn. 'Just joking.'

Marjorie and Daphne saw no place for joking about such serious matters.

'We had better get on, dear,' Marjorie said to Wyn. 'Daphne can start at the altar, and you do the choir screen ones again today, you have a real way with them.'

'Thank you,' said Wyn, gratified.

## 9

Quinta wasn't having an easy time with Alban. He was spending more and more days in London, and was gloomy and oppressive when he returned to Eyot.

'I suppose you'll be going on holiday soon,' he said glumly. 'With Phoebe. To some ghastly place that no civilized person would be seen dead in.'

'I choose places which Phoebe will enjoy, and which I can afford,' said Quinta equably.

'Come to Spain with me,' said Alban. 'In September. I have to go to Madrid, and then I'm planning to spend some time in Andalusia. I'm writing a guitar concerto; no, I haven't told you about it, you don't seem very interested in what I'm doing these days.'

Quinta felt guilty. It was true, she had been busy at work and she had all the usual practical difficulties of looking after Phoebe once her school had broken up. Most of all, she had begun work on Lydia's double-bass, and was rediscovering the intense pleasure of making something all her own.

'I'd love to go to Spain, Alban,' she said with a sigh. 'Anyone would.'

'I don't want to go to Spain with anyone,' said Alban crossly. 'I want to go to Spain with you.'

'I can't,' said Quinta. 'You know I can't. It's the start of a new school year, and Phoebe mustn't miss any school, you know how behind she is.'

'I didn't mean for Phoebe to come,' said Alban. 'She could stay with Louise. Just you and me. Two adults. Have you ever been to Spain? No, I know you haven't. I want to show you the Alhambra, and the plains, and Seville, and hill villages. I want you to enjoy the heat, the space, the wonderful colours, the sounds, the tastes. Delicious tapas, and then dinner outside at midnight . . .'

Quinta gazed out of the window, the courtyard barely visible through the rain which trickled dismally down the mullioned panes. What bliss it sounded.

'Think about it,' said Alban, crossly.

'Think about what?' said Phoebe, sidling into the kitchen clutching several books and a long-suffering cat.

'We were just talking about holidays,' said Quinta quickly.

'Oh?' said Phoebe. 'Can we go to the Caribbean?'

Alban let out a crack of rather malicious laughter.

'Phoebe, what are you thinking of?' said Quinta. 'Whatever put such an idea into your head? Of course we can't go to the Caribbean!'

'Louise is going. Her father's got a house there, and she's going there for the summer. Her mum's going to Italy with a friend. Her mum's got a lot of friends,' she went on, looking reproachfully at Quinta. 'Unlike some other people's mothers. This friend is a man, and she's very twiny with him, so they're going off to Italy together.'

Quinta couldn't help laughing. 'Twiny!' she said. 'Really, Phoebe, what do you mean?'

'They're always wrapped up together, you know.'

'Oh,' said Quinta.

'So why can't we go to the Caribbean?' asked Phoebe, sitting on the pew bench beside Alban and giving him a friendly shove. 'Move up, it's me and Madrigal here, two people need more room than one.'

Madrigal was the cat, who glared at Alban and moved on to his lap, just to annoy him.

'This cat's made of granite,' grumbled Alban. 'What do you give him to eat? He's going to cut off my circulation sitting here.'

'He's just a big cat,' said Quinta. She saw Phoebe opening her mouth to persist with the Caribbean theme, and knew she wasn't going to let the subject drop.

'It's quite different for Louise,' she said firmly. 'Naturally, if her father is there, she can go.'

'Well, where's my father?' demanded Phoebe. 'For all I know he might be in the Caribbean, too, or even . . .' she added, her face brightening 'somewhere more interesting, like the South Pole.'

'Your father is not at the South Pole,' said Quinta.

'Then where is he?'

'I don't know.' Quinta looked helplessly towards Alban, but he wasn't going to give her any help.

'Then he could easily be at the South Pole.'

Quinta did what she very rarely did, and lost her temper.

'Phoebe, that is enough. I don't want to talk about your father, he passed out of both our lives before you were born, and we certainly won't see him again. I am fixing up for us to go to a youth hostel, at Yntrig, which is not far from here, and is near the sea. I'm sorry if you two don't like my holiday plans, but that's the way it is.'

Alban and Phoebe sat silently as Quinta clashed dishes into the sink.

'I am now going to be late for work. Phoebe, get your things, you're going to Mrs Maddox this morning, and then Louise's mum will pick you up after lunch.'

'I hate Mrs Maddox,' said Phoebe rebelliously.

Alban came out of his cloud of self-absorption for long enough to see the tears starting in Quinta's eyes, and took pity on her.

'Grrr!' he said to Phoebe. 'I'm a large bear who will eat you if you aren't ready in five minutes. I'll take you to Mrs M, so you're in luck today.'

'You look tired,' Sam said when she finally arrived at the shop.

'I'm sorry I'm late,' said Quinta breathlessly. 'Bit of a domestic crisis.'

'I'm here, there's nothing for us to do, what does it matter if you're a few minutes late?' said Sam in his practical way. 'Don't go upstairs yet, get your breath back, I've just made coffee.' He pulled out a stool for Quinta and set down a mug of frothy coffee on the counter in front of her.

'Grated chocolate on top,' said Quinta appreciatively.

'Yes, chocolate is good for the morale if not the figure,' said Sam. 'Now, what's up? Trouble with Alban? Or life in general?'

'You are kind,' said Quinta. 'I'm lucky to have friends who take an interest.'

'Ah,' said Sam. 'Champagne day!'

Quinta stared at him. 'What are you talking about?'

'That's the first time I've ever heard you acknowledge that you needed friends. That makes it a red-letter day.'

'I've never said I didn't need friends,' protested Quinta.

'No, not in so many words. You're pleasant, yes, and friendly, and we have some good conversations, but it's sometimes like talking to a wall. And now,' went on Sam, 'there isn't a wall, or not so much.' He smiled widely at her. 'Much better for you. I told you this was going to be a time of change. When you let go a bit, stop resisting everyone, then all kinds of things happen.'

'I don't want anything to happen,' said Quinta, worried. 'My life is quite difficult enough as it is.'

'Yes, but if things are happening, there isn't anything you can do about it.'

'Are things happening?' said Quinta, sipping her coffee, and wiping the froth off her upper lip with the back of her hand.

'Yes, you know they are,' said Sam. 'Lydia coming, that was one thing. And that has led to you starting to make an instrument, not just work on other people's broken bits and pieces. She's been a catalyst.'

'Catalyst,' said Quinta thoughtfully. 'What a funny thing to call someone. Why should Lydia be a catalyst?'

'Because she brings change,' said Sam impatiently. 'Come on, Quinta, sharpen your wits, you must be able to see it. Your life isn't inside a cosy little cocoon any more, Lydia's broken the threads and you've had to come out.'

Quinta now had the giggles, and the infectious sound rang round the shop. 'Like a butterfly?' she managed to say.

Sam was laughing as well, unable to help himself. 'A slightly substantial butterfly,' he said.

'More a moth,' said Quinta.

The bell clanged and a customer came into the shop. It was Titus. He looked at them with a quizzical expression on his face. 'I'm sorry to interrupt,' he began.

Sam rose to his feet and swept the coffee cups away. 'No, no, we're to blame, it was just something very funny.'

Quinta was still smiling. 'Hello, Titus,' she said. 'How's chaos?'

Titus thought once again how good Quinta was to look at, particularly with a smile like that on her face.

'Chaos is in good order,' he said gravely.

'Ah, and my life which used to be in such good order is now in chaos,' said Quinta. 'Please excuse me, I must get back to my workshop.'

Quinta didn't know that after she had gone upstairs Titus had chatted idly to Sam as he flicked through some music. He was intrigued to learn that Quinta was a luthier. He had an intellectual's respect for people who could make things with their hands. Sam, who thought Titus very good-looking, was happy to gossip.

Perhaps I shouldn't have told him all those things about Quinta, Sam thought when Titus left. But it can't matter; he hardly knows her. He's got a good body, that man . . . and those eyes . . . and voice. What a pity he isn't one of us.

He bent down to open the drawer containing musical stationery and began to fill up the tub of keyboard pencils which stood on the counter.

We need to keep an eye on Quinta, though, he said to himself. Alban is being troublesome, he's much fonder of her than she realizes; it could be very difficult for her.

It was a Thursday. Rather to Quinta's surprise, Alban was at home when she got back from work. He didn't come out, but she could hear him in his studio, humming, swearing loudly from time to time, then working furiously at the piano before a period of quiet while he wrote his music down.

I'll make him a special dinner tonight, thought Quinta. She still felt guilty about him, she had felt guilty all day. Alban wanting her to go to Spain, Phoebe wanting to dash off to the West Indies, and demanding to know where her father was; it was all too much.

Quinta was exhausted by the time she had cooked the meal for herself and Alban, fed and entertained Phoebe and cleared the debris away. But she was determined to give Alban a pleasant evening; she could tell from the sounds emerging from the studio that his work wasn't going particularly well.

Think how history will judge me, she said to herself, if I turn out to have been a malign influence on the work of a great composer. A kind of anti-muse, that would be dreadful.

Alban cheered up at the sight of dinner. He looked round for Phoebe, and was relieved when Quinta said she'd been banished to bed so that they could have an evening to themselves.

'How did you manage that?' he asked, lighting the candles. 'It's usually impossible to get her to bed at a reasonable hour during the holidays.'

'Bribery,' said Quinta briefly.

Later, Quinta heaved a sigh of relief as Alban seemed his usual self in bed. He was in a good mood; a considerate lover always, he seemed to be especially tender tonight. Quinta wasn't too keen on that. She had always kept an emotional distance from Alban, and so she imagined, had he. She had thought you could keep the affairs of the body and the affairs of the heart separate.

Lydia, younger than she was but more worldly, had laughed at the idea. 'Nonsense,' she said. 'Men are capable of being all kinds of beastly things: two-faced, cunning, up to desperate tricks and stratagems to get what they want. But they often want heart as much as body, especially when they get to Alban's age.'

'That can't be right,' said Quinta. 'What about all these middle-aged men who run off with vibrant young things?'

'Ah, but they've been married for years, and are bored with their wives.' She thought for a moment. 'No, I think they run off because they realize their wives are bored with them.'

'You're very cynical.'

'Men like Alban, who've never married, they're different. They often have a romantic view of life, very sentimental.'

True, thought Quinta.

'Not always. Not your randy cleric, he clearly just liked young girls. He didn't need an affair or a holiday with his wife in exotic places. He needed a shrink. Probably still does. Probably never been near one, and has gone his selfish way. No doubt risen to high office in the Church, aren't some people humbugs?'

Quinta didn't like to think of him needing a shrink. To be the unfortunate victim of a man's uncontrollable passion was one thing. To be the victim of an unpleasant little complex was quite another.

Alban yawned, stretched and scratched his chest. Pleased with himself, thought Quinta.

'Are you going?'

'Yes,' he said, pulling the covers up round her. 'You go back to sleep.' He planted a kiss on her ruffled curls, wrapped himself in his voluminous silk dressing gown, made for him at great expense in the Burlington Arcade, and went off to his studio.

Quinta relaxed and reached out to turn the light off. There was a thud and the sensation of being walked on by rather too many feet as Madrigal settled himself happily down on the warm patch left by Alban. Quinta curled herself into a tight ball and fell thankfully asleep.

She didn't feel very relaxed the next morning when she discovered Phoebe's school report. She had forgotten all about it; it usually came home with Phoebe, nestling between projects, unidentifiable pieces of artwork and sundry items of clothing. All of those had duly arrived, to be hurled into the darkest corner of the cupboard by Phoebe, with a great shout of 'No more horrible, horrible school for weeks and weeks.'

Quinta strongly suspected that Phoebe had read her report, and had then hidden it in an old trainer. It was only by chance, when trying to sort out clean and dirty clothes to put in the washing machine before setting off for work, that Quinta had spotted it.

She sat down on the bed, and read it, with growing alarm. Alban, surprised by the silence and stillness, put his head round the door. 'I thought you'd gone,' he said. 'None of the usual whirlwind.' Then he saw Quinta's face.

'Quinta, darling, what is it?' he said, dropping down beside her and putting his arms round her.

She handed him the report.

'Oh, rubbish. Oh, what balls,' he said. 'Quinta, don't let this upset you. I never read such a lot of nonsense. This isn't Phoebe!'

'But Alban, look, they say I should consider getting advice

from a psychologist, that she might do better in a special school . . . perhaps her home circumstances . . . How could she . . .?'

'Don't you go blaming Phoebe,' said Alban at once.

'No, I meant the head, ghastly woman. I went to see her, not a month ago, everything was fine. She said that some children are slower to develop than others, no need to worry, would a visit from a social worker help me to sort out things at home at all . . . I said, there were no problems, everything at home was okay . . . And she must have been planning this even then!'

She grabbed the report and letter back from Alban. 'Look . . . inadvisable to take on full-time work. As a single parent . . .' Quinta sniffed and groped for one of Phoebe's special rabbit tissues.

'Your name will be mud if you use those,' Alban warned her. 'Come on, I'll make us a pot of coffee, ring up the shop and say you're going to be a bit late . . .'

'I can't,' wailed Quinta. 'I've already been late twice this week, it's always so tricky in the holidays . . .'

'Shut up,' said Alban, propelling her out of the room. 'Good thing Phoebe's gone off for a day's bird-watching, she mustn't see you upset like this over her report. It would make her feel dreadful.'

Alban rang the shop and spoke to Sam.

'There you are, Quinta. He says, why are you so worried about being late, which isn't often, when you work through most lunchtimes, and never put in for overtime? I told you so. It isn't even as if Gustav were about, so put it out of your mind and apply your intelligence to this. It's a problem; problems have solutions. We just have to find the best one.'

With unusual efficiency Alban made coffee, found some biscuits – you've had a shock, you need the sugar – and sat down opposite Quinta with a large sheet of blank paper in front of him.

'What's that for?' said Quinta suspiciously.

'Plans, ideas. Now, first, we need an educational psychologist.' Quickly, before Quinta could explode, he put a hand over her mouth. 'Not because Phoebe's subnormal, because she isn't, but in order to be able to wave it under this idiot's nose.'

Quinta subsided, and Alban removed his hand.

'That was unecessary,' she said crossly.

'No, it wasn't. You need to think with your brains now, not your stomach or your feet or whatever it is you use when you're upset. Okay, Simon's our man for that.'

'Simon! What does he know about this? He isn't an educational psychologist.'

'Of course not, but don't you remember him telling us about the trouble they were having with one of the choristers? One of the more difficult ones?'

'Oh, yes,' said Quinta. 'The one they found had carefully removed all those little panes of glass from windows in the practice room.'

'It was mediaeval glass,' said Alban. 'And that was one of his milder misdemeanours. They had to suspend him in the end, of course. There was a frightful stink, because he was one of Poughley's blue-eyed boys, son of that ghastly violin teacher who used to whack his pupils.'

'I remember. Poor child with a father like that.'

'Yes, so much for your stable homes,' said Alban grimly. 'Anyway, Simon arranged for him to see an educational psychologist, and he said the one they went to was pretty sound.'

'What happened to the boy?' asked Quinta. 'He left the choir for good, didn't he?'

'Yes, his pa removed him, I think he was going to try to get him a place in another choir, even though the psychologist said the problem was that the boy didn't actually want to sing, and hated being in the choir.'

'Poor kid,' said Quinta. 'Why force a child into that? It must be a miserable life if you don't enjoy it. I thought they tested them very carefully to make sure they're suited to being in the choir; it's not everyone's cup of tea.'

'Parents like it, think it gives them a head start in music, all these teachers want their sons to be the great musicians they've never been. I see a lot of it, pointless. They end up grinding away in some orchestra, excellent instrumentalists, totally uninterested in music, wishing they'd qualified as engineers or dental hygienists or anything not to do with music.'

Quinta's eyes grew dark with sympathy. 'Parents shouldn't decide what their children are going to do or be when they're little; how can you possibly know how they're going to turn out, what their interests are going to be?'

'Which brings us back to Phoebe,' said Alban firmly. He wrote on the paper: *Action points*, and underlined it. Then he started on a new line.

1 Ask Simon for name and number of psychologist.

'Okay, we can do that, and make an appointment as soon as possible.'

2 Find a new school.

Quinta protested. 'Alban, I can't take her away and send her to another school. She's happy there, and besides, it's supposed to be the best primary school in the city.'

'Listen,' said Alban patiently, 'she isn't happy there at all. She's stoical under all the drama, and she'll put up with a lot so as not to worry you. But, take it from me, she isn't happy there. And that school, by my reckoning, is a dud place. Who says it's the best?'

'Everyone. Parents, the local guide, the teachers at nursery school . . .'

'Then everyone is wrong,' said Alban. 'Come on, Quinta, she's learning nothing there.'

'How do you know what she's doing?' said Quinta, riled. 'What do you know about modern education?'

'Not much, but what I've seen doesn't impress,' said Alban. 'And take it from me, after what that old bag who runs the place has said about Phoebe in that report, there's no way she's going to get anywhere at that school. That's a lifetime's knowledge of human beings, Quinta, nothing to do with education at all, which tells me that.'

Quinta grew thoughtful. 'Perhaps you're right,' she said doubtfully. 'But what's the alternative? I went round all the local schools; honestly, I don't think Phoebe's going to do any better at any of them.'

'Then you'll have to go private.'

Quinta shook her head. 'No. I haven't got the money, and I'm never going to have the money, and quite apart from that, I don't believe in private education. Look what it did for me!'

'Yes, made sure you could read, write and add up, and taught you how to work so that you could concentrate enough to get yourself through three years of college with Phoebe clinging to your ankles.'

'That had nothing to do with my school.'

'More than you think.'

'In any case, I'd never send Phoebe to a school like mine. I didn't like it much, and what it would do to Phoebe . . .'

'We're getting somewhere,' said Alban. 'Not an all-girls school', he wrote under 'find a new school'. 'That's going to narrow it down a lot.'

'You may as well add: "find a school which is mad enough to take Phoebe on a scholarship", because there's no other way she could go to a fee-paying school.'

'I'll pay,' said Alban, looking up to the ceiling.

Quinta was touched. 'Alban, you know how expensive your life is; you couldn't undertake the education of a child. Education goes on; you can't drop it after a year or so. And it's clear from this report that Phoebe's never going to be bright enough to win an academic scholarship or anything like that.'

'Find out about bursaries and help with fees,' wrote Alban.

Quinta sighed, and got up from the table. 'This is all nonsense,' she said. 'Yes, you're right, she must go to a child psychologist, although I hate the thought of it.' She looked down at the school report which she was still holding clenched in her hand. 'They're professionals, Alban. They don't come out with all this without a reason. I've just got to face up to it, I've made a real mess of Phoebe. I knew I was hardly a perfect mother, but I've tried, I really have.'

Alban got up and twitched the report out of her hand. 'Give that to me. I'll keep it for you, out of Phoebe's reach.'

'I think she's probably read it,' said Quinta sadly. 'It was hidden, and the envelope looked as though it had been opened and then stuck back again.'

'I could kill that woman,' said Alban savagely. 'Now, Quinta, you are not to brood on this. Phoebe's probably in a real state about this, but you know she'll never let on. So you've got to pull yourself together, don't let her think you're at all bothered by it. Okay?'

'Okay,' said Quinta with a miserable smile.

'Right. Now, off you go, and don't worry. Have more faith in Phoebe; trust your own judgement. After all, you know far more about her than any teacher ever will.'

'I hate teachers,' said Quinta.

## 10

Although it was the end of July, with the summer term over, and even the choir had broken up for several weeks of holidays, the Cathedral School was far from closed. In a large office which overlooked the green, Mr Poughley, head of the Junior department, was expecting a visitor.

'The best china, Mrs Fitzackerley,' he said.

'Oh, are you offering her coffee?' said his secretary, surprised. It was a house rule, no coffee or tea for parents; it only encouraged them to linger. Mr Poughley maintained that this was done in the name of efficiency, he was such a busy man, so much to do, his day had to be scheduled down to the last ten minutes. The truth was that he loathed parents, especially mothers, and wanted to spend as little time as possible with them.

'Don't you know who Mrs Lennox-Smith is?' said Mr Poughley, in astonishment.

Mrs Fitzackerley shrugged. 'Just a parent. One son, eight, moving to the area. At least she didn't ask about scholarships, so perhaps they're well off, no trouble with the fees. She sounded all right on the phone, but the boy's called Milo; I thought that didn't sound too promising. A bit arty, if you know what I mean. I told her we had a long waiting list, but she said she'd come just the same.'

Mr Poughley was dancing with impatience as she spoke.

'This isn't just any parent! This is the new Bishop's wife. Her husband is the new Bishop of Eyot!'

Mrs Fitzackerley frowned. 'I thought he was in his fifties, isn't he a bit old to have a son of prep school age? Are you sure this is the same one?'

'Of course I'm sure. His chaplain rang to say that Mrs Lennox-Smith would be in touch over a place for her young son.'

'In that case,' said Mrs Fitzackerley, 'I'll move the card.'

'What do you mean?'

Mrs Fitzackerley gestured to some small filing boxes which were on a shelf behind her.

'This box here is the permanent waiting list; that's all the parents you feel doubtful about. Parents think their child is on the waiting list, but of course they always stay at the bottom of it; they'd never be offered a place unless we had a real crisis with numbers.'

She pointed to a second box. 'This one is the genuine waiting list, some of the children in here will be coming in the autumn or later in the year when there are places. This box is for the don't-knows. I put Mrs Trent in there, although I have to say I felt sure that she would end up in the doubtful box.'

She reached back and took a box down from the shelf. 'These cards here are for the ones you definitely want. You haven't interviewed them all, yet, of course. Some of them are coming next term, some of them won't be old enough for two or three years yet.'

Mrs Fitzackerley's fingers skipped swiftly through the cards in the box. 'There you are,' she said, inserting the new card. 'I've put Milo in there, in the definites box. Do you want the card dotted once or twice?'

'Eh?' said Mr Poughley.

'A blue dot is for an important or influential parent. A green dot is for a rich parent. Obviously the Bishop's son gets a blue dot, but is he rich as well? Or perhaps his mother is rich?'

Mr Poughley was flustered. He hated it when Mrs Fitzackerley spelt everything out in black and white like this. He liked to feel he was in charge, making decisions on a sound basis such as a lifetime's experience with young boys (not so convincing now the school had been forced to take girls as well), his fine qualifications (which wouldn't have allowed him anywhere near a state primary school) or, best of all, his intuition about the ability of children.

'I can tell at once,' he would say. 'The minute they come into my room, I know whether we've got a really good boy, I mean child. Never fails.'

Other members of staff, unblessed with Mr Poughley's special gift for selecting children, would sigh when they heard this, thinking of the time spent hauling some boy up to an adequate mark in his entrance exams, hearing the headmaster's words ringing in their ears. 'Brilliant boy, absolutely brilliant.' They knew all about the stars at sport, who disappeared into the third elevens of minor public schools, and the boys with 'Wonderful character, such powers of leadership,' who were ejected within a short space of time from whatever kind of school they went on to with cries from harassed headmasters of 'You've sent us a monster.'

Girls were less of a problem. Mr Poughley wasn't interested in them; he thought of them as unsatisfactory boys, and only wished they wouldn't grow up into tiresome mothers. He left it to the deputy head to assess them, or had done until the deputy head had left under a cloud. He wasn't sure how he was going to get on with the new deputy; being a woman, she would probably be hopeless. More work for me, he felt, suddenly full of self-pity.

Mrs Fitzackerley cast a knowing glance in his direction. Needs a new suit, she thought. Despite all the cross country running and swimming he did so ostentatiously, his tummy was getting decidedly bigger. A short, pale man, with a round, slightly startled face, he longed to be impressive: fit and lean, a leader. He saw himself as Napoleon, small in stature, but a dynamo among men. Everyone else saw him as Old Puffy.

Faustina Lennox-Smith wasn't impressed with what she saw. Mr Poughley strode up and down, laying on the charm. He had two main styles: urbane and sophisticated for parents from the south; tweedy and practical for the northerners.

What a pompous little man, thought Faustina. Oh, dear, I've had all these arguments about Milo not going away to boarding school at eight, and now I'm faced with this for a headmaster. As she smiled and talked in a friendly way, her heart sank.

Milo was led away by the school secretary to do some tests with Miss Wedmore. 'Routine, purely routine, I do assure you,' said Mr Poughley as he bustled incompetently with the coffee cups. 'I can see at once that young Milo is a bright boy, you can always tell. Now music, I have heard on the grapevine that you are something of a musician yourself, very good news, and I can assure you that you'll find Eyot a very musical place. Oh, yes, indeed, I can promise you a rich feast of music.' He gazed intently at Faustina, with his most charming smile plastered all over his face.

She smiled blandly back. 'Oh, good,' she said vaguely. 'I trained as a singer, but I don't sing professionally now.'

Mr Poughley was shocked. 'No, no, in your position, of course not.'

'But if you were asking about Milo's music, I have to say that he's not particularly interested in music of any kind.'

'I am sure you are mistaken, Mrs Lennox-Smith. Of course, we have special expertise in picking out musical children, and I have to say that we have some remarkable musicians among our boys. Three of our leavers this summer have achieved grade 8 distinction in their music exams, and all have taken major and valuable music scholarships here or to the best schools.'

'Commendable,' said Faustina, wanting to laugh as she realized she was beginning to talk like Mr Poughley. 'What about the girls?'

'Girls?' Mr Poughley was puzzled. 'Oh, do you have a daughter as well? I'm sorry, I didn't realize.'

'No, just sons. I only wondered whether the girls also took valuable music scholarships.'

'Ah, well, early days, our numbers aren't yet fifty-fifty, although the Dean does intend . . . I'm sure many girls have much to contribute to the school's full musical life.'

Do they train them to talk like this? Faustina asked herself. Is there a special headmasters' course? Or, horrific thought, perhaps all the teachers at this school were the same.

Mr Poughley's face brightened. 'Sons?' he said hopefully. 'I thought there was just the one boy . . .'

'Yes, well, no . . .'

I must pull myself together, Faustina told herself. 'I have three much older boys, grown up now.'

Mr Poughley looked a little taken aback, but Faustina was

used to that. She had married at seventeen, had twin sons at eighteen and another son at nineteen. She had then done some simple arithmetic, worked out that at this rate she could end up the mother of some twenty children, and had gone to a gynaecologist.

Clearly her husband wasn't going to do anything about it, as she had explained with some embarrassment. Matters had been arranged, and she had gratefully taken up the threads of her own life again, returning to music college to finish her training, while Lennox puzzled over his wife's apparent inability to have any more children.

Now, in her early forties, Faustina looked very young to have three grown-up sons. She had looked steadily younger ever since they had left home. The products of the best English schooling, they alternated between fear of women and contempt for them. Their mother mostly got the contempt, except when they were hurt by life's horrid blows and wanted to be little boys again. They then despised themselves for their weakness, and were even nastier to her.

'You must miss them, those charming boys. So like their father, so sporty, so splendid in every way,' said one of Faustina's friends.

'No,' said Faustina, who as she got older was beginning to bite on her tongue less and less. 'It's a great relief. Now I can enjoy Milo, who loathes sport, bless him, and who doesn't in the least want to go away to boarding school.'

'Oh, none of them want to at first, but when they do, they love it, absolutely love it. All mine did.'

Faustina thought of the somewhat chequered careers of her friend's children since they had left school, with one in a commune in India, one in jail in Spain for drugs dealing, one married to an American with very strange habits, and the fourth living in London within walking distance of the Tavistock Clinic, and said nothing.

'They must learn to stand on their own two feet,' her friend went on.

'My experience,' said Faustina, 'is that they learn to stand firmly on everybody's else's feet. No, I'm going to turn out one happy, balanced young person, who enjoys life and gets on with girls. That means day schools, and co-educational ones.'

However, her good intentions were starting to waver as she looked at Mr Poughley.

'Ah, much older boys. And they went to . . .? I assume you have Milo registered . . .? Naturally, one of our best schools . . . I believe the Bishop – the Bishop-to-be, I should say – is an Etonian . . .?'

He looks just like a dog waiting for a bone, thought Faustina distastefully. She smiled again. 'We haven't made any decisions about Milo. We want to wait and see how he turns out.'

'Of course, of course, how sensible, I wish more of my parents took such a sane view. And naturally, with your husband holding the position he does, provided we register in time, there should be no problem about a place . . .'

He beamed at Faustina, who was wondering when Milo was going to come back.

'I expect you would like to see round the school. Of course it is a sad and forlorn place, bereft of its young life as it is at this time of year, but I am sure you will be able to appreciate our fine facilities. I am afraid that I myself can't .. unfortunately, my many duties call me away, but by very good fortune, Miss Wedmore, who is to be our new deputy head, a very able woman, is here, as you know. Her appointment has only this week been confirmed by the Dean as representative of the Governors.'

'Yes, you had a spot of trouble with the previous deputy head, didn't you?' said Faustina cheerfully.

Mr Poughley winced.

'He moved on to higher things,' he said repressively.

'Oh?' said Faustina. 'I rather thought that lower things were his speciality.'

Mr Poughley looked at Faustina with some dislike. 'Of course, the papers exaggerated terribly, they always do. There was no harm in it at all, just normal, friendly warmth towards the boys . . .'

'And he was a keen amateur photographer and video man, wasn't he? You were mad to take him on,' said Faustina relentlessly. 'I was at the Royal College with Dodsy, and we all knew what he was like. I wouldn't have let him anywhere near my sons.'

Mr Poughley gave a weak laugh. Where was Miss Wedmore? Damn the woman, there was a place for Milo at the school even if he was a half-wit, surely she couldn't be fool enough to take the tests seriously. Ah, here she was at last.

'Well, Miss Wedmore, here you are, everything in order, I feel sure.' He beamed his special smile-for-boys at Milo, who gazed back at him with big, clear brown eyes.

'I'm Harriet Wedmore,' said the tall, athletic-looking woman who had accompanied Milo into the room. She felt she might have to wait a long time for the head to introduce them.

Annoyed by his social lapse, he waved a commanding hand at them, and pinned an insincere smile to his face as they shook hands. 'Now, Miss Wedmore, if you would care to show Mrs Lennox-Smith round the school, I'll ask my secretary to take Milo here across to Mr Praetorius.'

Harriet Wedmore smiled at Faustina. 'Oh, is he going to do a voice trial? I hadn't realized he was interested in becoming a chorister.'

Milo's mouth dropped open. 'I'm not,' he said quickly. 'Mum . . .'

'Is that Simon Praetorius, the Master of the Choristers?' asked Faustina.

'Yes, do you know him?'

'I've heard him play, in Cambridge. He's a very fine organist. I think it would be rather wasting his time hearing Milo, because, as I told you, music isn't really his thing.'

'You let us be the judge of that,' said Mr Poughley, his smile now switched into its patronizing mode. 'Your boy won't be long, Mr Praetorius will bring him back here and he'll be waiting for you when you have finished your tour.'

Faustina winked at Milo, who looked reassured, and obediently went off to the Cathedral with Mrs Fitzackerley. Harriet Wedmore led Faustina away towards the main school buildings, and Mr Poughley sank back into his comfortably upholstered swivel chair with a grunt of relief.

He felt quite ill. It was clear that Mrs Lennox-Smith was the kind of mother that he most disliked. Exactly the kind of mother that he didn't want to have anything to do with, and, of course, he had absolutely no choice. He knew, and she knew, and the Bishop-to-be and the Dean and Chapter knew, that even if the boy was half-witted and virtually ineducable, the school would have a place for him. Oh, well, he clearly wasn't half-witted, that was one thing, but God, thought Mr Poughley, sending up a rare genuine prayer, keep me from his mother. He groaned and reached in the drawer for an indigestion tablet.

Harriet Wedmore gave Faustina a quick sideways look as they crossed the cobbled yard. They paused by the main gate.

'Do you really want to see round the school?' she asked. 'Schools are very depressing places out of term time, and I get the feeling you aren't very keen.'

Faustina laughed. 'Is it so obvious? Of course, you're quite right. Actually, to be honest, I feel very disheartened. I do so want Milo to go to a day school, but it has to be one which prepares the pupils for Common Entrance. I don't care about that, but my husband insists. I want him to go to a school which has girls, and so . . . well, if this doesn't work out, it's all going to be very difficult.'

She paused, and shook her head in irritation. 'I think it's the only school my husband will approve of; it's suitable, you see, a son at the Cathedral School.'

'But you're worried about what kind of a school it is,' Harriet Wedmore finished for her. 'Don't. Mr Poughley is very much a figurehead. He's away a lot these days; he's quite good at the PR side, believe it or not. And actually it's not such a bad school, from what I have seen. I'm fussy about where I work, and I can tell you in confidence that I've been brought in to tighten things up a bit. The school's had one or two scandals, so I think they're going to make sure that they get everything right from now on.'

She paused, watching conflicting thoughts cross Faustina's face. Experiences with her three eldest boys, and with Milo in his three years at the local primary school, had made her wary of teachers, and unwilling to trust them. This Miss Wedmore seemed excellent in every way . . . but then so had others.

'We'd like to have Milo,' Miss Wedmore went on. 'His work

seems well up to standard, a few gaps in maths, but nothing we can't put right. I like him, I'd like to teach him, I think he has an interesting mind.'

What suckers mothers are for anyone who's nice about their children, thought Faustina bitterly.

'Art's his special thing,' she said. 'He's very keen, and I think is going to be good.'

Harriet Wedmore laughed. 'I can't introduce you to the art master, because he's just started a jail sentence for stealing illuminated manuscripts from some books in the Cathedral library. He was one of the lay clerks, and used to nip in there and help himself between services.'

Faustina gave in. If the woman could be so pleasant, and frank, and laugh like that, then it was probably going to be all right.

'I suppose you are replacing the art master?' she enquired.

'Yes, indeed. A local artist, who is a teacher as well as a good painter, is coming to give lessons to those children who are seriously interested. And we have a general art teacher who will also teach tennis in the summer joining us as well. So Milo will be well looked after.'

She looked at Faustina, who still had a worried expression on her face, and smiled.

'Now, I think Milo is going to be longer than Mr Poughley predicted, because I happen to know that Mr Praetorius is in a meeting which doesn't finish for a while yet. Don't worry about Milo, they'll show him round the crypt, that's what they usually do, and the children all love it. Bones, you know, and even a mummified knight.'

Faustina smiled. 'He'd love a mummified knight.'

'So I suggest you go across to Flora's, which as you probably know, is the best coffee place in Eyot, and wait for Milo there. I'll bring him over. And please don't worry,' she added. 'The school will be much better than you think.'

Faustina shook the rain off her umbrella and put it in the handsome brass umbrella stand inside the cafe door. The carpet was thick underfoot, the waitress in her black and white outfit was smiling and helpful. The smell of coffee, of chocolates, of cinnamon toast soothed her senses as she slid into her seat at a table set in the corner.

The two sides of the cafe here were glass from wall to ceiling. From where Faustina was sitting she could see along Leofric Street, which led to an ancient stone bridge across the river; to her left, she looked out on to St Wulfstan's Square, with its pretty old fountain in the middle and the old shops all around. Even in the steady drizzle it managed to look attractive.

Bedraggled tourists, enveloped in light-coloured macs, peered disconsolately into shop windows. The newspaper man on the corner of the square held out a soggy copy of the first edition of the evening paper as the rain trickled down his placards.

It's very different from Cambridge, thought Faustina as she sipped a cup of rich Sumatra coffee. Although clearly just as wet. For a moment she let her mind drift to memories of warmer places, of ease and sunlight and laughter. Then she jerked herself back. These were no thoughts for an English clergyman's wife.

Locals, clad in darker clothes, and moving briskly with a purpose, went backwards and forwards across the square. A cluster of giggly girls made faces at the people sitting at their tables in Flora's as they went past the windows. Other people looked up from their coffee and frowned. Faustina didn't; she smiled at them, and gave them a cheerful little wave. Surprised, they paused a moment, and then grinned back at her and waved in return.

How nice it would have been to have had a daughter, thought Faustina. She adored Milo, and had been as warm and good a mother to her three eldest sons as she could; but she had often wished that one of them had been a daughter. On the other hand . . .

I know no-one here, she said to herself, as she poured out a second cup of coffee. And none of these people hurrying past know who I am. Yet, in a few months, in a year perhaps, if I'm sitting here, I'm sure I'll know some of them, and others will recognize me, mention that they saw the Bishop's wife having a coffee in Flora's.

She sighed. Not, 'I saw Mrs Lennox-Smith,' or better, just Mrs Smith (so ridiculous of Lennox to hyphenate his name; so pretentious), or, best of all, Faustina. No, from now on, it would be mostly 'the Bishop's wife', as though I had no separate existence.

A man drew out of a crowd of people heading towards the bridge. Faustina tensed. Surely it was . . . No, what tricks the grey light played on one's imagination. She returned to her coffee and her dim thoughts, and at that very moment the door of the cafe was opened with great force and a tall man swept in. He surged past the tables and sat down dramatically opposite Faustina.

'Titus! It is you! I thought I saw you outside in the square. Titus, how good to see you.'

Titus looked her up and down, and then smiled, satisfied. 'You see, Fausty, you're better-looking than ever.' He lowered his voice. 'Now, where can we find a bed?'

Faustina let out a shout of laughter, and the two old dears at the next table snuffled disapprovingly into their Flora's best coffee blend.

'I mean it, I can't wait, we must go to bed at once.'

'Sssh,' said Faustina. 'And that is so like you, Titus. You walk out of my life for what, more than eight years, and then here you are, saying come to bed.'

Titus's dark eyes grew even darker. 'What, you mean to say you don't want to go to bed with me?'

'Titus, it's been eight years, it's not that . . . you don't understand.'

A clear voice piped across the restaurant. 'There's mum. I'll be okay now, thank you very much, Miss Wedmore.'

Faustina turned her head to see Milo making his way purposefully towards her, only briefly halting by the trolley of cream cakes. She rose to thank Harriet Wedmore, but she just raised a hand in salutation at the door and vanished.

'She's got to see someone,' explained Milo. Then he looked at Titus. 'Hello,' he said in his friendly way. 'Who are you?'

Quinta had had to take an extended lunch-break in order to go shopping. Phoebe's feet had grown, and she needed new Wellingtons. How horrible to have to buy rubber boots for your summer holiday, thought Quinta. What a way to live.

'I need some new shorts, too,' said Phoebe, eyeing a brightly coloured pair in a shop window. 'I like those ones there, look.'

'Yes, they're very nice, but I expect they're very expensive, and I think jeans or cords will be better for your holiday this year.'

'Louise's mum bought her a bikini, and all kinds of tops, as well as shorts like these ones in the shop window. Sandals, too, beach towels, oh, lots of things.'

'Yes, Louise is a very lucky girl, but you don't need that for where we're going.'

'I think perhaps we're going to the South Pole after all,' observed Phoebe, as Quinta set off to look for a warm jumper. 'And I've got those jumpers which Pauline passed on to me, those ones which Gavin's grown out of. It was nice of her, because Peter is smaller than me, and he could have had them.'

Quinta thought grimly of the threadbare relics which her friend had bestowed on her with such great benevolence.

'I don't think Pauline would let Peter be seen dead in those old jerseys, Phoebe. I put them in the bin.'

'Oh,' said Phoebe, unsurprised. 'I thought I hadn't seen them for a while.'

Phoebe dawdled past her favourite shop, full of baroque swags, fat little cherubim and ornate Venetian candlesticks.

'When I grow up, I'm going to be very rich and have a house full of things like this,' she said wistfully.

Quinta remembered the things she had longed for as a child, her plans, and look what had happened to her.

'I don't think we often grow up to have what we want,' she said rather sadly.

'What a depressing thought,' said a familiar voice behind her.

'Hello, Simon,' said Quinta. 'Come along, Phoebe, you've got to be at the library for the art session in five minutes, and I've got to get back to work. Sorry, Simon, but I have to dash.'

Simon's face fell, but at that moment a roly-poly little woman who was sweeping along with two children of about Phoebe's age in tow stopped beside them.

'Hello,' she cried. 'It's Quinta and Phoebe, isn't it? We met at patchwork quilts on Wednesday morning. I think Phoebe quite enjoyed that, didn't you, Phoebe?'

Phoebe beamed at her. 'Yes. Are Jonas and Gail coming to the art session now?'

'Yes, indeed, and I'm staying to help.' She smiled happily at Quinta. 'You're always busy, aren't you? I don't know how you manage it, a full-time job, Phoebe, and no husband. Shall I take Phoebe along with us?'

'Yes,' said Simon, promptly. Quinta couldn't help laughing at him; the roly-poly woman laughed as well, for no particular reason, although she looked as though she laughed a lot just for the fun of it. She bore Phoebe off, and Quinta found herself with Simon gazing dotingly at her.

'You look like one of those angels there, adoring an unseen Being,' she said crossly.

'I am adoring you,' said Simon. 'You know I adore you, oh, Quinta, why won't you let me get near you?'

'I'm not quite sure what you mean,' said Quinta. 'If you mean I don't talk about my deepest thoughts and feelings to you, no of course I don't, not to you or to anyone else. If you mean you want to get close to me physically, I've told you often enough, no, I won't go to bed with you.'

'Why not? You go to bed with Alban.'

Quinta was furious. 'You share everything in your family, do you?' she enquired nastily. 'Look, what I do with Alban is between me and Alban, it's nothing to do with you. And it doesn't mean that I'm available to all the other men in his family.'

'Not all the men, just me. You aren't in love with Alban, I know you're not.'

Quinta sighed. 'Simon, why do we have this conversation over and over again? Look, I'm going to be late back at the shop, I must go.'

Simon took her arm, and drew her back into a wide shop entrance, away from the flow of damp people. 'I want to kiss you,' he said urgently.

Quinta shook herself free. 'Simon, you're mad. Quite apart from the fact that, although I like you very much – or I would if you didn't keep on at me all the time – I don't want to kiss you, think of who you are and where you are. The Cathedral's not five minutes away, canons and minor clergy passing up and down, for heaven's sake!'

'I don't care about the canons,' said Simon sulkily.

Quinta looked at him in exasperation. How could a man in his forties behave like a surly adolescent suffering the pangs of unrequited love?

'And try to remember that you're a married man with a family.'

'Is that the only reason you won't sleep with me? I'll leave home tomorrow, get a divorce, if you'd come away with me.'

'Oh, grow up,' said Quinta. 'I'm not coming away with you whatever you do.'

'Other women sleep with men who are married,' said Simon relentlessly.

'I don't.'

'Alban may not be married, but what about the woman he keeps in his flat in London? You don't seem to mind that.'

Quinta was astonished, and it showed in her face.

'Ah, you didn't know about Hermione, then?' said Simon triumphantly. 'Perhaps that will make you change your mind, maybe you haven't wanted to be unfaithful to Alban. It might be different now you know he's unfaithful to you every time he goes to London.'

Quinta pulled herself together. She was surprised, but not, she realized, hurt or offended by this revelation about Alban. What a complicated life Alban has, then, she thought. Much more so than I had realized. I wonder if Lucy Praetorius knows about this Hermione, what does she think of her son with two mistresses at opposite ends of the country? More respectable than bigamy or adultery, I suppose.

'It makes no difference, Simon. I'm sorry, but really, it has nothing to do with this.'

To her relief, Quinta spotted Titus walking up the street with a woman she didn't know and a little boy. Titus was leaning down towards the woman, his face alight with pleasure. What a warm, generous look, thought Quinta as she noticed them. I wonder who she is; someone close, for him to look at her in that way. But thank goodness, Titus will stop and say hello to Simon, and I can get away.

'Bugger,' said Simon, as Titus stopped to greet him.

'Faustina, this is Simon Praetorius. And Quinta, a friend of his brother's.'

Friend of his brother's!

Simon glowered at Titus and Faustina. Then he recognized Milo, and was overcome with embarrassment.

'Oh, God, you're that one,' he said incoherently.

Milo fixed him with a disapproving look. 'This is the man I was telling you about Mum, that wanted me to sing silly things to the piano.'

Titus looked at Milo, and at Simon. 'I heard Milo might be coming to the school here. I didn't realize he was going to be a chorister.'

'He's not,' said Faustina and Simon together. Simon stared at Faustina. 'Don't you want him to be a chorister?'

'No,' said Faustina. 'He can't sing. He isn't in the least musical. He'd be hopeless, and he'd hate it. I can't think why that headmaster got the idea into his head.'

Simon gave a great sigh of relief. 'I've just had the most terrible row with old Puffy. He said I had to take Milo here into the choir – it's considered a great honour to be in the choir, you understand – because he was the Bishop's son, and it would please the Bishop. I said I wouldn't, and he got very cross.'

'Oh, dear,' said Faustina. 'I'm sorry, what a silly misunderstanding. But surely you have the final say on which boys go into the choir.'

Simon gave a contemptuous laugh. 'Oh, in theory, yes. In practice, Puffy usually decides. The choristerships are the only scholarships the school gives for boys of this age, so of course, when Puffy's keen on a boy, he wants them to be in the choir. At the moment I've got a boy who can't sing, another one who can't read words, let alone music, and one who's so wild he should be in the zoo. I don't mind average boys; if they're keen, you can usually train them to make a reasonable sound, but some of them are completely hopeless. How can a boy with a lisp sing the psalms, or Latin, for God's sake?'

Quinta was enthralled by these fascinating insights into the glorious and dignified world of the Cathedral choir, and she let out a squeak of mirth. Faustina grinned too. 'It sounds as if you have a hard time of it,' she said sympathetically.

'You don't know how hard,' said Simon gloomily.

'The men's voices are good,' said Titus in bracing tones, and got a dark look from Simon for his trouble. 'And, Simon, while we're on the subject of singing, Faustina has a very good voice. Royal College, only she doesn't do it professionally any more.'

Simon looked more cheerful. 'That's good news. We have the Oratorio Society, of course, for the usual things, Messiah, big Requiems, occasionally something a little more adventurous when I can get away with it. But I want to start a chamber choir, be a little bit more ambitious. When you're settled, come and join us.'

'Thank you, I'd love to.'

Titus gave her a quizzical look. 'A chamber choir is a suitable hobby for a Bishop's wife, is it?'

'Oh, yes,' said Faustina gravely. 'I'm sure Simon will include sacred works, I shan't wear low-cut dresses, and all the Cathedral biddies will thoroughly approve.'

Quinta thought with a quick flash of envy that Faustina would look magnificent in a low-cut dress. She felt unusually aware of her tatty jeans and sweatshirt, worn with an old mac of Alban's thrown on top.

'You don't look like a bishop's wife,' she said frankly to Faustina.

Faustina sighed. 'No, and I don't behave like one, either. Of course I'm not really a bishop's wife yet, not until the autumn, but I know a lot of my husband's colleagues don't think I'm a very suitable wife for a senior member of the clergy. Unfortunately, he can't trade me in for a better model.'

'No,' said Titus seriously. 'It's funny, most men of his age who aren't clergymen, leave their wives to go off with lissome young things of half their age. Now, what the Bishop needs is someone older than you, much dowdier, with a pleasant but distant expression, and a keen interest in gardening.'

'Yes, and no artistic leanings,' said Faustina. 'I'm afraid I don't score very highly on the list of approved features. Never mind, Lennox hasn't done too badly, even with me for a wife.'

Simon had sunk back into his Hamlet mood. Quinta looked at him, exasperated, said her goodbyes quickly to him and the others, and fled before he could say anything.

'She seems a charming girl,' said Faustina. 'Not pretty, but an interesting face and lots of vitality.'

'Yes,' said Titus. 'Very young, of course. She has a daughter, Phoebe, about your Milo's age. No husband, but she lives with Simon's brother.'

Faustina liked to get things straight. 'Is your brother the child's father, then?'

'No,' said Simon shortly.

Titus didn't wonder what was bothering Simon; all the men in the choir knew about Simon's hopeless passion for Quinta.

Faustina had been thinking. She looked at Simon. 'Your brother must be Alban Praetorius, the composer.'

'Yes,' said Simon. 'He's the famous one,' he added bitterly.

'So you're a musical family. You're married with children, I know, because I've read about you in concert programmes. Are your children musical?'

Simon saw the amused look on Titus's face and flushed, aware that he was making a fool of himself. He forced a smile. 'Early days to say.'

'I hear Quinta's daughter is musical,' said Titus. 'Don't you teach her, Simon?'

'Yes, I give her piano lessons when Quinta lets me, but she's proud, can't afford to pay me for the lessons the child needs, won't let me do more than the minimum.'

'That's a shame,' said Faustina. 'Does she do a lot of music at school?'

'I don't think so,' said Simon. 'Goes to one of these modern primary schools, lots of group work and happy times, but I don't think she learns anything very much. Worries Quinta, I know that.'

'You should have girls in the choir,' said Faustina to Simon. 'Then she could have one of Mr Poughley's scholarships.'

Simon closed his eyes in horror, he hated the thought of girls in the choir. 'No danger of that, thank God,' he said.

'You mustn't utter such heresies,' Titus said to Faustina. 'The merest mention of girls in the choir stalls makes the Dean and Chapter and the lay clerks go pale with horror and look up the order of words for cleansing the premises of pollution.'

'I know,' she said. 'Still, if you're all so traditional, you really ought to go back to castrati, oughtn't you?'

Milo, who had discovered a model shop, burrowed his way in between them. 'Mum, I've been very good, and I've hurt my brain doing all those sums at that school, so do you think I've earned a present? Please?'

Faustina gave him a hug. 'I think you have. Say goodbye to Mr Praetorius and Titus, and we'll go in and have a look.'

She shook hands with Simon, and Titus bent down to kiss her on the cheek. He held her hands for a moment. 'Goodbye for now, Faustina; when are you moving into the Palace?'

'In the autumn,' she said. 'We'll let you know, Lennox will be so pleased to see you again.'

'Mmm,' said Titus.


'Well,' said Marjorie. 'That's most interesting, I must say. You do keep your eyes open, Wyn,' she added graciously.

'So Mr Praetorius actually took her arm?' said Marjorie. 'Physically laid hands on her?'

Wyn nodded her head vigorously. 'Yes. They were standing just off the street, in a doorway, and there was no need, the rain had stopped.'

'Doorway!' said Marjorie, summoning up images of dark deeds in Georgian streets, with harlots and strumpets lolling in doorways as they waited for custom.

'Of course, she is almost family,' said Daphne.

'She is no such thing,' said Marjorie, affronted.

'If she lives with Mr Praetorius's brother, then . . .'

'Then, as Christians, we disapprove, but we have to give her the benefit of the doubt. She may just be his housekeeper. It may be just a business arrangement. But I, for one, don't believe this story about a husband somewhere.'

'I never heard about any husband,' said Wyn. She tightened the nut on the large flower stand which she had been cleaning. 'There.'

Marjorie was binding cones on to a long pole. She cut the tape with pleased savagery. 'That should hold. Hurry up with the tea, Daphne, I'm parched. And you're sniffing again.'

'Sorry,' said Daphne automatically. She pulled a paper hanky from her sleeve and gave her nose a half-hearted blow.

'Lady Wray was talking about Quinta,' Marjorie went on. 'She's apparently an old school friend of Lydia's.'

There were a few moments of silence while the three of them chewed over this fact.

'Lydia must have gone to a very good school,' ventured Wyn at last.

'Yes, Grisewood,' said Marjorie. 'One of the very top ones.'

'Of course, Quinta might have been a scholarship girl,' said Daphne.

It was possible, they would need to find out.

'In any case, Lady Wray was asking Lydia about her friend.'

'Quite right, too,' put in Daphne. 'You can't be too careful these days.'

'Lydia said she had a husband, abroad. An officer of some kind.'

'Her friend has been leading her on. There's never been a sign of the father of that child, always supposing it isn't Alban Praetorius.'

'He wouldn't keep quiet about it if she was his,' said Marjorie. 'He's very bold about things like that, quite Bohemian in his ways.'

'I blame his mother. She's a very strange woman, and living abroad, it's not what you'd expect from that kind of a family.'

'Perhaps Lydia made it up, about the husband,' said Wyn, dipping her ginger biscuit into her tea cup.

'I've told you before, dear,' said Marjorie, 'that's not a very nice way to eat your biscuit.'

Wyn apologized and ate the rest of it in a more seemly fashion.

'I'm sure Lydia would never dream of making up stories like that, certainly not to deceive her grandmother.'

'No,' agreed Daphne. 'You can see, she's a very straightforward girl, she would never resort to anything underhand.'

'No, perhaps not,' said Wyn, doubtfully, remembering herself when she was that age. Had Marjorie and Daphne really never lied to their families about their less suitable friends? Had Marjorie and Daphne ever been that age? Some people were born middle-aged; maybe Marjorie and Daphne had never been young, had never slipped out to meet undesirable young men.

Lydia was in fact being thoroughly underhand where her grandmother was concerned. Lady Wray was pleased that Lydia and Adam had met at last, and seemed to get along so well together. 'Perhaps he'll invite her out to the cinema,' she said to her friend Sybil.

'I expect so, or a night club, or wherever these young people like to spend their time. The bid is with you, Wilhelmina, I think.'

'I'm so sorry, two clubs.'

'Where is your granddaughter this afternoon?' asked one of the other bridge players.

'She has gone to a talk which is being given by a colleague of Adam's. Something Roman, how intellectual these young girls are these days.'

'No bid,' said Sybil. 'Yes, she's gone with Adam, I think, very suitable.'

They all agreed, with pleased expressions on their faces at the thought of two young people embarking on a suitable courtship.

Courtship would not have been the appropriate word to

describe what Adam and Lydia were in fact doing at that moment. Lydia found Adam a delightfully vigorous and experienced lover, although she did have some slight qualms about some of his tastes.

'Oh,' she said. No qualms about this. 'Oh, I like that, mmm.'

'I love your body,' said Adam, nuzzling her back. He ran his hands down her in a very possessive way. 'So slim, such a gorgeous taut, trim bottom. Like a boy's arse.'

Lydia twisted round very swiftly. 'Boy's arse? You don't like boys, do you?'

'Of course not. Otherwise why I would be here doing this with you?'

His hands flickered in exciting places, and Lydia forgot about her momentary worry as she set about doing some exploring of her own.

Afterwards, she lay, looking exactly like an abandoned Diana, flushed and content. She watched Adam as he stretched and went over to the window. He's got a lovely body, too, she thought. Reddy gold hair all over his body, even his pubic hair. Very impressive, altogether.

'I hope you're not a berserk, or a shape-changer,' she said suddenly.

'What?' he said, surprised.

'Like in the sagas. The Viking who had a very good friend, only you had to be careful with him, because he was a berserk, and another one who was great in the morning, but you didn't visit him in the evening, because he was a shape-changer.'

'Oh, I see,' said Adam, who was not a literary man. 'I don't know the sagas very well. No, I'm not a shape-changer, nor a berserk. On the other hand,' he said, picking her up and falling back on to the bed with her, 'I do have some wild habits, as you will shortly discover.'

'Oh, good,' said Lydia.

## 12

Quinta was fascinated to hear about Lydia's affair with Adam. They were sitting on a Saturday afternoon in Wesley's Ice Cream Parlour, and Lydia was working her way through the biggest ice Quinta had ever seen.

'It's all the sex,' explained Lydia as she sucked up chocolate sauce with her straw. 'It makes me very hungry, and it's hard work with Adam, lots of action.'

'Tiring, then?' said Quinta, who was enjoying her rather smaller ice.

'Exhausting, but certainly more-ish. He's big, bigger than Angus. Very rewarding. Lots of muscles, but he's not one of your boring heave-ho men, he has lots of interesting ideas. Bizarre, some of them,' she added thoughtfully.

Quinta was waiting for Phoebe, who was with the educational psychologist. Quinta had wanted to stay, but she had been shooed away. 'Go and have a cup of coffee, I'll be at least an hour and a half.'

'You're worried about her, aren't you?' said Lydia. It must be awful to have children, she thought, and not only to lose all your freedom, but to have to live through all their mishaps and problems as well as your own.

'How's my double-bass getting on?' she went on, hoping to take Quinta's mind off Phoebe.

'Oh, oh, yes, look, I brought this to show you.' Quinta rummaged about in her satchel-like bag and pulled out a sketch-pad. She flipped over the pages and laid a drawing in front of Lydia. 'What do you think?'

Lydia bent her head over to look closely at the drawing. Then she pushed back her hair from her forehead, and gave Quinta a pleased smile.

'Quinta, it's just right. A dragon's head, oh, I can't wait. Can you really do this?'

Quinta nodded, pleased that Lydia liked the design.

'How big will it be?'

Quinta demonstrated with her hands. 'The pegs will come here, you see. And I'll do these hatched areas in gold.'

'Terrific,' said Lydia.

The doors swung open and Adam was with them. Quinta hadn't met him before. Goodness, he's huge, she thought, and then, unable to repress the thought, she smiled; of course he had a big prick, how ridiculous he would look naked if he hadn't.

She kept this thought to herself, as Lydia showed him the dragon's head. He looked at Quinta with new interest.

'You can certainly draw, this is meticulous.'

'Yes, because it's the one I'll work from.'

'And you'll carve it yourself?'

'Of course,' said Quinta.

Adam went to the counter and got himself a vast bowl of assorted ices. He poured various sauces on top and returned to the little marble-topped table.

'Where did you learn to draw?' he asked, pulling the pad towards him to look at the dragon's head again.

'At college. Part of the training.'

'Hmm,' said Adam.

'Quinta's going to start work on the scroll as soon as she comes back from her holiday,' said Lydia. 'Where are you going, Quinta? You never said, just that it was somewhere near the sea so that Phoebe could play on the beach.'

Quinta pulled a face. 'That was the plan. We were going to go to Yntrig. Unfortunately, the youth hostel is booked up, a block booking they said. So I've got to find somewhere else, which is going to be difficult, because it isn't long now, and I can't change my holiday dates.'

Lydia gave Quinta a surprised look. 'What a coincidence. That's where Adam's dig is, that's where I'm going.'

'I'm afraid we're to blame for the lack of space at the youth hostel,' said Adam. 'We've booked most of it for the volunteers.

It's an emergency dig, the site is rapidly disappearing into the sea, so we need as many people as we can get.' He started to say something else, but hesitated.

Lydia looked at him with her sleepy eyes. 'Out with it, Adam. What were you going to say?'

'It's only a suggestion.' He turned to Quinta. 'You see, one of my technical people, who does the drawing work on site, can't come. She rang me this morning. It's going to be impossible to find anyone else at such short notice . . .'

Lydia's face lit up. 'Oh, and you think Quinta could do it.'

Adam quelled Lydia's enthusiasm with a cold blue look. 'She could do it, I am sure, because she has the skill, but it isn't fair to ask.'

'Why not?' said Lydia.

'Because,' and he turned his attention full on Quinta, who was thoughtfully finishing her ice, 'because I think your friend Quinta works very hard, and when she has a holiday, then she needs to relax, not to work many hours a day as will be the case on site.'

'Actually,' said Quinta, 'I'd love to do it. Holidays with Phoebe aren't much of a rest, in fact. I only get any time to myself at half term when I take her to Butlin's.'

'Butlin's?' Lydia was shocked.

Quinta grinned. 'Sounds dreadful, doesn't it? But Phoebe adores it, any child of her age would. Endless things to do, you don't have to pay for anything separately, it's all included in the price. She's supervised all the time, and enjoys every minute.'

'But what about you?' Lydia just couldn't see Quinta at a Butlin's holiday camp. 'Do you stay in one of those horrid little chalets and go to Bingo and dance competitions in the evenings?'

'I do stay in one of those chalets, which aren't at all bad, if basic. And no, I don't go to anything at all while I'm there, that's what's so wonderful, I can spend all my time reading. That's why it's such a holiday for me.'

Adam regarded her with respect. 'It isn't easy bringing up a child single-handed, is it?'

No sympathy, thought Quinta, but a lot of understanding. I wonder why he makes me feel so uneasy.

'At least I've only got one,' she said lightly. 'Think of those poor mothers left with three or four to bring up on their own.' She looked at Adam thoughtfully. 'Tell me more about what's involved.'

She listened intently, as Adam explained. 'It sounds interesting,' she said. 'I could do that.'

'No money,' said Adam. 'Everyone's a volunteer on this one. But you could have Cathy's room at the lodge – that's where several of us are staying. Phoebe would have to share with you. And you'd get breakfast and an evening meal, that's laid on.'

'What about Phoebe?' said Quinta. 'She'd be a nuisance, she'd want to help, but not for more than half an hour, and she would probably cause chaos.'

Adam shook his head. 'No problem. There'll be quite a few children there, and several people are coming with husbands and wives who won't be involved with the dig. Your daughter would have a whale of a time.'

'Done,' said Quinta. 'Can I speak to this Cathy person on the phone, make sure I bring what I need, get some more information about it?'

'Sure,' said Adam. 'I'll give Lydia her number. And I'm very grateful.'

'Don't be,' said Quinta with ready good-humour. 'You're doing me a favour.' She looked at her watch. 'Heavens, if that's the time, I must go. Phoebe will have finished by now.'

'Let me know what she says,' Lydia called after her as she flew out of the door. Then she turned her attention back to Adam. 'Finish your ice-cream quickly,' she said, looking at him with bed-hungry eyes. 'I've got to be back for five o'clock.'

'An hour,' said Adam, getting up from the table.

'You haven't finished your ice,' protested Lydia, as he took her by the hand.

'There are some things I like even better than ice-cream,' he said.

Phoebe was full of self-importance after her session with the psychologist. Quinta had hoped to speak to the woman who had done the tests, but she merely handed Phoebe over with a smile. 'I don't think you've got very much to worry about with this one,' she said. 'I'll send the full report in a week or two, and then if you've got any questions, give me a ring. However, perhaps you should start thinking about a different school. I don't feel that her present school is the best place for her.'

Dismissed, Quinta walked home with Phoebe. She was relieved; obviously Phoebe wasn't as bad as her head had said, but what on earth was she going to do about a different school?

'Of course, she should go to the Cathedral School,' Pauline said in her bossy way as she came round to pick up Phoebe on Sunday evening.

'That's all very well,' said Quinta, 'but you know I can't afford the fees.'

'You'll have to swallow your pride and ask your parents to help.'

Quinta shook her head. 'No. They'd pay all right, but they'd say she had to go away to board somewhere horrible, and then they'd want her in the holidays.'

Pauline pursed her lips. 'Beggars can't be choosers. Phoebe's obviously got serious educational problems, it needs to be sorted out. I think you should put your child's best interests before your own feelings.'

Why is Pauline always so right and yet invariably wrong, thought Quinta as she stuffed Phoebe's pyjamas into her rucksack.

Phoebe had been boot-faced about spending the night with Pauline. 'Gavin's a drip, and Peter's just a baby,' she said scornfully. 'And Pauline makes me eat food for supper that's good for me, and I hate it, because it makes me feel sick.'

'Tough,' said Alban, who had wandered out of his studio looking for refreshment. 'It does you good to have to eat what you don't like, that'll make you appreciate your mother's cooking.'

'How are you going to manage without me?' said Phoebe darkly. 'I mean, Q, just what are you going to do without me here? It'll be very boring, and Alban's going to be in London. You'll be really lonely.'

'I'll manage,' said Quinta, thinking what bliss it would be to have an evening entirely to herself. 'I've got to get things ready for our holiday.'

'I'll pack my things,' said Phoebe. 'You might forget the things that really matter, like books, and my black velvet owls!'

'Yes,' said Quinta, as Phoebe vanished to her room to start piling things on the floor. 'But I'll remember the unimportant things like knickers and socks.'

'I suppose you've got a list,' Phoebe shouted contemptuously from her room.

'No, actually, Phoebe, I haven't,' Quinta shouted back.

Now, as she saw Phoebe off, she felt guilty. Phoebe gave her a reproachful look, and then ran back to wrap her arms round her neck and give her a ferocious hug.

'Have a good time at Water-World tomorrow,' Quinta called after her, and watched until Pauline's car had turned the corner.

She supposed they did need to set off to Water-World very early the next morning, which was why Phoebe had gone to spend the night there.

'You'll never get her to us on time, Quinta,' Pauline had said. 'You're getting very lax these days, I had hopes of you for a while, because you seemed to be getting quite organized. You mustn't let yourself slip. I know everyone goes on about how hard life is for single mothers these days, but it's hard for the rest of us, too, and you don't hear me complaining. We all have to organize our lives.'

I am much more disorganized than I used to be, thought Quinta. I haven't made a list for days, and I certainly need one quickly if we're going away on Friday. Help!

She closed the door, and made a face at the huge old clock which ticked away in the hall. It had a sun face, with moon and sun at the bottom. Round the edge of the face were written some words from a poem by Herrick:

> The glorious lamp of heaven, the sun
> The higher he's a-getting
> The sooner will his race be run
> And nearer he's to setting.

How true, thought Quinta, as she always did; the words made

her feel that she was wasting time, the hours were sliding past, and so was her life.

Quarter past five. Alban would be off shortly, and then, oh joy, an evening all to herself. As long as Simon didn't know that Alban was away and decide to pay a visit. Or Pauline ring up once the children were in bed to harangue her or nag her into doing something she didn't want to do.

To her surprise, Alban was still in the kitchen. He raised an expressive eyebrow at her, then opened the fridge and took out a bottle of cold water. He poured himself a glass and leant against the fridge.

'We've got to have a talk, Quinta,' he said.

Oh, no, thought Quinta. 'We often talk,' she pointed out.

'Yes, but not about anything that matters.'

'You talk about your music. Doesn't that matter?'

Alban looked surprised. 'Of course it matters, really it's the only thing that matters in the end. No, that's not what I mean, other things do matter, I realize that.'

Unusually, he seemed ill at ease. He fiddled with his glass, then put it down on the table.

'Quinta, I've been thinking. We ought to get married.'

Quinta was so surprised she dropped the pan she was drying up. It landed with a resounding clang on the tile floor.

'Now look what you've made me do,' she said reproachfully. 'It's chipped the corner off the tile!'

'It can be replaced,' said Alban.

'That is so like you,' said Quinta. 'These tiles cost a fortune, aren't you worried about the cost of anything?'

Alban looked surprised. 'I'm certainly not worried about the cost of one tile. Come on, Quinta, you're losing your sense of proportion. And anyway,' he went on, working himself up into a temper, 'it's bloody rude. I ask you to marry me, and you witter on about a floor tile.'

'You didn't exactly ask me to marry you,' said Quinta. 'You said "we ought to get married", as though it were an obligation or a duty, not anything you much wanted to do.'

'I'm sorry. Do you want me to take you out to dinner, crawl on my knees? I'll do that if you want.'

'I don't want that,' said Quinta vehemently. 'I'm very fond of you, Alban, you know that, but I don't want to get married, not to you or to anyone else.'

Alban was silent for a few moments. Quinta methodically finished drying the pans and hung them on their hooks.

'This is no good,' Alban burst out. 'Fond of me! You've never been as close to me as I'd like. You're always so reserved, I never know what you're really thinking or feeling. Now you're slipping away from me even more, I don't know why . . . but I'm not going to lose you. I've offered to marry you, and you say no, without even thinking about it. I suppose if Phoebe's bloody father turned up, you'd go off with him without a backward glance. Yes, and you'd marry him, too, if he'd got rid of his wife, wouldn't you? People say I'm too old for you, but he must be old enough to be your grandfather. Probably too old to get it up any more, but you wouldn't care about that, would you, because you're still in love with him, after all this time, and after what he did to you, and I don't suppose you're capable of ever loving anyone else. It makes me sick.'

He flung out of the room, only to reappear almost immediately. 'And what about Phoebe? She needs a proper father, have you ever thought about that? No, you struggle on, the devoted single mother, and Phoebe has to do without all kinds of things that she deserves, like a decent school and proper music lessons – all because of your stupid pride and your misplaced passion for the bastard who debauched you when you weren't old enough to know any better.'

Quinta's eyes were round with shock; Alban had never spoken like this to her before. She ran her damp hands through her hair, making it flare into a halo around her head.

'Oh, Quinta,' said Alban. 'Quinta, please.'

Quinta was furious. 'Oh, yes, marry me, all home comforts at no cost, and you've always got a cosy little mistress down in London when it gets boring at home. What's the advantage, Alban? Four nights a week with me instead of two, and then three nights down there with Hermione. Terrific for you, and all done because you care so much about Phoebe!'

The scorn in her voice made Alban wince. 'Hermione? What's Hermione got to do with this? If we get married, Hermione will have to go. She wouldn't want to stay, anyhow. And how did you find out about Hermione?'

'Simon told me,' said Quinta.

'Bloody Simon,' said Alban furiously. 'It comes to something when your own brother . . . Well, never mind that. The point is, Quinta, we can't go on like this.'

Oh, God, thought Quinta. What's going to happen to us now? If Alban felt like this, how could she go on living in his house? And how would she manage if she had to find somewhere else to live? She could barely make ends meet as it was.

She ran out of the kitchen, tears streaming down her face, and locked herself in her room. Alban knocked and banged, and called desperately to her; in the end he went away, leaving her alone with her damp and depressing thoughts.

A little later she heard the door bang as he left the house on his way to the station.

So much for my wonderful, peaceful evening alone, thought Quinta as she lay in the darkness of the chill summer night. Even the cats had deserted her, and she could feel the empty silence of the house all around her.

Thoughts ran round and round in her head. If she left Alban, and the Manor House, and it might well come to that, where could she go? How would it affect Phoebe, who had enough problems in her young life as it was?

This was the only home Phoebe had ever known. And she had always had Alban there: would it be very traumatic not to see him again? Because it would have to be a clean break, if he was feeling like this. Perhaps she should leave Eyot altogether. Her heart went cold at the thought; it wasn't only Phoebe who had found a home here. Besides, could she get a job anywhere else? Money was tight, even now with the minimal rent Alban charged her in return for housekeeping.

Then there was the double-bass for Lydia. Of course, she'd finish it, whatever happened, but she had formed a plan of making some more instruments . . . It would be soul-destroying to have to go back to just repairing instruments.

In those dark hours, Quinta felt more alone than she had ever been in Eyot. She looked at the foundations of her life, and realized how fragile they were. And how they weren't just her foundations, but Phoebe's as well. She felt a stab of fear at the thought of how much Phoebe depended on her, how sure she was that Quinta had the answers, could make everything all right.

And I can't, thought Quinta wretchedly, as a restless sleep finally came to her with the grey light of dawn. I can't.

Quinta was so busy for the remaining few days before they went on holiday that she didn't have time to think properly about Alban. It was a problem, it would have to be solved, she could see her life having to change, and not for the better; but for the moment she pushed the whole matter firmly to the back of her mind. Phoebe's holiday came first, and she wanted her to enjoy it all. Phoebe knew when Quinta was depressed or worried, and hated it, so Quinta, who had learned to keep her worries and problems to herself, was successfully able to hide the fact that their future suddenly looked so uncertain.

Phoebe passed her days in an orgy of holiday activities, while Quinta finished off everything she could at work. She put in as much time as she could on Lydia's double-bass; although she was looking forward to her holiday, she hated the thought of leaving it. I'm becoming obsessed with it, she told herself. Probably because, when I'm working on it, I forget about everything else.

'Even Phoebe,' she confessed guiltily to Lucy Praetorius on the phone. Lucy had rung up to talk to Alban.

'He's not here,' said Quinta. 'He was due back, but there's no sign of him, and he hasn't rung. Have you tried him in London?'

'I just get the answerphone,' said his mother. 'I'm sure he's there all the time, listening to me. You can listen in, can't you, with these modern ones? You can filter out the people you don't want to speak to. I left a very sharp message last time I rang, but he still hasn't telephoned me.'

'Oh dear,' said Quinta. 'I hope he's all right.'

'If he won't speak to anyone, including me, then either he's in the throes of a major composition, you know how he is then, or he's in a huff and is afraid I'll tell him not to be so silly.'

Quinta thought for a moment. She felt guilty, he had gone off without a word; was he really so upset?

'What about Hermione?' she said. 'Wouldn't she answer the phone?'

There was silence at the other end. Then: 'Ah, so you know about Hermione, do you? I wondered if you did. Did Alban tell you about her?'

'No, Simon did, in a fit of pique.'

'To have one idiotic son is bad enough,' said Lucy, in decidedly unmotherly tones, 'but two is an ordeal. I'd like to knock their heads together.' She paused. 'Hermione goes back a long way, before he met you.'

Quinta hastened to reassure her. 'It doesn't bother me at all, really, Alban's free to do whatever he wants.'

'She's the most depressing creature,' said Lucy. 'She stopped growing when she was about eighteen. I don't mean physically, goodness, she's a great tall thing, but mentally and emotionally. She's never grown up properly, which is always so disheartening. Then, she worships Alban in exactly the way she did when she was barely out of adolescence, and it's very bad for him. She waits on him hand and foot. She's a flautist, you know, plays in one of the London orchestras. Alban always says orchestral players have a mental age of about fifteen; but he doesn't seem to mind it in Hermione. Really, he is tiresome, I wish he'd grow up and get married.'

'He wants to marry me,' said Quinta, rather nervously.

Lucy laughed, and Quinta could tell it was with genuine amusement.

'I said no. I'm so sorry, if you wanted him to get married, but I just don't want to marry him.'

'Quite right, too,' said Lucy briskly. 'I'm so fond of you and Phoebe, you know I am, and I'd love to have you for a daughter-in-law, but in the long term Alban isn't right for you. One son with a disastrous marriage is enough, I knew from the beginning that it would be a mistake for Simon to marry Evie. Such a silly woman with her endless ridiculous fads – and never original ones, either; always what everyone else is doing. She's going on retreats now, says she wants to become a deacon. Can you believe it?'

'Oh,' was all Quinta could say.

'Well, never mind that. When Alban reappears, will you tell him he must telephone me? I'll be coming to England in September.'

'He's going to Spain in September,' said Quinta. 'And I don't know when I'll see him again, unless he's back in the next day or too. I'm taking Phoebe on holiday, you see, and I'll be away for three weeks.'

'How annoying. If he isn't there, who's going to look after the cats?'

'I'll have to put them in the cattery,' said Quinta. 'For three weeks, they'll hate that. And I'm a bit worried about leaving the house empty for so long . . . I wish Alban hadn't chosen just now to vanish. I suppose it's my fault, we had rather an argument . . .' She sighed.

'Nonsense,' said Lucy. 'You aren't responsible for anything Alban thinks or does, he's quite old enough to behave properly. And it's no excuse being an artist; in fact, I think creative people need to be more disciplined than the rest of us, not less. You go off and enjoy your holiday. Find someone to house-sit if you possibly can, although that might be difficult at such short notice. I'll see you in September, we'll have a lovely long talk.'

She rang off, leaving Quinta feeling a little better. She bent down to pick up a sock of Phoebe's which was lurking behind the chest where the telephone sat, and found an unopened letter lurking behind the radiator. Postmarked nearly a week ago, she thought. Not from Alban, which had been her first thought. Thank goodness for that. She opened it, and let out a whoop of joy.

'What's up?' asked Phoebe, emerging from her room.

Quinta was back on the phone dialling furiously. 'It's Harriet, oh you won't remember Harriet, she looked after me when I first came here, before you were born. Good news, she's coming to work in Eyot, heavens, I am pleased.'

# 13

'You see,' Quinta told Lydia as they packed all her and Phoebe's belongings into the back of the Land Rover, 'it's worked out beautifully. She's coming to teach at the Cathedral School in the autumn, so she needs somewhere to stay while she's house-hunting; it's such a relief, and she likes the cats.'

'Won't Alban mind if he turns up and finds a stranger in his house?' said Lydia.

'He knows Harriet, and he gets on well with her, except he can't understand how anyone can spend all that time running. So that's all right.'

She bent down to pick up a large floppy sun hat which had fallen out of an over-full carrier bag and was claimed with loud shrieks by Phoebe.

'Besides, he knew I was going away, and he didn't bother to make any arrangements about the house, so it's tough if he doesn't like it.'

Lydia felt slightly jealous for a moment of this other old friend appearing in Quinta's life, and then she laughed at herself. Quinta didn't have so many friends – even if you included Pauline on the list – that she could do without any of them.

'How old is this Harriet?'

'Early thirties, I suppose,' said Quinta. 'She rescued me when I arrived here in the middle of the night on a coach, took me home, looked after me, held my hand while I was having Phoebe . . .'

She laughed, remembering Harriet afterwards, expressing her heartfelt determination never to have any children of her own.

'You'll like her, Lydia, she's straightforward, and has a good sense of humour. Also, she's very astute about people. She has such a clear mind that it's always helpful to talk to her when you're in a muddle. She walks into your mind, brushes it down, tidies it up, and then you wonder why on earth whatever it was seemed so complicated.'

'Hmm,' said Lydia. 'Well, I'm glad she's coming here if it's going to stop you worrying about the house all the time you're away. You never used to worry, did you, from what I can remember? You seem to worry a lot these days.'

'I've got a lot to worry about,' said Quinta in dark tones. Then she laughed. 'But not now, I feel as excited as Phoebe does about this holiday.'

'I think that's the lot,' said Lydia, flinging Phoebe's Wellingtons on top of the heap of things in the back of the Land Rover and surveying the empty pavement. 'I don't know how Phoebe's going to fit in, it's going to be a dreadful squash.'

'Oh, she's used to that,' said Quinta. 'I'll just take Harriet's key to Mrs Maddox round the corner, she'll be arriving later today; pity I'll miss her, but it can't be helped.'

A few minutes later she swung herself into the driver's seat. 'I've never driven one of these before, wonder how it works.'

Lydia settled Phoebe more or less comfortably in the back, and then climbed in beside Quinta. 'I haven't got a clue,' she said. 'That's why you're driving, you're supposed to know. Adam didn't trust me in a strange vehicle like this, although he said he'll teach me to drive it while we're on the dig.'

'I didn't think you had a licence,' said Phoebe from the back. 'So how can you drive?'

'I can drive,' said Lydia. 'I mean, I know how to, but I haven't taken a test yet, they couldn't book me in until October. But I can drive as long as someone who does have a driving licence is in the car with me.'

'So why doesn't Adam trust you?' said Phoebe persistently.

'He thinks Quinta's had more experience. She drives the van, remember.'

'Badly,' muttered Phoebe, as Quinta jerked uneasily into gear and drove slowly away from the kerb.

'Quiet,' said Lydia, laughing. 'You are so rude, Phoebe.

Now, just enjoy the drive, and be glad to be off on holi-day.'

'I suppose it's better than going on the train with millions of people, like we usually do,' said Phoebe.

'Ungracious child,' said Quinta, concentrating furiously on her driving. 'And if you're not excited at the prospect of going on holiday, I am.'

'And so am I,' added Lydia. 'Three weeks without grandmama nagging at me, what heaven!'

'I know all the young people these days are very casual about that kind of thing, they think nothing of going off together, single men and girls, no married people with them . . .'

Marjorie manhandled an enormous clump of greenery out of the back of her small estate car.

'But, and I don't say this to criticize Lady Wray, but, young people simply cannot be trusted together.'

'There will be a lot of them there, safety in numbers, don't you think?' murmured Wyn, trailing along behind with a box of strange-looking poppy heads which had been stiffened and sprayed and subdued by Marjorie's skilful hands.

'There are a lot of people at orgies,' said Marjorie. 'Not, of course, that I have ever been to one.'

'No, naturally not,' said Wyn, trying in vain to imagine Marjorie in a veil and harem trousers. The word orgy always wafted her to the mysterious East, with sultry palaces and sloe-eyed houris spread with abandon on cushions set about a marble fountain. It was a happy thought, but Wyn was brought back to the north of England with a bump by Daphne, who remarked that one's aim with young people must be to foresee every opportunity for misbehaviour and to make sure they were gainfully occupied elsewhere instead.

'We shouldn't always think the worst,' said Wyn. 'And they aren't so young, none of them teenagers; in their twenties, I think, most of them. Apart from the children.'

Marjorie and Daphne regarded Wyn warily over the foliage.

'They have more ideas when they get a bit older,' said Daphne. 'Dangerous ideas.'

'They think they can handle anything, and of course they

can't,' said Marjorie. 'No, if I were Lady Wray, I would have put my foot down.'

'I don't suppose Lydia would have paid any attention if she had,' said Wyn, determined to stand her ground, just for once. 'Lydia is only her granddaughter, and she's of age; there really is nothing for Lady Wray to say about it.'

'She can ring up her mother, tell her what Lydia's up to. Or her father.'

'No, Daphne, not her father. He's a man of very loose morals, very lax, he'd just laugh and tell her to enjoy herself.'

'Is he a nice man?' enquired Wyn. 'I've got your wire here, Marjorie, if that's what you're looking for.'

'Thank you dear, I find it helpful if everyone puts all the things we need down on the table straight away. Then one can find everything as soon as one wants it. No,' she went on, 'he is not a nice man. I think we mentioned to you that he ran away with the cook.'

Wyn laughed. 'Fortunate man to have a cook to run away with.'

Marjorie and Daphne were shocked by Wyn's levity. Marjorie lowered her voice. 'We are in a sacred place, Wyn,' she said in a patient voice. 'Lydia's mother was very much upset by the whole business. The cook was one of these girls who come to help out; they took her on when things were particularly busy at the hospital. It was a shocking affair, shocking.'

She twisted a large branch of greenery and broke it off with a firm snap.

'Lady Wray was very put out about it. She tries to discourage Lydia from seeing her father, and since he lives abroad, Lydia can't see him that often. But she's been very wilful about it, and I believe went to stay with him – and the other woman . . .'

'The cook,' said Wyn helpfully.

'Yes, the cook, she's been to stay with them several times while she was at the University.'

'She may have inherited some of his, well, propensities,' said Daphne, her face lighting up at this pleasurable thought.

'I certainly hope not,' said Marjorie. 'It's all very well for a man, and quite bad enough, but it's much worse for a girl to be like that. However, we must give her the benefit of the doubt.

Now she's here, in Eyot, which is a long way from London, and where such goings-on are fortunately rare, I expect she'll settle down. She should marry Adam and start a family, he's a most suitable young man, and then she will do no-one any harm by going off with him.'

'No, indeed,' said Wyn brightly. 'It would be quite expected of them then. To go away together, I mean, and do things together that they aren't supposed to do now . . . if they are doing anything, which of course we can't know.'

The Vicar of the church where they were helping out with the flower festival bustled into the vestry.

'Good morning, good morning, ladies, how good to see you. Enjoying a gossip, are you? I know you ladies, always tearing your friends and acquaintances to pieces.'

Marjorie drew herself up to her full height; she was a tall woman, and looked imposing enough to quell any number of vicars.

'We never gossip,' she said with superb aplomb. 'Come, Daphne, come, Wyn.' She glared at the Vicar. 'Are you doing an arrangement, Vicar?'

'Oh, dear me, no. I leave all that to the ladies, let the experts do it, I say. No, I shall just sit in the entrance here, with my own little floral arts, working away, and those who are interested may watch.'

'What are his little floral arts?' asked Wyn, interested, as the Vicar went off to waylay a verger.

'Icing sugar,' said Marjorie in a voice rich with contempt. 'He makes little flowers, leaves, that kind of thing, out of icing sugar.'

'He's very good at it,' said Daphne, who hated to see any man of the cloth belittled. 'Exquisite, little masterpieces in miniature, that's what I call them.'

'Tush,' said Marjorie.

There weren't nearly as many lurid goings-on at the dig as the three graces liked to imagine. For one thing the weather, having had a few days of watery sunshine and some temperatures within a few degrees of the seasonal norm, reverted to the sullen state of the rest of the summer. Cold winds, pouring rain and low, heavy grey clouds were not conducive to sultry thoughts.

Lydia grumbled to Quinta as they sat in the sitting room of the house Adam had been lent, trying to coax some life into the fire. It had been a shooting lodge, and was built in the baronial style. 'What a ghastly place,' Lydia had exclaimed when she arrived.

'I wish they'd taken the stuffed heads and gloomy pictures with them when they left,' said Quinta.

'It would seem unfurnished without them,' said Lydia gravely. 'After all, camp beds and rucksacks aren't exactly in keeping with the surroundings. Do you think it's this place which is having such a dampening effect on Adam?'

'Not the ardour you expected?' said Quinta, blowing rather hopelessly at a little patch of red which glowed under a smoking log.

'Certainly not what I had hoped for,' said Lydia disconsolately. 'He's preoccupied, hardly says a word to me all day, then in the evening, it's talk, talk talk; not with me, but with the archaeologists, and then telephoning people, writing notes . . . you'd think he was writing a book the amount he writes. He doesn't come to bed until about two o'clock in the morning, and then it's all a bit perfunctory, he's obviously dying to get to sleep.'

'In Eyot, he had plenty of time for amorous pursuits,' Quinta pointed out. 'Here, he's on duty as it were. He's tucking this excavation around his normal work, you heard him say so. He hasn't got time to dally with you as well as fight the weather and the mud and the encroaching sea.'

Lydia giggled at Quinta's poetic language. She raised her arms above her head and stretched langorously. 'It's wonderful just to get inside at the end of the day and get clean and warm again.'

'Yes,' said Quinta, who was getting used to working underneath a huge fishing umbrella, propped up in a makeshift way around a box which acted as a table. It kept her papers dry, but the water trickled down her neck and arms. 'I think I have a damp soul by now,' she said. 'Is it ever going to stop raining?'

'I hope so,' said Lydia, yawning. 'Look at me, half past ten, and I'm dying to go to bed. Dreadful. It's boredom, I think, I had no idea it was going to be so boring. Nothing happens, each day is the same. No exciting finds, nothing unexpected. I shall be glad when it's over.'

Quinta looked at her, and wished she was slim and effortlessly elegant in the way that Lydia seemed able to be, even in her scruffiest clothes. 'When it's over, presumably Adam will be back in Cambridge,' she said practically.

Lydia sat up. 'True, and I will hardly ever see him.'

'You could always follow him to Cambridge,' suggested Quinta, her eyes noting a sudden wariness in Lydia. Lydia swore that all there was between her and Adam was sex: was that really the case? Could Lydia possibly be falling in love with Adam? It was a thought that worried Quinta, who wasn't sure whether her unease was founded on her suspicion that Adam was not exactly what he seemed, or whether she was just envious of her friend having such a carefree attitude to men and sex.

It was difficult to judge how Adam felt. He was carelessly possessive about Lydia, making no secret of his relationship with her. He would give her bottom a casual caress as she walked past, bend over and bite her neck while she was sitting at a table, swing his arm round her as they stood and talked about some detail of work.

No, surely there wasn't any more to it than that. It was merely a summer affair . . . but would he embark on a mere summer affair with Lady Wray's granddaughter, of all people – and right under the noses of the two grandmothers? That suggested something more serious. Perhaps Adam felt it was time he got married; people started talking after a while if a good-looking young man remained single.

Did he have another girlfriend in Cambridge? That was a side of his life about which, according to Lydia, he never spoke. Would Adam care what anybody said? Quinta thought not. She just felt, on no particular grounds, that whatever there was between Adam and Lydia, it wasn't going to be very long-lasting.

'Who can tell?' said Lydia. 'People are inseparable for years, wonderfully suited, all kinds of bonds and then, pouf, they go their different ways and never see each other again. While others seem to have no more than a casual or superficial friendship, and there they are, heading for Darby and Joan happiness.'

She got slowly to her feet. 'No point in fighting the inevitable, I'm going to bed. Is Phoebe asleep?'

'Ages ago,' said Quinta. 'She sleeps like a log, all the fresh air and companionship, it's doing her the world of good.'

'Those kids are the only ones having a good time,' said Lydia. 'Oh, my back. There's one job that isn't for me: digger.'

Quinta laughed. 'I don't think either of us has found our metier. I like doing the recording work, but Adam's very impatient and critical, I can see he misses that Cathy person.'

'Nonsense, he's lucky to have you,' said Lydia. 'Goodnight.'

'Goodnight,' said Quinta. 'Let's hope tomorrow brings some excitement.'

Tomorrow did. First, Phoebe, during one of her brief forays into the dig proper, found a Roman shoe. She was disappointed by it, 'Horrid, dirty thing, I don't believe any Roman wore anything like that.'

The experts were pleased; Lydia, grubbing away at a wall, heard them talking. She wiped her forehead with a damp and muddy hand. What am I doing here? she thought. I could be in Greece, in the sun . . . Only you couldn't, she told herself firmly, because Angus is there with horrible Selina, he didn't want you. But I've got Adam now, bigger, better in bed . . . and yet.

Yet what? Lydia said to herself as she scraped away at a peculiar bump in the wall with the point of her little trowel. Yet, there was something missing with Adam that had been there with Angus. What? Like many people, Lydia found it very hard to think clearly about emotional matters – at least, about her own.

Had she felt more strongly about Angus than she did about Adam? Reluctantly, she had to admit that she had. Sex with Adam was certainly very exciting. So it wasn't that. Was Angus warmer? Was it that she had thought they were friends as well as lovers? Well, going off with Selina wasn't very friendly. Had

Angus been more fun to be with? Yes, but he was younger. Adam was grown up. She could laugh at Angus, could she laugh at Adam?

On reflection, she didn't think she'd want to. Perhaps it was that Angus had been part of growing up, a fling, although quite a long-lasting one, amazingly so, really, when you considered most university friendships. Or was it, and the chilling little thought crept unbidden into her mind; was it that she was afraid of Adam? It was difficult to laugh at someone who made you afraid.

'You shouldn't be shivering,' said Quinta who was passing by. 'It's almost warm today, and I do believe the sun may be going to come out.'

A nearby volunteer raised his tousled head from a trench. 'Sssh, if you show that you've noticed, the sun'll go straight back behind a cloud.'

'I wasn't cold,' said Lydia. 'I had a grim thought, suddenly.'

The head reappeared above the trench again. 'Bad, if you have those in broad daylight,' he said. 'Those are hour-of-the-wolf thoughts.'

'Hour-of-the-wolf?'

'Yup. The early hours of the morning. The time when people die and the witches come and the wolves howl in the wilderness.'

Quinta's eyes creased with amusement. 'He's right, that's the time for grisly thoughts.' Her eye was caught by something in the earth. 'What's this?' she asked, bending over to pick it up.

'Don't touch it,' called the head from the trench. He sprang out, and came over to them. He crouched down beside Lydia, and took her trowel.

'Coins!' said Lydia.

'Yes, a cache,' he said with great satisfaction as he deftly brushed the earth away from the little heap of dull metal. 'This will please Adam. Don't touch, I'll get him.'

'Never a word of thanks to us for finding the wretched things,' complained Lydia as she and Quinta sat eating their lunch together. 'Just yak, yak with his fellow earthies.'

'I think it's team effort, individuals don't really count for much.'

'You're right of course. Still, he praised Phoebe when she found the shoe; that was kind of him.'

'Yes,' said Quinta. 'He's good with children.'

Lydia finished her apple and lay back against the rock. The sun had come out and there was warmth in the air. The site was balanced on the edge of a cliff, and gulls wheeled round their heads, hoping for scraps. The sea was calmer than it had been, but still restless and grey.

'I wouldn't like to have been a Viking,' said Lydia lazily. 'Imagine being out on that, day after day.'

'No wonder they were wild when they came ashore,' said Quinta. 'Sheer relief.'

'Grim times to live in,' said Lydia. 'In our civilized times, here, busy on scholarly work, or in Eyot, say, those Vikings seem utterly remote. Not just of another age, but a different species.'

'I wouldn't be too sure,' said Quinta, peeling off her socks. 'Oh, how wonderful not to have damp feet for once.' She wriggled her toes. 'I'm sure that whatever kind of people there have been since the Stone Age, oh, since before then, they're still here among us. And there are probably highly evolved people here too, what mankind might be like in ten or twenty thousand years from now.'

'Are you sure they'll be more civilized than we are?'

'You said yourself, not many Vikings marauding around Eyot. And we don't hang children, or burn witches.'

'They do in some places.'

'But it isn't the norm. People protest, know it's wrong. And we're horrified when we hear or see bloodthirsty happenings in the news. We're appalled; well, we probably wouldn't have been three hundred years ago.'

Lydia was unconvinced. She didn't share Quinta's optimism, and pointed out that the world would no doubt have blown itself up long before ten or twenty thousand years had passed. Quinta thought not, what a waste of time it would all have been, she argued.

'So, who's watching?' said Lydia. 'Who does care about us?

Less than ants in the greater scheme of things, that's what we are. Not that there is a greater scheme of things.'

'Music,' said Quinta, closing her eyes and enjoying the warmth on her face

'Music?' echoed Lydia, puzzled.

'Music. If there weren't a greater scheme of some kind, there would be no music. No species that produces Mozart can be ants. Shakespeare knew all about music. Harmonies of the universe, all that.'

Lydia thought about it. 'You could be right,' she admitted. She followed Quinta's example and took her socks off. 'Heaven,' she said, 'to have dry toes.' She looked down at their feet. 'Aren't feet horrible?'

'Babies' feet aren't. They're delightful.' Quinta sat up and looked at Lydia's feet. She groaned. 'Slim, elegant feet, just like the rest of you, wouldn't you know it?'

'Don't be silly,' said Lydia, lying back. 'Are women ever foot-fetishists, or is it only men?'

Quinta considered. 'I don't know any foot-fetishists, male or female.'

Lydia opened a lazy eye. 'You think you don't know any, but how can you tell? That's the thing about perversions and strange habits, isn't it? Mostly, the people who have them appear to be perfectly normal.' She yawned, and closed her eyes again. 'I had a cousin who was one.'

'One what?'

'Foot-fetishist. He bought dozens and dozens of pairs of shoes for his wife, extraordinary shoes. He couldn't make love to her unless she was wearing these very strange and exotic shoes.'

'How did she feel about that?'

'She got very fed up. She liked wearing trainers, boots, sandals, not spiky, high-heeled numbers with sequins and what-not on them. She said they made rips in the bedclothes for one thing, and besides, he was never quite sure what size her feet were, he usually bought them too small.'

'Goodness,' said Quinta. 'What happened?'

'She left him. They got divorced, and he married a woman who worked in a shoe shop.'

'Perhaps the Duke of Wellington was one,' said Quinta.

Lydia looked at her with half-closed eyes. 'Why? Because of the boots? I thought those were merely practical.'

'Not those ones, his own boots. Don't you remember? He did his wife the honour with his boots on.'

'Randy rather than a fetishist, I'd say.'

Quinta's laugh rang out above the sound of the squalling gulls. Then she sighed. 'Nobody would be keen on my feet, not even a fetishist,' she said. 'Peasant's feet, that's what I've got.'

'I think they're rather pretty feet, actually,' said a voice above them. 'May I join you?'

'Hello, Titus,' said Quinta in surprise. 'What are you doing here?'

'Visiting,' he said. 'You've found a pleasant spot here. Shouldn't you be hard at work? Doesn't Adam keep your noses to the grindstone?'

'Not if he doesn't know where we are,' said Lydia. 'Do you know Adam?'

'Our paths have crossed in Cambridge,' said Titus unexpansively. 'I just gave a lift to a couple of friends of his. I was coming this way, so I said I'd drop them off.'

Lydia got to her feet. 'Does Adam know they're coming?' she asked.

'They seemed to think he was expecting them, or at least one of them. They're a brother and sister,' he explained. 'I think the brother is the one who knows Adam. Striking-looking pair.'

'He never mentioned them,' said Lydia. 'I'll go and find him.'

Titus slid down beside Quinta.

'I'd better get back to my drawing board,' said Quinta.

'Much nicer here,' said Titus.'

'You're right, but duty calls.'

'Have five minutes more lying in the sun, it'll do you good, you've got dark shadows under your eyes. Do you lead a wild life or do you just not sleep very well?'

Quinta looked at him in surprise. 'Things worry me rather at night,' she admitted.

'Then relax while you can,' said Titus. 'Tell me, are your friend Lydia and Adam an item?'

'You could say that, yes.'

'That's what I'd heard.'

'Why do you ask?'

'I find it surprising, that's all.'

'Why?'

Titus said nothing for a minute, but gazed out to sea. 'Oh, no particular reason. Lydia didn't strike me as his type, that's all.'

'They make a very handsome pair,' said Quinta.

'Handsome is as handsome does,' said Titus annoyingly. He got up and wandered closer to the edge of the cliff.

'Careful,' cried Quinta.

'It's all right, I have no intention of hurtling over. Tremendous erosion on this bit of coast.'

'That's why they're excavating,' said Quinta. 'They think this whole piece of cliff will vanish in the next year or so, taking the Roman fort with it.'

'Sooner than that, I'd say,' remarked Titus. 'I wouldn't eat my lunch here again if I were you. This could disappear any time.'

Quinta was collecting her things and stuffing them into her rucksack. She pulled her socks back on, wrinkling up her nose as she felt the wet wool on her skin.

'Thank you for the warning,' she said politely.

'Tell the children, too,' he said. 'Phoebe's here, isn't she? I saw her as I came up with some other children.'

'They know about the cliff,' said Quinta. 'Adam doesn't think there's any immediate danger. He's a responsible kind of person, he'd move everyone away very quickly if there were any danger.'

'Responsible? I suppose so,' said Titus thoughtfully. He held out his hand to Quinta to pull her up. 'Come on, show me round this fort before it plunges over the cliff and out of history.'

## 14

Quinta enjoyed showing Titus round. Here, on a summer's day, with warm breezes blowing across the short, cliff-top grass, she felt more relaxed in his company than she had before. He was an easy companion, with a quirky sense of humour: Quinta had a soft spot for a witty man. Alban doesn't make me laugh very often, she thought, as she showed Titus the bath house. Perhaps that's why I've never been completely comfortable with him.

She discussed this with Lydia later on, as she sat on the edge of Lydia's bath, waiting for her to finish. Lydia swirled the bubbly water with her hands.

'I'm the sea, washing that beastly fort over the cliff, whoosh!'

'Lydia!' said Quinta reprovingly. 'Think of the loss to scholarship. And you an historian.'

'That's why I'm not a very good one,' said Lydia candidly. 'History to me is people, not heaps of rubble marked Hypocaust; Bath House; Probable Site of Latrines . . .'

She slid down into the bath and blew into the bubbles. 'Funny you should say that about Alban making you laugh,' she went on. 'I was thinking about Adam and Angus and men with a sense of humour today while I was digging out that wall.'

'And?'

'I don't think I do like witty men, not especially. They leave me feeling at a loss, I'm not quick enough for them, not like you.'

'Don't be ridiculous,' protested Quinta. 'You're much cleverer than I am.'

'I wouldn't be too sure about that,' said Lydia. 'I have a good, steady mind, when I can be bothered to use it. But it isn't an original mind, and I don't find things funny the way you do. You like people's absurdities; with me, either I don't notice them, or I find them annoying.'

'Most of the time I don't think Alban knows what makes me laugh,' said Quinta. 'But he likes people to laugh,' she added loyally. 'He isn't a killjoy.'

'I like complex men,' said Lydia. 'Men that you never feel you know entirely.'

'Like Adam. He's very secretive, isn't he?'

'Mmm, he is rather. And that's why you're lucky to have Alban, you can see he's a very complicated person, lots of depth. That's what makes him interesting.'

'Oh, do you think so?' said Quinta, who felt that Alban was in many ways like his brother, simply an overgrown schoolboy.

'Titus, now, he's very urbane, very easy to get on with, but a bit superficial, wouldn't you say?'

'No,' said Quinta thoughtfully. 'No, I don't agree, I don't think Titus is at all superficial. I think he's an interesting man. Very clever.'

'Wonder what he's like as a lover,' said Lydia, idly inspecting a blister on her toe.

Quinta laughed. 'Neither of us is going to find out, we aren't old enough for him.'

'True. He must have a mother complex.'

'Potted psychology,' said Quinta. 'Actually, I think Titus is remarkably free of complexes, I never knew a man so at ease with himself.'

'Who's his latest?'

'I don't know, I haven't seen him with anyone recently. Come on, Lydia, do hurry up, I must have a bath, and I said I'd give a hand with the cooking, all these extra people.'

Lydia sat up abruptly, sending a wave of water over the edge of the bath. 'Which extra people?'

'You've soaked me,' said Quinta, seizing Lydia's towel.

'Never mind. Tell!'

'Titus is staying overnight, wants to talk to Adam and that other chap. Mathematics, chaos and archaeology, I daresay; what a mixture. And so are that brother and sister who turned up.'

'What? Oh, God, they're not staying, are they? I thought they were just here for the afternoon. Oh, bother. Where will they all sleep?'

'In the children's room, I suppose, since Phoebe and the others are away for the night. They're staying overnight with Lara's grandparents, they live near here and have a swimming pool. So the sister can come in with me and have Phoebe's bed.'

'I don't like these friends,' said Lydia as she got out of the bath.

'I haven't met them yet,' said Quinta, letting Lydia's bath out. 'What are they like?'

'Just as Titus said, striking-looking. Closed, Etruscan faces, with slanting eyes and fey smiles. Amazing dark Titian hair. Not your sort of coppery red, but very dazzling, especially with creamy skin. Ugh! They're twins, apparently. Felix and Zoe. I wish they hadn't come.'

'We could do with some lively company,' said Quinta. 'It's been a bit dull in the evenings, perhaps they'll liven things up.'

'Perhaps they won't,' said Lydia darkly. 'Use my bath oil if you like, Quinta.'

'Thank you,' said Quinta. 'What luxury. If you're down before I am, tell the kitchen I won't be long.'

But when Quinta emerged from the bathroom, she found Lydia fuming in the passage, in a way most unlike her normal placid self.

'What's on earth's the matter?' said Quinta. 'Come to my room, I'm freezing here.'

'This is the matter,' said Lydia, sitting on Phoebe's bed and patting it.

'Calm down and say what you mean,' said Quinta, briskly towelling her hair.

'Adam has thrown me out,' said Lydia dramatically.

'What?'

'Yes, I'm to sleep in here with you, if you please! Felix is sharing Adam's room.'

'Is that all?' said Quinta. 'It won't do you any harm to have a good night's sleep for once, and you can hardly feel deprived, you've had nights and nights with Adam.'

'Yes, but not frightfully active ones, I told you that.'

'Bit strange, though, sharing a double bed,' said Quinta.

'It's two singles pushed together.'

'That's quite sensible, then.'

'Why can't Titus sleep in there?'

'What's the difference?' said Quinta. 'You wouldn't want to sleep between them, would you?'

'No,' said Lydia. 'But I would rather it was Titus in there, I tell you, I just don't like this Felix. He's oh-so-friendly, but if you ask me, he's a bit of a creep. He could perfectly well share the children's room with Titus, and Zoe could come in here.'

'Where is Zoe going to sleep?' asked Quinta, who was not really very interested in all these arrangements.

'Adam says he'll move a camp bed into one of the attics for her.'

'She'll be cold up there.'

'Good,' said Lydia. 'Then she'll want to go, and she and her brother can push off back to Cambridge or wherever they've come from.'

'They'll have to move on tomorrow, in any case,' said Quinta pacifically. 'The others will be back.'

Titus duly went back to Eyot the next day, but Felix and Zoe stayed. Lydia found herself squeezed into Quinta's room on a camp bed, and she expressed herself forcibly to Adam.

He laughed and caressed the back of her neck. 'Very flattering,' he said, 'I like to hear that you can't do without me. However, a little abstention will do you no harm, and I'll make up for it when we get back to Eyot, just you wait.'

Lydia kissed him with hungry ardour, and he responded with enthusiasm. 'Pity there are so many people around,' he said. 'Or we could get down to something more serious.'

'I thought abstention was good for me.'

'It is, but not for me.'

'Then you shouldn't share a room with Felix.'

She leant against him; she could feel that he had an erection and she slid her hands down towards him. He twisted back. 'Enough,' he said, holding her away by the wrists.

'Ouch,' said Lydia. 'Let go, you're hurting me.'

'Only a few days more,' said Adam. 'And make an effort to

get to know Felix and Zoe. Felix is a very old friend of mine, and although I haven't met Zoe before, she seems good fun. And you'll see more of them, Felix is going to be spending some time in Eyot over the next few months.'

'Oh,' said Lydia. 'How nice.'

After an all-too-brief spell of warmth, the August weather reverted to its nasty display of storm and tempest. The volunteers did their best, but were usually driven to find shelter in the small hut which had been put up on site. They huddled over an inadequate stove, doubtless, someone remarked, poisoning themselves with fumes, thus wiping out several brilliant academic careers.

'I don't think I want to be an archaeologist any more,' said a young man, sniffing uncomfortably.

'It's made my mind up for me,' said another girl brightly. 'No more northern Europe for me, I'm specializing in somewhere warm.'

'Italy,' said someone with longing in her voice.

'Turkey.'

'Anywhere that isn't here.'

Adam seemed impervious to the bad weather. Wrapped in an enormous waterproof, he lasted out on site for longer than anyone, and would thrust his head into the hut, look round at the miserable, wet faces and chase them back to work.

'Bloody slavedriver.'

'Glad I'm not in his department.'

'Don't know why he's so keen, this isn't even his field. What's he got to prove?'

'He really pisses me off. The sooner this lot tumbles into the sea, the happier I'll be.'

Despite being wet and thoroughly uncomfortable, Quinta was in a strange way enjoying herself. She saw hardly anything of Phoebe, who had made some firm friends and spent every moment she could with them. Quinta was worried that she was being a nuisance, but when she remonstrated with Lara, who was the wife of the photographer, she was laughed at.

'More the merrier,' said Lara, who was an earth mother with a remarkably good temper. 'They're easier to deal with if there's a crowd of them. Besides, it isn't safe here, anyone can see that, you wouldn't be able to concentrate on your work if Phoebe was hanging around with nothing to do. She'll be all right with me.'

Quinta could see that Phoebe was indeed all right, and as a result she felt freer than she had ever done. It was like being suspended in time: Eyot, the problems with Phoebe's school, Alban, her work: they all seemed to belong to another world. Here, on the stormy coast, she was just herself.

She tried to explain it to Lydia. 'For a while, not to be a mother, or a mistress, or an employee, it's a great relief, you see.'

Lydia looked at her friend. Wrapped up in her own affairs, and more and more put out by Adam's seeming indifference, she hadn't noticed how happy Quinta was looking.

'It's true,' she said, looking at her critically. 'You look much more relaxed, and you smile all the time, like you used to, and your hair is all wild and flying out from your head. That's the damp, I suppose . . . You look more positive, less guilt-ridden. I know what it is, you've given up those horrid little lists.'

Quinta, grinning, produced a list from her pocket. 'No, I haven't, see!'

'Different sort of list,' said Lydia. 'Notes rather than a list. Practical, not desperate.'

Quinta stared at her. 'Do you think my lists were desperate?'

'Definitely,' said Lydia. 'So don't start again when we get back. Oh, I can't wait, only a few more days of this dump. I shall be so glad to get back to Eyot.'

'What, to your grandmother, and yes, no, three bags full?'

'Yes, but also to more of Adam, I do hope; they can't live in each other's pockets in Eyot the way they do here,' said Lydia gloomily.

'Everyone except you likes them,' said Quinta. 'They have a lot of charm.'

'That's all they do have. They don't help at all, just idle around in the lodge all day. Zoe sometimes does a bit of washing up, but you have to ask her.'

'Adam says Felix has been working terribly hard, he needs a rest. He's in business, isn't he?'

'So Adam says, although I'm not clear exactly what business,' said Lydia crossly. 'Something foxy, don't you think the pair of them look like foxes?'

'No, really, I don't,' said Quinta, laughing so hard she had to put her cup down. 'You're jealous, Lydia, that's all it is. Adam's what, twenty-eight? He's bound to have friends from before he met you. I mean, he's only known you for five minutes, and didn't he say he was at school with Felix?'

'He wasn't at school with Zoe, she's been in America for ages. Their parents are divorced, and she went off to California with her mother. And Adam's all over her.'

Quinta had noticed that Adam's eyes were warm when they rested on Zoe, but she was such an attractive creature, it was hardly surprising. Quite different from Lydia, though, it would be strange for a man to like such opposite types. True, Zoe was slim, lucky her, thought Quinta enviously, but she was like an elf, very unlike tall Lydia.

She wasn't going to say anything, though; Lydia was worked up enough already. Quinta still couldn't make Adam out, but if Lydia was as keen on him as she appeared to be, then she hoped for her sake that Felix and Zoe wouldn't continue to engross Adam's interest.

That afternoon the sky was as black as a winter's day, and the wind howled about their ears. The sea was purple with endless white crests on high waves as far as the horizon where it merged with the sulphurous clouds. Above the sound of the winds they could hear the waves roaring and crashing on the rocks at the foot of the cliffs.

The volunteers had had enough, but Adam wouldn't hear of them stopping. 'We haven't got enough time left to do the job properly as it is,' he shouted against the wind. 'There's definitely no time to knock off early today. A bit of wind won't hurt anyone.'

At about three o'clock Lara came and found Quinta. 'It isn't safe here,' she said baldly. 'I've heard the forecast, there's a severe weather warning out, storms and high tides in this area. I'll take the children to my mother's, but Quinta, if I were you, I'd leave right now yourself.'

'Is Mike going?' asked Quinta, straining to stand up in the wind.

'No,' said Lara. 'He can't, not until Adam calls a halt, and God knows when he'll do that. You see, Mike relies on word-of-mouth recommendation, he can't afford to get on the wrong side of Adam.'

'He's got young children,' shouted Quinta, shocked. 'Adam shouldn't expect anyone to stay, he couldn't hold it against Mike if he went.'

'He's a vindictive man,' said Lara. 'Not one to cross, he cares for no-one and nothing. But it's different for you, you can't keep going in this weather. Come with us, I'll squeeze you in, or I could come back for you.'

'You are kind,' said Quinta gratefully. 'But Lydia won't go while Adam's here, so I feel I ought to stay.'

Lara looked at her approvingly. 'She's lucky to have a friend like you. She'll need all the friends she's got if she's involved with Adam Stixwould, I can tell you that for nothing. And another thing . . .'

'What?' screamed Quinta, but Lara's words were carried away by the wind.

Quinta struggled over to where Lydia was struggling with a tarpaulin. 'Adam wants this covered,' she gasped. 'Can you give me a hand?'

'It's pointless,' said Quinta. Was it her imagination, or did the sea seem louder?

'I hate storms,' said Lydia. 'It's going to thunder, I know it is.'

'Thunder?' yelled Quinta. 'Who'd notice, with this lot blowing the way it is? Come on, Lydia, let's go back to the lodge.'

'Adam said to stay until he said we could go.'

'To hell with Adam; come on, Lydia, this isn't school, we don't have to do what the man says. If he wants to play captains and go down with his fort, then let him.'

'I don't want to leave him here,' said Lydia.

Quinta could see Adam through the murky darkness, a huge, commanding figure. He looks like something out of another time, Quinta thought; a great untamed spirit of the north.

'No, just mad.'

Quinta spun round. It was Titus. He hurled himself towards where shadowy figures were darting to and fro at Adam's orders, and let fly in an astonishing voice which carried even above that wind.

'Go,' he said. 'All of you. Right now. Not to the lodge, it isn't safe there. Never mind your kit, don't wait for anything. This cliff is sliding away, that's the rumbling you can hear. Get as far back from here as you can. That direction, head for that light there, and you'll be all right.'

Adam turned on him in fury. 'How dare you come and tell my workers what to do?' he began.

'Oh, bugger off,' said Titus irritably. 'You idiot, putting these people's lives at risk through sheer pig-headedness. What does this fort matter? It was unimportant in Roman times, it's unimportant now.'

Adam glared, and then started off towards the lodge.

'Not that way, you fool. The cliff is already going there.'

Adam turned, his face white in the rain. 'The cliff near the lodge? Going? But Felix and Zoe are there, I must get to them.'

'They'll have left long since, the police have been round.'

But Adam didn't hear him, he was running along the cliff with long, striding steps.

Titus hesitated for a moment, then shrugged, heard a deepening series of thunderous rumbles from the cliff edge, and took himself smartly off after the others.

He found them taking shelter in a farmhouse, the farmer's wife clucking with disapproval at the stupid things that people from the city got up to.

'University folk? Aye, I can believe that, and with nowt more of sense than my four-year-old upstairs there.'

Lydia was sitting stiff and trembling. 'Adam?' she said, as Titus came in, the wind blowing the door behind him with a bang.

'He's gone off towards the lodge, silly bugger,' he said. 'No, I don't know if he'll be all right, he thinks he's gone to rescue Felix and Zoe. They won't be there, of course, they'll have cleared out hours ago. I never saw a pair better able to look after their own skins.'

'But Titus; oh, Adam . . .' began Lydia.

'Don't Oh, Adam me,' said Titus. 'I've had enough of that man. If you ask me he's indestructible. If he isn't, there's nothing you can do about it. I expect the coastguards will have to rescue him, at great risk to themselves.'

'I've never seen Sybil Stixwould in a state like that, before,' said Marjorie.

'He is her only grandson,' said Daphne.

'She must be so proud of him.' Marjorie rammed the top firmly into the cafetière, sending little puddles of coffee on to the white tablecloth. 'Really, I don't know why they have these, the old-fashioned coffee pots were much more sensible.'

'These are supposed to make better coffee,' said Wyn, mopping up the spillage with her napkin.

'Nonsense,' said Marjorie.

They were so excited by the happenings at Yntrig that by common consent they had adjourned to Flora's for a nice cup of coffee. For once, the flowers could wait.

Wyn had found a newspaper, and she opened it, inadvertently giving Daphne a smart blow with the wooden pole which nestled inside it.

'Sorry,' she said.

'I can't see why they have poles in newspapers,' said Daphne, very put out.

'It's so that they can hang them from those hooks by the door, dear,' said Marjorie. 'Does it say anything about it, Wyn?'

'Dramatic clifftop rescue . . . Drama on the coast as house and Roman fort slide into the sea . . . Archaeologist risks his life to save friends.'

'Well,' said Marjorie. 'Such bravery!'

'Yes, but the friends weren't there,' pointed out Wyn. 'They'd very sensibly left much earlier. The coastguards were the real heroes, and the RAF, fancy flying a helicopter in that weather.'

Marjorie and Daphne weren't interested in the coastguards or the RAF. They didn't know them, whereas they did know, if not Adam, at least his grandmother.

'I heard,' said Wyn, 'that the one who saved all the diggers was Titus.'

'What, the lay clerk?' said Daphne.

'What did he have to do with it?' said Marjorie suspiciously.

'He had been up to the site earlier in the week, and when all the storm warnings were given, and the radio said about the dangers from high tides, he put two and two together, realized they'd be in danger and went off to warn them. The police were evacuating houses around and about, but they didn't know that anyone was working up at the site.'

'Well, it was their business to know.'

'Perhaps it didn't occur to them that anyone would be foolhardy enough to be there in such atrocious conditions.'

'Foolhardy! Dedicated, that's what I call it,' said Marjorie indignantly. 'Very few people take their work as seriously as Adam clearly does.'

'It's rather funny, isn't it?' said Wyn, rustling the pages of the paper as she looked for the pictures on page five. 'Him being plucked off the top of the chicken house just as it was sliding after the lodge and about to disappear over the cliff. Not very dignified for a professional man.'

Daphne shuddered. 'I can't bear to think about it. Pour the coffee, Marjorie, and I'd like the paper, Wyn, if you've finished with it.'

## 15

Titus brought Quinta home the next morning, after an uncomfortable night on the farmhouse kitchen floor. Most of the
volunteers had been anxious to get away as soon as they
could, but a brief foray into the storm, and a few minutes
listening to the portentous warnings on the radio, persuaded
them to stay.

'Tail end of a hurricane,' said the farmer's wife, who took
things as she found them. 'It'll blow itself out soon enough,
and we'll see it fairing up in the morning.'

'I think she looks on us as a kind of livestock,' Quinta
whispered to Titus. 'You know, lambs in the kitchen sheltering
from spring snow, early calves in the barn . . .'

'I certainly know how animals must feel in one of those
lorries,' grumbled Titus, wedged between a table and the
cheerful young archaeologist. 'I suppose this house will stand,
that's a terrible wind out there.'

'Stood four hundred years, won't go just yet,' said the farmer's
wife from the door. 'I'll be turning the lights out now, you'll be
wanting your sleep.'

'Wanting isn't getting,' muttered another volunteer. 'Oh, for
a hot bath.'

Quinta echoed his words as she opened the door and fell over
Harriet, who had heard people arriving and had come out to
see who it was.

'Quinta, I was so worried about you, it was on the news,
that fort sliding into the sea. They said all the volunteers were
accounted for, but you never know what they were counting.'

'That's a ghoulish thought,' observed Titus as he followed them inside. 'I gather that, despite the appalling storms, the only victim was an old dear who got into such a temper when she couldn't watch her favourite programme on the telly that she had a fit and expired.'

Harriet raised an eyebrow at him.

'I'm sorry,' said Quinta wearily. 'Harriet, this is Titus, who rescued us all. Harriet's an old friend from when I first came to Eyot, Titus. Come to think of it,' she said, remembering, 'she rescued me then, so you're both my rescuers. Harriet, do I smell coffee?'

'Yes,' said Harriet. 'Quinta, you'd better change out of those clothes. Go and have a hot shower or a bath, and I'll get some breakfast for both of you.'

'Good idea,' said Titus. 'The farmer's wife in the farm where we spent last night was very hospitable, all things considered, but she could hardly be expected to feed a dozen of us.'

'How did you get back?' asked Harriet, as the door closed behind Quinta. 'It said on the news that most roads in that area were impassable.'

'Oh, we did a few detours,' said Titus. 'I had to get back; I've got a meeting this afternoon which I can't miss.'

'Where's Phoebe?'

'With friends who have a house on the other side of Yntrig. Quinta spoke to them this morning, Phoebe slept right through the storm last night, she must be the only person in the county who did. She didn't want to leave, and they're happy to have her for another day, so I told Quinta to leave her there. She'll be better off without having to cope with Phoebe just at the moment.'

'Very sensible,' said Harriet, pouring coffee. 'Black? White? Sugar?'

'White, no sugar, but I'll have a biscuit if you've got one.'

'In that tin,' said Harriet. 'I'll start breakfast, I don't suppose Quinta will be long.'

Titus lolled against the archway, his offers of help politely refused by Harriet. 'How did you rescue Quinta?' he asked.

Harriet laughed. 'Quinta exaggerates,' she said. 'I just gave her house room when she first came to Eyot.'

'How old was she then?' asked Titus.

Harriet flashed him a glance as she peeled strips of bacon on to the grill pan.

'It was nearly nine years ago, two or three months before Phoebe was born.'

'And Phoebe's father? Was he with her then?'

'You'll have to ask Quinta about him,' said Harriet noncommittally. 'Why all the questions?'

'Sheer curiosity,' said Titus blandly. 'I like to know about people.'

'So do I,' said Harriet. 'Tell me about yourself.'

Titus bowed. 'Another man would take that for a set-down, but I take it as a compliment. It's always pleasant to have other people interested in one, don't you think? And, like all men, I love talking about myself.'

Harriet smiled. 'Go on, then. Why are you in Eyot?'

'Work,' said Titus. 'I'm at the university, scrabbling about on the wilder shores of chaos theory. You won't have heard about it, because it's all very new and has not yet hit the popular magazines.'

'Wrong,' said Harriet. 'I have heard about it. I've been sharing a flat with Isobel Warrender for the last two years.'

Now Titus's eyebrows rose. 'Have you just?'

'Yes, indeed, and you can take that nosy look off your face, yes, Isobel and I are more than flatmates, no, I am not a wild seducer of women, I have no designs on Quinta. As it happens, I value friendship more than anything, certainly more than my sex life.'

'Ah,' said Titus, nonplussed.

'So you,' Harriet went on inexorably, 'must be Titus Croscombe. You're here in Eyot instead of in Cambridge or America where you really belong, because of a boozy old crock called Halliday, who has roosted at the university here ever since it opened and refuses to go anywhere else.'

Titus smiled. 'How right you are.'

'Has he the answers?'

'No, not at all. He's too old, for one thing. But he asks all the right questions, and someone working with him is more likely to find the answers – at least to the questions I want answered – than anyone else.'

'How old are you?'

'Thirty-two.'

'Old for a mathematician.'

'Yes, but I'm not, strictly speaking, a mathematician. Thankfully not, they're a sad bunch, mathematicians. Not your Isobel, she's in a class of her own. So what brings you to Eyot?'

'I'm a teacher,' said Harriet. 'I've got a job at the Cathedral School. In the Junior Department.'

Titus's eyes narrowed. 'Come on! Something tells me that you're far too high-powered for that place. It's a nightmare of a school: Dickens out of Evelyn Waugh rewritten as a sitcom.'

'So I gather, but I've been brought in to tidy it up a bit.'

Titus thoughtfully sipped his coffee, thinking it over. Then he shook his head. 'I don't believe you,' he said. 'No-one would come to work here, in that school, unless they were desperate.'

'Or unless they wanted to be in Eyot to train with Walter Hatchett, and the Dean and Chapter offered a very good financial package because they were so worried about the school.'

'Ah,' said Titus, with a satisfied grunt. 'Of course, look at you. You're a runner.'

'I am. And teaching is one of the few jobs you can do while training.'

'Do you have time?'

'I do. No family, only myself to look after, I shall find a house or flat that needs very little doing to it, and I will employ someone to keep it clean for me . . . Even with homework to mark, I shall have all the time I want to train.'

She went to the door and opened it. 'Quinta!' she called. 'Breakfast's ready.'

Quinta padded into the kitchen, her wet hair curling wildly about her face, her feet bare, her skin rosy and her body encased in a huge silk dressing gown.

'Alban's,' she said, as she slid into a pew. 'Goodness, what a treat, breakfast cooked by someone else.'

'What do you mean, Alban's?' said Titus, sitting across the

table from her. 'Ouch, what on earth? Damn it, there's a cat here, and it's bitten me.'

'That's Madrigal,' said Quinta, laughing. 'It's affection, he must like you if he bit you.'

'Thank you,' said Titus, sucking the side of his hand.

'The dressing gown belongs to Alban,' Quinta continued as she reached for the coffee. 'I could see you looking at it and thinking, what an extraordinary garment for me to wear.'

'I was, actually,' said Titus. 'It's superb, where did Alban get it?'

'Burlington Arcade, I think,' said Quinta. 'Or Jermyn Street, somewhere like that. He has several, he wears them when he's composing, you see.'

'It suits you,' said Titus after looking reflectively at her for a moment. 'Very Burne-Jones. You should always wear clothes in those colours. Preferably made of silk. Velvets, too, in rich colours; brocades . . .'

'Hardly practical on a limited budget,' remarked Harriet, putting large platefuls of food in front of each of them.

'Goodness,' said Quinta happily. 'What a wonderful breakfast. Everything I like and shouldn't eat. Where did all this food come from?'

'I guessed you'd be back some time today, and I thought you'd be hungry, so I nipped out first thing and got some food, the kind of thing you can eat at any time of day,' said Harriet. 'Luckily, I got enough for two,' she added, watching Titus launch himself into a sausage.

'Good thinking, that,' said Titus with his mouth full. 'Excellent bacon, you've been to Gumble's.'

'I have,' said Harriet. 'It hasn't changed a bit since I was last here.'

'I never go there,' said Quinta cheerfully. 'Far too expensive.'

By the time Quinta had eaten her large plate of food, followed by several fresh rolls with some thick, fruity jam which Harriet had also bought, her eyes were drooping, and she yawned widely. 'Four more days' holiday,' she said sleepily. 'I'll have to think of something to do with Phoebe. Poor child, what a wretched holiday.'

'Not at all,' said Titus. 'From what I can see, she's had a very good time. It must have been nice for her to get away from you.'

Quinta blinked, too tired to take in the full harshness of the remark, but vaguely upset by it.

'It's the only time I can really spend properly with Phoebe, when we're on holiday,' she explained. 'When I'm working I try, but I'm too busy.'

'What makes you think she wants you to devote yourself to her?' inquired Titus. 'In my experience children just want a solid base that they can come back to; they hate having a parent hanging around them all the time.'

Quinta stared at him. 'You haven't got any children.'

'No, but I have hordes of nephews and nieces, and I was a child once, with a doting widowed mother. Lord, how guilty she made me feel, because I wanted to be off with my friends, doing interesting things with new people, not plastered dutifully to her side.'

Quinta yawned again. 'I'm sure you're wrong; children do best with the undivided attention of their mothers, everyone knows that.'

'Everyone knows that,' he said mockingly. 'Very unsound. Mostly what everyone knows is hopelessly wrong. What do you think, Harriet?'

'I think Quinta should go and get some sleep,' said Harriet calmly. 'I think you may be right, but it's hardly the time to say so.'

'Mmm,' said Quinta. 'Yes, I am going to go and sleep, if you don't mind, Harriet. I'm suddenly totally exhausted.'

Titus and Harriet sat by the log fire with another pot of coffee.

'Ridiculous, a fire in August,' said Titus.

'Necessary,' said Harriet. 'It isn't warm at all, and it's cheerful for Quinta when she wakes up.'

'She needs to sleep for several hours,' said Titus.

'Don't you? Haven't you been up all night as well?'

'No, I can sleep anywhere,' said Titus. 'And I don't worry all the time, like Quinta does. Tiring, worrying. She's been working very hard on this dig, although I think she actually liked not having to run round after the child for a while, however much she denies it.'

'Maybe,' said Harriet. 'Does Quinta devote herself to Phoebe?'

'Lives for her, as far as I can see,' said Titus.

'What's your interest in Quinta?' asked Harriet suspiciously.

'Friendship,' said Titus, with a warm smile. 'Like you, I value friendship very highly. Quinta interests me, I feel she's a trapped spirit, wasting her life away. It is, by the way, a purely platonic interest,' he added. 'My tastes run to mature women. And Quinta has Alban.'

'Has she just?' said Harriet.

'Where is Alban?' went on Titus, looking round as though he expected to see him crouching in the log basket.

'America,' said Harriet shortly. 'He rang. Something came up, he won't be back for some time, because he's going straight on to Spain. He asked me to tell Quinta.'

'Oh,' said Titus.

'I think perhaps there's a problem there,' said Harriet. 'I think I've come at a very good time, I can see there's some sorting out to be done.'

'Never interfere with other people's love lives,' said Titus, stretching his legs out towards the fire. 'Always a disaster, people have to make their own mistakes.'

'Quinta has,' said Harriet cryptically. 'And I don't think, from what I know of him, that Alban should be Quinta's love life.'

'Do you know him? From when you were in Eyot before?'

'Yes. He was very kind to Quinta, that's what started it all. Kindness isn't a bad basis for a relationship, but . . .'

'Quinta needs something more full-blooded than that, in my opinion,' said Titus, as he got to his feet. He stretched and yawned loudly, running his fingers through his hair.

'Thank you for the breakfast and the coffee; I'll see you again, I feel sure.'

'I expect so.'

Despite his slept-in clothes and roughly dried hair, Titus still managed to look well put-together as he pulled on a crumpled jacket and made his way out of the house. Harriet, who was a non-participating connoisseur of male looks, had to admire his elegance. And an unusual man, she thought; it was rare to find a man with so little vanity.

She mentioned this to a tousled Quinta, who emerged several hours later, full of apologies, but looking much better for a refreshing sleep.

'Yes, I like Titus, he doesn't oppress, but he's very effective.'

'Effective?

'Yes. He isn't exactly bossy, but people tend to jump when he tells them to.'

'Authority.'

'That's the one,' agreed Quinta. 'I'd better phone Lara, have a word with Phoebe.'

'Ring this evening, to say goodnight,' suggested Harriet.

Quinta laughed. 'You're as bad as Titus. That was a bit near the bone, wasn't it? I suppose I do rather cling to Phoebe, but after all, I've got to supply the care and affection of two parents.'

Harriet said nothing, and Quinta, who had slid to the carpet in front of the fire, looked up at her, her eyes glinting.

'Oh, oh, you agree with him, I can see it in your face. I don't care what you two think or anyone else, somebody's got to care about Phoebe. That reminds me, is there any post?'

As she flicked through the envelopes, she told Harriet about Phoebe's school and the psychologist. Harriet approved. 'Have you had the report?'

'No, I'm seeing if it's here. Oh, listen,' said Quinta, momentarily diverted by a circular in a fat brown envelope. 'Cyclists! Pamper your bottoms!' She went off into a peal of laughter. 'Look, Harriet, a catalogue full of things nobody could possibly want. I wish I had lots of money, I'd love to buy people absurd presents from catalogues like this.'

'How old are you?' said Harriet, twitching the letters out of her hands. 'Concentrate. This must be the one you want, it's from the Institute.'

Quinta opened it, a sinking feeling in her stomach. As she read through the pages, she frowned, and looked more and more puzzled. Finally she handed it to Harriet. 'You read it. You may be able to make sense of it,' she said with an uneasy laugh. 'It doesn't seem very clear to me.'

'Perfectly clear,' said Harriet briskly a few minutes later.

Quinta looked up from the fire.

'Phoebe is clearly a highly intelligent child. Not a conformist personality, but then you aren't much of a conformist yourself, are you? Take this to Phoebe's headteacher, I imagine she'll change her tune when she sees this.'

Quinta brightened. 'Do you really think so? Alban said that whatever the psychologist's verdict was, the head's attitude to Phoebe wouldn't change.'

'He could be right, but I don't think so,' said Harriet. 'She's a professional woman, she has to take notice of this.' She handed the papers back to Quinta. 'Well, that's one thing less for you to worry about.'

'It is a relief,' admitted Quinta. 'The psychologist said when I picked Phoebe up after the tests that there was nothing to worry about.'

'You've been worrying just the same.'

'Naturally,' said Quinta, her mouth creasing into a smile. 'I always worry about Phoebe.' She stretched and got to her feet. 'She doesn't go back until Tuesday. I'll make an appointment to see the head and show her this. I was dreading having to find her a new school.'

'That's all right then,' said Harriet. 'Is that today's local paper? Pass it over, Quinta, I haven't seen it.'

Quinta obligingly found the *Eyot Gazette*.

'House-hunting,' said Harriet as she took the paper and opened it. 'I can't stay here for ever.'

'Oh dear,' said Quinta, her eyes clouding over. 'Nor can I.'

'Why not?' said Harriet, her eyes travelling swiftly down the columns of advertisements.

'Oh, things are a bit tense with Alban,' said Quinta. 'I think it would be better if I didn't live here any more. It's going to be difficult though, I can only afford somewhere very modest, probably a long way from the centre. And this is Phoebe's home, she loves it here, and she's fond of Alban.'

'Things have a way of working out,' said Harriet, reaching for a pen and ringing several advertisements. 'And you don't have to do anything in a hurry, Alban's going to be away for several weeks.'

'Oh, is he?' said Quinta surprised.

'Yes, he rang from America. He's going straight on to Spain, he said, rather than coming back to England first.'

'Oh,' said Quinta again. 'Was there any other message for me?'

Harriet looked at her in a kindly way. 'No. If you ask me, from what he didn't say, I think he's feeling very hurt.'

'Bother,' said Quinta. 'Still?'

'Did you have a quarrel?'

Quinta nodded. 'He wants to marry me, and I said no. So he's brooding.'

'I expect he enjoys it. Maybe it will be good for his composing. Perhaps he'll come back with a masterpiece stirring in his mind.'

Quinta laughed. 'I don't think his music ever goes near his mind. The only thing that stirs in his mind is grumbles.'

'Sounds very tiresome,' said Harriet. 'You're wise not to marry him; I don't think it would work. Mind if I use the phone? I'm keeping a record of my calls.'

'I shouldn't worry about it,' said Quinta. 'You've been doing Alban a favour, he doesn't like his house to be empty, thinks a gang is going to break in and swipe his manuscripts and leave with the grand piano by the back door.'

'He hasn't changed, by the sound of it,' said Harriet reaching out for the telephone which began to ring just as she was going to pick it up.

'Hello,' she said. 'Quinta? Yes, she's here.'

Quinta took the phone. 'Oh, oh I see. Yes, I have slept, yes, I agree, it makes everything seem quite different . . . No, Phoebe's staying with Lara's parents for another night . . . Oh, Lydia, I really can't, Harriet's here, and . . .'

'Don't mind about me,' hissed Harriet.

Quinta put her hand over the receiver. 'It's Lydia. She says she's got to get away from her grandmother's this evening. I can't think why she's in such a state, she's only been back there for a few hours. She wants to meet me for a drink.'

'Go ahead,' said Harriet. 'If she needs to talk, then you can't say no.'

'Lydia? Can I bring Harriet? No, she isn't in the least bit like your grandmother, of course not . . . No, very good company, and full of good advice. All right, by the bridge, eight o'clock. See you, bye.'

Quinta put the phone down and looked at Harriet. 'You don't mind, do you, Harriet? We can go to a pub . . .'

'I'd like to meet this Lydia,' said Harriet. 'Let's go to a wine bar rather than a pub. I'll treat you to a meal.'

Quinta's face lit up. 'Do you know, I never go out for a meal? But I'll pay for myself, I'm not that hard up.'

'I offered first,' said Harriet. 'It'll do you good to get out, by the sound of it, and no Phoebe to worry about.'

'I don't know any wine bars,' said Quinta. 'But I think Lydia does.'

She looked thoughtfully at Harriet. 'Do you know, I wouldn't have thought you were a wine bar kind of person.'

'Too much of the puritan?' Harriet shook her head. 'No, I drink a lot of wine, at least when I'm not in training. I spent a lot of time in wine bars in Cambridge, and I find the proprietors are usually very clued-up people. I can put the word around that I'm looking for somewhere to rent.'

'Cambridge?' said Quinta. 'I didn't know you'd been in Cambridge, I've only got a London address.'

'Yes, that's my mother's house. But I've been living in Cambridge for a couple of years.'

Quinta's eyes narrowed. 'Did you ever come across a man called Adam Stixwould?'

'Adam Stixwould?' Harriet suddenly became very alert. 'Now, how do you know Adam Stixwould?'

Quinta explained about Lydia, and then about the Stixwoulds and finally she told her about Felix and Zoe.

'Well, this is all very interesting,' said Harriet. 'I think your friend Lydia may have taken on more than she can handle. What's she like? Impetuous? Does she have a lot of boyfriends?'

Quinta considered. 'No, I don't think so. She had a long-time boyfriend at Oxford, and then he suddenly ditched her, at the end of her last term. They were going to go to Greece, but he went with someone else, and now he's going to marry her. The someone else, I mean. That's why she came up here, she was at a bit of a loose end.' She paused, leaning forward to put another log on the fire. 'What's she like?' Quinta thought for a moment. 'Indolent, tall, economical in her movements, languid. Very beautiful,' said Quinta a little sadly. 'I wish I looked like her.'

'Hmm,' said Harriet. 'So she took up with Adam Stixwould on the rebound, did she?'

'Not really. She met him because their grandmothers are such good friends; he came up to Eyot for this dig. He has a house here, which he lets out.' Quinta sat bolt upright as a thought suddenly occurred to her. 'I wonder . . .'

Harriet shook her head. 'No way would I have Adam Stixwould for a landlord,' she said firmly. 'Have the grandmothers got their eyes on something permanent there?' she asked.

'Between Adam and Lydia? Getting married, you mean?' Quinta thought for a moment. 'I suppose they might. That generation, I don't think they realize that Adam and Lydia are sleeping together.'

'They may realize more than you think,' said Harriet dryly. 'I would certainly imagine that Adam's grandmother would like to see him married to a young and suitable girl.'

'I'm not sure that Lydia would want to marry him,' said Quinta, thinking about it.

'Do you like Adam?'

Quinta shook his head. 'No, I don't. He made me feel uneasy when I first met him, and the way he behaved on the dig . . . He's a monster. Cold, and I think a bit unhinged.'

Harriet looked at her approvingly. 'Yes, that's his reputation in Cambridge. He has some unpleasant habits by all accounts, your friend would do well to steer clear of him.'

'I don't think she will,' said Quinta doubtfully. 'I think she's crazy about him, even after the way he behaved on the dig.'

'Bad news,' said Lydia glumly as they settled themselves round a barrel tucked away in a dark corner of the wine bar. 'Grandmama is all over this Felix and Zoe. Sybil Stixwould brought them round to her this morning, could grandmama put them up for a day or two? She can't, because she's got men in, dry rot or rats or something. So they're staying with us, and they are ghastly. Grandmama and Sybil croon over them, lovely manners, such charming young people . . . ugh!'

'How did you manage to get away this evening?' asked Quinta. 'Didn't your grandmother think it a bit odd?'

'I said it was a long-standing engagement, and she said it couldn't be, because I should still have been on the dig if it hadn't been for the storm and everything. So I said I had been coming into Eyot with you, Quinta, this evening anyway, even if we'd still been on that wretched dig, to meet an old friend who was only in Eyot for one night . . . goodness, the lies I tell!'

'Where's Adam?'

'In hospital still, they're keeping an eye on him because he's got bruised ribs or something. I went to see him this afternoon, but I didn't stay long, I was too cross. He said to thank my grandmother for having his friends to stay, and that as soon as he's out of hospital, which I expect will be tomorrow – they throw you out really quickly these days, don't they? – as soon as he's back home, Felix and Zoe can move into his house. He'll be up two or three days a week from Cambridge, apparently.'

Harriet and Quinta looked at each other.

Lydia gave a loud and undignified sniff. 'And I don't think he's spending that much time in Eyot because of me, I think he wants to see them.'

'Calm down,' said Harriet. 'Have some wine. Tell me about this brother and sister. Why have they come to Eyot?'

'Oh, it's bad news all round,' said Lydia. 'Felix runs a shop in London, importing exotica from eastern Europe: antiques, hand-made ethnic clothes, porcelain . . . you know the kind of thing. It's doing very well, so he's looking for other towns to open shops in.'

Lydia took a swig of wine and looked disconsolately round the arched cellars of the wine bar.

'And another thing, this new Bishop is their uncle, believe it or not. So of course Sybil Stixwould and my grandmother think that's wonderful. The Bishop and his family don't move into the Palace until next week, unfortunately,' she said in Felix's drawling voice, 'otherwise, we could have stayed with Uncle Lennox, he's a splendid old boy.'

Quinta giggled, which drew her a reproachful look from Lydia.

197 •

'It may not seem important to you,' she said tragically, 'but it matters to me. It matters a lot.'

'Let's order some food,' said Harriet. 'I had no idea Eyot was going to be such a lively place. I am glad I'm coming to live here, I can see there's never going to be a quiet moment.'

'She seems all right,' whispered Lydia as Harriet went to the bar to get some menus.

'She is,' said Quinta. 'I told you you'd like her. Now, what are we going to do about the heavenly twins?'

## 16

Lydia wasn't the only one to dislike Felix and Zoe; their Aunt Faustina wasn't too keen on them either. She didn't know them at all, because their mother, the Bishop's sister, had moved to America when they were small. But she had her doubts about a nephew and niece who had ignored their uncle for years, only to pop up full of family feeling when he moved into what the guidebooks called the most splendid bishop's palace in England.

It was splendid, she had to admit that. It was built on the banks of the Eyot, and the view over vast lawns, across the river and on to the distant fells was breathtaking. Faustina wondered how much the magnificent gardens cost to keep up, but the Bishop's Chaplain earnestly assured her that the hefty fees charged to the public for admittance covered most of the costs.

Faustina wasn't too keen on the public, either. Not that she grudged them the gardens, and the weekly chance to walk through the official rooms, it was just that she wished the whole house was open to the public and she didn't have to live there. The Bishop revelled in it all. He couldn't wait to be spotted as he took an episcopal stroll, chatting amiably to 'what after all, my dear, are really parishioners. It is just that we now have so wide and big a parish.'

Rich, thought Faustina, considering that he had never been a parish priest. Destined for high office from his ordination, he had followed the comfortable path of a clerical high flyer, taking in a royal chaplaincy and headship of a theological college along the way.

'It's all rather distasteful,' she confided to Titus as they walked along the river bank by the university campus. She hadn't come to see Titus, so she told him, but to visit the music department. 'I thought I might enrol for an MA.'

'You'll be too busy as the Bishop's wife, Lennox will want you by his side.'

'Oh no, he won't,' said Faustina firmly. 'We came to an arrangement some time ago. He knows how I feel about this bishopric, and if he's got any sense, he won't push his luck. He can play the Bishop, I've got Milo and my music.'

'When does Milo start at school?' asked Titus.

'Next week.' She sighed. 'I do hope he likes it. It seems an odd school, and I've heard mixed things about it.'

'Send him somewhere else,' said Titus.

'Somewhere else would be boarding school. Lennox has very conventional ideas about schools.'

'There's a good deputy head starting at the school,' said Titus, thinking of Harriet.

'I know,' said Faustina. 'I met her when I took Milo for an interview. But one good teacher doesn't make a good school.'

'Stop worrying about him,' said Titus. 'He's got plenty of character, he'll do all right wherever he goes. At least he'll be at home, so you can keep your eye on things. You can kick up a fuss if you don't like what's going on, as the Bishop's wife they'll have to take notice of you.'

Fautina smiled widely. 'Yes, and that dreadful headmaster knows it; it made him frightfully cross when I was there.'

Titus stopped and looked down at her. Then he looked quickly around. Term hadn't begun, and there was nobody about. 'Come on,' he said urgently. 'This way.' Taking her by the hand he led her, protesting, at a great pace across a mock Gothic quadrangle and up the stairs.

'Titus, let go,' said Faustina. 'Where are we going?'

'Pictures,' said Titus inventively. 'Fine gallery here, I know you like pictures.'

'Titus, I don't in the least . . .'

He opened a heavy door and pushed her firmly inside. He closed the door behind him and leant on it, his face alight with laughter as he saw the expression on Faustina's face.

'Titus, this is outrageous, these are your rooms.'

'Yes, they are,' said Titus, wrapping himself round her and propelling her towards another door. 'And this is my bedroom.'

'Titus, this is impossible. We can't possibly . . .'

'You'd be amazed what we can possibly,' said Titus, cutting off her protests with a lingering kiss while his hands were busy elsewhere.

'Titus, said Faustina, as she collapsed on the bed. 'Titus, this is a small community, I'm the Bishop's wife; it was all very well eight years ago, but . . .'

'Oh, shut up,' said Titus. 'God, you're so voluptuous, Fausty, I have missed you.'

'I've missed you, too,' said Faustina, her face buried in his neck. 'Oh, Titus, quick, quick, oh, Titus!'

Good body, thought Faustina later as she watched him strolling across the room. He's like a big cat, so relaxed. I think that's what is so attractive about him, no hang-ups, no neuroticism about anything.

'Hang-ups about you,' said Titus, joining her on the bed.

'I must go swimming or take up running,' said Faustina. 'Look at your firm stomach; mine is like a cushion.'

'Yes,' said Titus, blowing an affectionate rasberry on it, 'that's what I like about it.'

'Stop it,' said Faustina, 'it tickles, and I don't want to make a noise.'

'Tell me,' said Titus, retrieving a pillow from the floor and leaning against it with his hands comfortably behind his head. 'Tell me, how is that husband of yours?' Faustina rolled over and looked at him.

'What do you mean?'

'I get the impression that perhaps you don't go to bed with him very often. Is he worn out by his pious round?'

Faustina sighed. 'No, but he's taken up celibacy.'

Titus sat up straight and gave a yelp of laughter.

'You can't be serious!'

'I can. I never really listened to his reasoning, it all seemed very half-baked to me. I don't think he's ever been very logical, and theology is so far-fetched at the best of times, isn't it?'

'Oh, it's on religious grounds, is it? What about his duty to his wife and all that?'

'I think he believes he's done his duty to his wife. I thought it was because, well, I'm not a slim young thing any more, and perhaps he had interests elsewhere, but he's too ambitious to risk anything like that these days. But of course I've realized it's actually because he's impotent.'

'What?' said Titus incredulously.

Faustina nodded. 'I feel sorry for him in a way. He won't admit it to me. I know everyone has bad moments, and I didn't think much about it. I wasn't very well when I was expecting Milo, and besides . . . Then afterwards, it wasn't any better. So . . .'

'Do you mean he's been like this for more than eight years?' Titus was astonished. 'Why didn't he get medical help?'

'I shouldn't really be telling you about this,' said Fasutina guiltily. 'But it's difficult never being able to talk about it with anyone. He won't discuss it at all, not with anyone; that would mean he'd have to admit there was a problem. Much better to have had a surge of religious fervour.'

'I'd rather stick to the other kind of surge,' said Titus. 'Was it Milo that tipped him over the edge?'

'It might have been,' said Faustina. 'I did ask a psychiatrist friend of mine, in a roundabout way, but of course he knew who I was talking about. He thought perhaps Lennox had had some trauma connected with his sexuality at about that time, which had given him . . .'

'The droops,' said Titus brutally. 'Oh, Fausty, why ever did you marry him?'

Faustina looked surprised. 'Because I was in love with him, of course. He was quite a bit older than me, charismatic . . . well, you know he is . . . There's a feeling of power about him. He was tremendously attractive. He still is, I suppose, but after the madness wears off and you get to know someone better, the attractiveness isn't quite so important . . . The twins and Charles didn't exactly help, either. They're so like him, I could see all the things I didn't like about Lennox steadily developing in them.'

'Milo isn't like his brothers at all, from what I can see,' said Titus consolingly.

Faustina paused before answering, in an expressionless voice, 'No, he isn't. Luckily, he takes after me.'

'These twins, Felix and Zoe, they don't seem very like Lennox, either.'

'No, not at all. They're his sister's children. She was much younger than him, so I don't think she ever knew him very well. She never gets in touch with him, she hasn't in all the time I've been married to him. I met her once at a party, an odd woman. She married a friend of Lennox's and then divorced him when the twins were little. Then she married again, an American, and went to live in California.'

'That's why Zoe has an American accent.'

'Yes, their father insisted on a traditional English public school education for the boy, but he didn't care tuppence about the girl, so she stayed with her mother and went to school in the States. Did law or something, she's supposed to be very clever.'

'She didn't strike me as being very bright when I met her,' said Titus. 'She's obviously very close to her brother.'

'Yes, it's surprising, really, when you consider they didn't grow up together.'

'Why don't you like them?'

Faustina considered for a moment. 'I'm not sure. Too good to be true? Those astonishing looks, the dark red hair, stunning complexions, deep blue eyes. And he's so poised and sure of himself, he's arrogant. I don't like his hairdo, either.'

Titus dissolved in laughter, and Faustina thumped him in a friendly way.

'Oof,' he said, his hand reaching out towards her. She wriggled away and slid off the edge of the bed.

'Come back,' he said, his hand groping for her.

'No, really, I can't,' said Faustina. 'I've been away long enough, I must pick Milo up from the Sports Centre . . .' She looked at her watch, let out a gasp and flew about the room picking up her clothes.

'Late?' inquired Titus.

'Very,' said Faustina. 'I should be there now. Oh, hell. Titus, could you ring them, tell them to hang on to him until I get there, say I've been delayed.'

'They will anyway,' said Titus comfortably. 'I bet most of the mothers are late . . .'

But Faustina had gone.

'Blast,' said Titus, padding into the other room. 'I never fixed up with her for next time.'

'Yes, it was definitely the Bishop's wife,' said Daphne. 'Mrs Gridlock says she'd seen her picture in the paper. She was walking with Titus along by the river, and then . . .' she paused to draw breath, 'then, they went into his rooms.'

Wyn was unimpressed. 'They're old family friends,' she pointed out. 'And more than grown-up. Titus lives at the university, it's not as though they had an assignation in a friend's flat or anything like that.'

Marjorie shook her head in disapproval. 'You still don't understand our Eyot ways, Wyn,' she said. 'This isn't London, or Paris, where people live very loose lives, and no-one worries about it. Here, we're quite old-fashioned in our outlook.'

'What was Mrs Gridlock doing at the university?' asked Wyn. 'Did she have an illicit meeting lined up with one of the dons?'

Since Mrs Gridlock was defiantly middle-aged, with a fifty-inch waistline, horrendous varicose veins and a demonic squint, this was less than kind. But Wyn was feeling out of sorts, she had treated herself to a jar of summer fruits in champagne from Gumble's for pudding the previous night, together with a very rich ice cream, and now she was regretting it.

'Mrs Gridlock's cousin works in the canteen,' said Daphne stiffly. 'Mrs Gridlock was giving a hand. She is a very reliable source.'

'You must see, Wyn,' said Marjorie, in what Wyn considered patronizing tones, 'that the Bishop's wife, like Caesar, must be above suspicion.'

'Like Caesar's *wife*,' said Wyn.

'I beg your pardon?'

'You said, above suspicion, like Caesar. Caesar, being a man, could do what he liked. It was his poor wife who wasn't allowed to put a foot wrong.'

'That's my point,' said Marjorie. 'It's not whether the Bishop's wife is up to anything she shouldn't be or not, it's that her reputation must be unsullied. As a loyal member of the Church of England, dear, you must see the truth of this.'

'I never heard or read anything in the Prayer Book or the Bible about bishops' wives not being allowed to visit old family friends,' said Wyn. 'So I don't see that it's got anything to do with the Church of England. I just think it's nastiness and gossip, always thinking the worst.'

With that, she swept a pile of greenery off the bench, took her bucket of flowers in her other hand and swept out of the flower room.

'Wyn, where are you going?' said Marjorie, thundering after her.

'I'm going to do the flowers in the Bishop's Chapel,' said Wyn, without looking round. 'It's peaceful in there, silent prayers only, and NO gossip.'

'Well!' said Daphne and Marjorie, staring after her.

'And she's using honeysuckle; Canon Feverfew is taking the service in there tonight, and honeysuckle brings on his asthma.'

'She shouldn't have brought that honeysuckle in at all,' said Marjorie at her most magisterial. 'It is of a lax habit, and most unsuitable for a Cathedral chapel.'

To Faustina's relief, Milo was larking about on the rubber mats with two other children when she got to the Sports Centre. A young woman with a flame of curly red hair and a friendly smile got up from a stool as she came in, and came towards her. Faustina frowned. Who was she?

'Quinta,' she said helpfully. 'We met in the rain the other day, you were with Titus.'

'Oh, yes, er, Titus,' said Faustina guiltily, pushing her driving glasses back up her nose. 'Have you waited with Milo? That's very kind of you.'

She called to him, and he made a face. 'Mum, I'm having a smashing time,' he said. 'Do I have to go?'

'Come on, Phoebe and Peter,' shouted Quinta. 'Time to go.'

The three of them trailed reluctantly over towards the two women.

'It was no trouble,' said Quinta. 'The instructor had to leave, and I didn't like to see a little boy left alone, so I said I'd wait.'

She gave Faustina a beaming smile as she spoke, robbing the words of any criticism Faustina might have read into them. 'I know what's it's like, rushing about trying to pick them up on time,' Quinta went on. 'Phoebe has lists of what to do if I'm late sewn into all her pockets.'

'No, I haven't,' muttered Phoebe. 'I'm not stupid, I know what to do, and I've torn the lists out; I hate lists.'

'What was that, Phoebe?' said Quinta.

'Oh, nothing. Q, can Milo come back with us? We were having a really good game, him and me. Peter was the victim.'

'I always am,' said Peter rather dolefully.

'That would be nice,' said Quinta briskly, 'but I expect Milo has other things to do, and you know we're going out to Midwinter when we've taken Peter back home.'

'Oh, goodie, I like going there,' said Phoebe.

Faustina smiled at her. What a striking child, she thought, with those dark eyes and her mother's hair.

'This is Phoebe, by the way,' said Quinta. 'And Peter, who is a friend's son.'

'Peter's going to that school next term,' Milo told his mother. 'The one I'm going to. His brother's there already. He says it's a dump, and they put your head down the lavatories.'

Faustina looked at Peter with horror.

'Peter, nobody has ever put Gavin's head down the lavatory,' said Quinta at once. 'You know if they had your mother would have found out about it, and someone would have been in awful trouble. Gavin's just trying to scare you.'

Milo looked relieved.

'Well, it's very nice to have met a friend before you start,' said Faustina.

'Yes, but Phoebe's much more fun, and she doesn't go there,' pointed out Milo.

Quinta laughed. 'No, Phoebe goes to our local primary school,

Milo, but I expect we'll be able to see something of you in the holidays at least.'

'I'm going to be a probationer,' said Peter importantly.

'What's that?' asked Milo suspiciously.

'It's practising to be a chorister. When I'm nine, I get to be a real chorister, with a white coat.'

'Surplice,' said Faustina, laughing.

Milo's eyes were round. 'Oh, you poor thing,' he said in a sepulchral voice. 'You mean they make you sing every day in the Cathedral. Did your mum say you had to be one?'

'No, I want to be a chorister,' said Peter indignantly. 'Choristers are special. It's always Gavin this, Gavin that, and we can't do that because of Gavin's choir, and we must be in at this time, because Gavin's got a choir rehearsal. Now they'll have to say it about me as well.'

'Do you like singing?' asked Faustina, amused.

'I don't sing very much,' said Peter, 'but I suppose it's all right. I learnt a hymn by heart for my voice trial, that was very boring, the singing teacher my mum got for me went on and on about this and that. But I did very well, because they turned lots of boys down.'

'I'm sure,' said Faustina gravely, trying not to catch Quinta's eye.

'Peter's mother, Pauline, takes music very seriously,' said Quinta.

'Is she a professional?' said Faustina.

'She was. At least, she did music at college, but she more or less gave it up when she got married. She's very keen on music for children.'

'I see,' said Faustina. 'Well, Peter, I'm afraid Milo isn't very keen on music.'

'Nor am I, really,' said Peter, with devastating honesty. 'I think it's boring.'

'Then why do you want to be a chorister?' said Phoebe, glowering at him.

'That's different,' said Peter, with unimpaired calm.

'Stupid,' muttered Phoebe, and got a sharp look from Quinta.

'Come on, Milo,' said Faustina. 'Quinta, I'm so glad to have met you again. I'll give you a ring, I'm sure Milo and Phoebe would like to get together before the end of the holidays.'

'And me,' piped up Peter.

Quinta pushed Phoebe on in front of her before she could say anything.

'Are you in the phone book?'

'Yes,' said Quinta. 'Under Praetorius. A, not S.'

'Of course,' said Faustina. 'I'll look forward to seeing you again, Phoebe.'

'Bye, Milo,' said Phoebe, with a wave. 'We'll really clobber him next time.'

As soon as everyone had given up expecting any summer at all and had fled abroad or gone home to look out their winter clothes, the weather had cheered up. The sun was shining over Eyot, the river had retreated to its normal level, and people had emerged in light summer clothes, thronging the streets of the old town in bright colours, and planning outings to the coast.

'Far too late to be any use to you, duckie,' said Sam when he bumped into Quinta outside Gumble's. 'You have had an exciting time, though, can't wait for you to get back and tell us all about it. I was worried about Phoebe, I can tell you, but Denzil, my hairdresser, you know; well, he does Mrs Thrumby's hair. She told him that her daughter Lara was on that dig, looking after all the young ones, and that no harm would ever come to any child who was in her care. Are you going in?' He gestured towards the entrance to the shop.

'No, of course not,' said Quinta. 'My week's budget would go in a second if I so much as put my foot through the door.'

'I'll treat you to something,' said Sam.

'No, you won't, and I don't do as badly as all that, because whenever Alban does the shopping, he heads straight here and buys all kinds of exotic delicacies.'

'Nice,' said Sam. 'Where is Alban? He hasn't been in the shop for ages, he usually comes in to have a chat when you're away. He gets lonely without you.'

'Oh, dear,' said Quinta. 'He's in Spain, I think. He's gone to gather local material, songs and so forth, I suppose. He's writing a guitar concerto.'

'Spain,' said Sam. 'Think what a wonderful tan he'll have when he gets back. I do envy him.'

Sam, who had a heart of gold, would have loved to go abroad for his holidays, but he had an elderly mother to whom he was devoted, and who didn't like abroad, so he dutifully spent all his holidays with her.

'I have suggested she move somewhere better,' said Sam. 'She could afford to, and really, Scarborough is rather down-market these days, all the riff-raff go there. But she's used to it, and has her friends, and one shouldn't uproot old people.'

'You are kind,' said Quinta warmly. 'You'll be away in October, won't you? It could be lovely, look how the weather's changed.'

'Yes, I'm looking forward to a holiday.'

'Have you been busy?' asked Quinta. 'It must have been difficult on your own.'

'No, Gustav was in for the fortnight. He's raving about your double-bass, by the way.'

Quinta looked uneasy. 'Oh. I didn't really want him to see it, at least not yet.'

Sam laughed. 'He could hardly miss it. He says if it turns out as good as it looks, he'll get some more commissions for you. I told him, straight out, that in that case he would have to come to a proper financial arrangement with you.'

'Oh, Sam, you didn't!'

'I did, of course I did. Doing repairs and helping with the shop isn't nearly such skilled work as making instruments. It will bring him more customers, too, if you get a reputation.'

'If,' said Quinta. 'And it's a big if. Oh well, I'm quite looking forward to getting back to it next week.'

'Here's Phoebe,' said Sam as Phoebe rocketed out of the stationers where she had been carefully selecting a pencil as a present for Sylvester.

'Hi, Sam,' she said. 'How's life?'

'Good, thank you,' said Sam. 'You look after your mum, now, Phoebe, make sure she enjoys the rest of her holiday.'

'It's my holiday, too,' pointed out Phoebe.

'Yes, but you always have lovely roses in your cheeks,' said

Sam, giving them a friendly pinch. 'We want to see some in your mum's face.'

'Okay, mate,' said Phoebe obligingly.

'And when Alban turns up, tell him the music he ordered has come in,' said Sam, as he pushed open the door to Gumble's.

'Amazing smell,' said Quinta, as an aroma of cheese and hams and roasting coffee floated out.

'It's horrible, ugh,' said Phoebe, tugging at her mother's sleeve. 'Come on, we can go now I've got Sylvester's present.'

'And a lovely present it is too,' said Sylvester as Phoebe gave it to him with a flourish.

'It's for your music, so you can make squiggles on it,' explained Phoebe. 'Look, it's got Beethoven's signature on it, I knew you'd like that. And a rubber on the end for when you make mistakes.'

'Plenty of those,' said Lily. 'Upstairs now, Phoebe, and I'll show you and your mum your rooms.'

Lily had suggested to Sylvester that he invite Quinta and Phoebe to stay overnight, and he had been delighted with the idea. Gabriel was away playing at a festival in Spain, and he hated it when the house was empty.

'It'll give Quinta a break,' said Lily. 'Phoebe can help me, plenty for her to do here, she won't be bored. And Quinta can sit on the terrace or in the garden and do nothing, which I daresay is what she never gets the chance to do.'

Sylvester bore Phoebe off to play some music to her and Quinta sat on the terrace in a blissful stupor.

'Do you know,' she said to Lily, 'I never do this? Just lie and think about nothing at all.'

'No, and you'd worry about things a lot less if you did it more often,' said Lily, plonking an iced drink on the table beside her. 'It's hard bringing up a child on your own, especially a handful like Phoebe. And that Alban's been hassling you, hasn't he? I suppose he wants to get married. Take my advice and don't even think about it.'

Quinta laughed. 'How do you know so much, Lily?'

'I've got eyes, and I know a lot about men. Particularly artists, I've always had a lot to do with artists. Best avoided, at least as husbands. All right in bed, some of them, but that's as far as it goes.' She paused and looked at Quinta. 'And that isn't so hot, either, is it? What with you being tired, and Alban being selfish and jealous, well it doesn't make for a lot of fun between the sheets. You find someone closer to your own age, someone with a lot of go in him. Make the most of it while you're young.'

'I like older men, if I like them at all, which I don't think I really do,' said Quinta thoughtfully.

'That's because you never got over what Phoebe's father did to you, you're still hoping another one like that will come along. One of those is enough for any life, take my word for it. Look how he ruined your life, and I don't suppose he ever gave it a second thought.'

'He didn't ruin my life,' said Quinta defensively. 'I wouldn't be without Phoebe for anything.'

'No, I daresay not, but nobody needs a baby, however nice, at the age when you were lumbered with one. Carrying on with a girl of fourteen, wicked, that's what it was. And I don't suppose you were the only one, either. If he got his kicks that way, he wouldn't stop at just the one.'

'How do you know I was only fourteen?' said Quinta.

'I know Harriet very well, and she told me at the time. Don't worry, I've never told another soul, and nor has she. She talked it over with me, because she was wondering whether it would be best for you if some effort was made to get hold of Phoebe's father, make him pay.'

'I never told her who the father was.'

'No, of course you didn't, your sort is always loyal, and particularly to men who don't deserve it. But there are ways and means of getting information about almost anybody. We could have found out all right. We didn't, though, I said it was best to let it lie, and Harriet agreed with me. Got a lot of sense, has Harriet. Is she still staying with you?'

'On and off,' said Quinta, lying back again and closing her eyes. 'She's in Cambridge this week, but she'll be back at the weekend. She's found a house, she'll move in there quite soon.'

'Well, it's good for you to have another friend in Eyot,' said Lily. She bent over to pick up a newspaper which had slid to the ground from Quinta's lap. 'That other friend of yours, Lydia, she's a nice girl. Getting into deep water, from what I hear. She's going to need her friends soon, no question.'

Sylvester calls her a witch, thought Quinta. He's quite right. She drifted away into a dozing sleep, achingly haunted by the image of Phoebe's father, looking down at her as he had done when they made love so deliriously.

Funny, thought Quinta, in her half-awake state, how all my erotic dreams are still about him. Funny how soft men's faces and mouths go when they're making love, however firm they are normally. Funny, the whole business of making love. Bizarre, when you thought about it in cold blood. Which you didn't, of course, that was the trouble.

She was dragged out of her reverie by shouts from Phoebe, announcing her arrival from some way away. She yawned, and sat up as Phoebe hurled herself into her lap.

'Oof, Phoebe, you weigh a ton.'

'Sorry, Q. Listen, Sylvester let me play his cello, he did really. It's fantastic, it makes heavenly sounds which go right through your tummy. Q, listen,' went on Phoebe, holding Quinta's head between her hands and making her look straight in her face. 'Listen, I've got to learn the cello, I've just got to.'

'Phoebe, look, you've spilled my drink all down my front, oh bother. Get up a moment, *please*, Phoebe.'

Quinta dabbed rather inefficiently at her T shirt with the remnants of a tissue from her pocket. Lily appeared as if by magic with a cloth, just as Sylvester came across the terrace, beaming.

He lifted another chair effortlessly in one huge hand and sat himself down by the table.

'Quinta, early days yet, but do you know, I think Phoebe is going to be good at the cello. Really good, it's clear she's got an instinct for it.'

Quinta sank back into her seat, and shut her eyes for a moment.

'Don't say anything,' said Lily. 'If Sylvester thinks she's got talent and Phoebe's keen, they'll find a way between them, save your breath and give in right away.'

'Open your eyes, Q,' said Phoebe, pulling painfully at Quinta's eyelashes. 'I know you haven't really fainted, has she, Sylvester?'

'All right, all right,' said Quinta, rubbing her eyes. 'Sylvester, this isn't practical!'

'No, perhaps not,' said Sylvester with vast good humour. 'But then music isn't very practical at all. She is musical, your Phoebe, no question about it, and I think the cello is her instrument. Now, I don't usually teach beginners, especially not young ones, because you have to deal with their invariably appalling parents. But in Phoebe's case, well, I shouldn't care to see her wrongly taught, it would worry me greatly to see her having lessons with that cack-handed fellow who most of the young ones go to.'

'I thought all his pupils had a wonderful technique,' said Quinta. 'That's what people say when they come to the shop.'

'Technique!' said Sylvester with scorn. 'I'll give him technique. No, no, it wouldn't do at all, not for Phoebe. I'll teach Phoebe.'

Quinta had to smile, he was so enthusiastic. 'It's impossible, of course,' she said. 'There's no way I could afford lessons with you, Sylvester, I can't imagine what you must charge. I couldn't even afford lessons with the cello teacher you despise so much.'

'You can afford me,' said Sylvester, making a sweeping gesture as he spoke that knocked over Quinta's glass for a second time. 'Oh, sorry,' he said as he noticed. 'Lily! Lily! Bring a cloth.'

'I'm here,' said Lily behind his left ear. 'And I've got a cloth. You make work for me, that's what you do.'

She mopped ferociously, and then stood, with one hand on her hip, looking at Quinta. 'No, Phoebe,' she said, seeing the child was about to express her own opinions at full volume, 'I am talking.'

Phoebe subsided, she always did what Lily told her.

'Sylvester will teach her for nothing, for three months. Then he can say how much promise she really has, and if she is as good as he thinks, then he'll go on teaching her. For nothing,' she added.

'That's right, Lily,' said Sylvester approvingly. 'I couldn't have put it better myself.'

'Mind you,' went on Lily, 'it's a foregone conclusion, because I've never known Sylvester wrong about a musician yet, whatever age they are. Now, that's enough, Phoebe, your mum doesn't want you crawling all over her that like. You're coming with me, because it's time for your supper. No, you aren't going to eat it with the grown-ups; your mum and Sylvester are going to have a peaceful meal by themselves.'

She turned to Sylvester, 'I'll lay the table here on the terrace,' she said. 'It's warm enough for about the first time this summer.'

Quinta looked at Sylvester, saying nothing. Sylvester gave his booming laugh.

'Don't you look so suspicious, young Quinta. This is cause for celebration, not for worrying, so you can take that anxious expression off your face.'

'Sylvester,' began Quinta, 'look, it's very kind of you, but . . .'

'No buts. It's settled. You have no right to deny this to Phoebe, and besides, I won't let you. End of discussion. Have another drink.'

'She'll need a cello,' said Quinta in despair. 'I haven't got the money to buy her one, even small ones cost a lot, and although I expect Gustav would give me a discount, I still couldn't afford it.'

'No problem,' said Sylvester, 'You can make her one, when you've finished that fancy bass. Won't take you long. Meanwhile, Gustav can lend you one, I'll have a word with him. Good for business, because once other mothers see Phoebe having lessons with me on a cello made by you, they'll all want one. You mark my words. Now, I wonder what Lily's giving us for dinner.'

## 17

Quinta was still feeling very light-hearted when she got back to Eyot the following afternoon. Pampered by Lily and kept constantly amused by Sylvester, she had enjoyed her brief stay immensely. Sylvester had said she must come again, often, for weekends when Gabriel was there, or when they had friends up from London.

And three months ago, thought Quinta, six weeks, even, I wouldn't have dreamt of going to Midwinter Hall to stay with anyone. Now I'd go any time. In fact, I like being with other people, how surprising.

Firmly vetoing Phoebe's impassioned pleas to go now, this very instant, to the shop to get a cello, she headed for the kitchen. Food, she thought. There's time to get to the supermarket before Phoebe has a bath.

Phoebe's voice drifted through the door. 'Mum, what are you doing?'

'Making a list,' Quinta called back.

Phoebe appeared at the door. 'Oh, no, not lists again!'

'This is a harmless list, a shopping list, everyone has them,' said Quinta.

Phoebe watched her open the fridge and jot some things on the list. 'Milk, nearly out of butter . . . Phoebe, would you like sausages for supper?'

'Okay,' said Phoebe. 'Oh, there's someone on the phone. They sound a bit strange.'

'Phoebe, you wretch, why didn't you say? They'll have hung up.'

Quinta flew to the phone on the wall of the kitchen. 'Hello?

Hello? Phoebe, go and put the other phone down, I can't understand what they're saying.'

'Peculiar,' said Phoebe. 'I told you.'

'I'm so sorry,' Quinta was saying into the phone. 'Mr Praetorius? Alban Praetorius? No, I'm afraid he's away. Can I take a message?'

She held the receiver away from her ear and stared at it for a moment. It wasn't the telephone that made the person on the other end difficult to understand, it was the language. She wasn't quite sure what language he was speaking, but whatever it was, she didn't understand it.

French. He wasn't speaking French, but he might understand it, foreigners were so much better at languages than the English. She would try French. She haltingly asked the madman at the other end to explain himself. Ah, he spoke French, no better than she did, but it was comprehensible . . . more or less. But who was he? And what on earth was he talking about? Ane . . . wasn't that a donkey? And why was he talking about 'éteindre la linge'? Quinta wracked her brains. Surely that was something to do with washing. Now he was talking about someone called Achilles. Quinta gave a great sigh, as Phoebe buzzed back into the kitchen, big with news.

'Sssh,' said Quinta, without looking round. 'I'm trying to understand what this man is saying, I can't make head or tail of it. I think he must be Spanish, at least that's what it sounds like when he isn't trying to speak French.'

A firm hand took the phone from her. 'May I? If it's Spanish, I can help.'

It was Lucy Praetorius. Quinta gratefully handed the phone to her, and motioned furiously to Phoebe to be quiet. Clearly, something was up; if it was Spanish, then the person was probably calling from Spain and it must be to do with Alban. Had he got himself put in jail? Was he lost? But why all the gibberish about donkeys and laundries?

Lucy finally put the phone down, and tried to detach herself from Phoebe so that she could greet Quinta. Phoebe adored Alban's mother.

Quinta kissed her. 'What are you doing here?' she asked. 'I

thought you weren't coming until next month. Oh, I am pleased to see you!'

'A friend was driving over and offered me a lift, I thought I would come and see how you are; I had a feeling all was not well with my two incompetent sons, and you see, I was quite right. Yes, Phoebe, there's a present for you, of course there is.'

'Is Alban all right?' asked Quinta anxiously. 'I couldn't understand what on earth that man was trying to say.'

'Well, he is and he isn't,' said Lucy. 'Oh, I must sit down, and I shouldn't laugh, it must be very painful for him. Really, it's so silly.'

'What's happened?'

'Alban's injured his leg, a tendon, by the sound of it, so uncomfortable, poor boy. He was on a donkey . . .'

'A donkey?' said Quinta incredulously. 'Why ever was he on a donkey? He was going to hire a car.'

'Yes, but for some reason he was riding through this little hill town on a donkey. You know how narrow the streets in such places are.'

'I don't,' said Quinta, 'for I've never been, but I know what you mean.'

'The women hang their washing on lines across the street. They have a pulley system for getting the washing up and down. It seems that the pulley slipped, or something happened, and the washing line came down just as Alban was underneath on the donkey. Of course the donkey panicked and got itself completely wrapped in the washing, and Alban got tied up in the line and was dragged off. He fell awkwardly, well, he would in the circumstances, don't you think? When he tried to get up, he couldn't.'

'Oh, poor Alban,' said Quinta, in fits. 'Oh, I shouldn't laugh, but it is funny. That's what the man was on about, of course, his Achilles tendon.'

Phoebe was listening with great interest to all this. 'One of our teachers at school did his Achilles tendon in,' she said informatively. 'He had to have it in plaster, and go round in a wheelchair. For weeks and weeks.'

Lucy and Quinta looked at each other with dawning horror.

'Wheelchair!' said Quinta.

'Weeks and weeks! Oh, dear,' said his mother. 'He's the most terrible hypochondriac.'

'I know,' said Quinta grimly. And then, practically, 'How is he going to get back?'

'It wasn't entirely clear. I think there's another Englishman there who's going to bring him back. Is he insured?'

Quinta thought for a moment, and then breathed a sigh of relief. 'Yes, yes, of course he is. He was joking about it, because someone at the record company that does his music insisted that he took out very full insurance, he has it on a yearly basis, in case he has to go abroad at short notice. Alban said they were a lot of old fusspots, and he'd been travelling for years without any insurance, and he'd never been ill or had any accidents, and the only thing he'd ever lost was a spongebag. He left it in a hut in Finland.'

'What was he doing in . . .' began Lucy. 'Oh, never mind. I wonder if there's anyone in the embassy who could help? There must be a consul nearby, and presumably he's in hospital. That'll give us a few days' grace, time to think up a plan and get things sorted out.'

They weren't to be so lucky. Lucy's attempts to get any information from the embassy were fruitless, but late in the evening they had a phone call from Sylvester. Gabriel had rung him. He had been in Seville, working; someone had contacted him about Alban's accident. He was coming home tomorrow, and would accompany Alban.

'Sylvester says the insurance people are laying on ambulances and things, so there's nothing to do at this end,' Lucy reported. 'And,' she went on with a smile, 'he said to keep your pecker up and not let this bugger things up for you.'

Quinta grinned at that, but all the light-heartedness of the morning had evaporated. Alban at home was difficult in any case. Alban with a leg in plaster and a wheelchair was a disaster.

Could you make love with a sprained Achilles tendon in a plaster? thought Quinta as she made her way round the supermarket, trying to think of food to tempt an injured Alban.

Probably; nothing short of death ever seemed to put men off sex, she thought gloomily.

Something seems to have put the man in my life off sex, thought Lydia resentfully, as she spooned yet another helping of mousse into her mouth. Her grandmother was animadverting on Felix and Zoe; her opinion of them had undergone a radical change after a few days of their company.

'I don't trust them,' she said. 'I don't know why Adam spends so much time with them, and it's strange, him offering to lend them his house. He doesn't charge them any rent, Sybil says. Of course, Sybil thinks they're wonderful.'

She jabbed at her mouth with her napkin. 'Finish that up, Lydia. We'll have coffee in the drawing room.'

She continued with her theme as they drank their coffee in the big, formal room.

'I rarely disagree with Sybil, but I'm not impressed by that pair at all. I know the boy was at Eton, but they let in all sorts these days, I'm told, provided they can pay the fees. And she seems a perfect dimwit, with that sly smile. I don't approve of his business, either, importing pretty objects from Hungary and Czechoslovakia. It doesn't seem a very useful way to earn a living.'

'No, grandmama,' said Lydia, her mind full of thoughts of Adam. She hadn't seen him for ten days, and she was torn between a determination never to see him again and a desperate longing to jump into bed with him. Now that her grandmother had taken against the twins she didn't want to invite Adam to the house.

'He'd turn up with those two trailing along, he has no sense of how to behave,' Lady Wray said crossly. 'I'm glad you didn't see too much of him, Lydia, it would have been a mistake to become attached to him.'

'Yes, grandmama,' said Lydia, as she rose from her seat.

'Where are you going, Lydia?' said her grandmother.

'Just to make a phone call, if that's all right, grandmama.'

'Yes, of course, but don't talk for hours. It's a very idle way to spend your time, you know, talking on the phone when you could be doing something more useful.'

'Yes, grandmama, I mean, no grandmama,' said Lydia.

And what have I got to do that's more useful? thought Lydia as she drifted out of the room. Her grandmother didn't approve of the phone, so it stayed in the hall, with an uncomfortable little chair beside it, to discourage lengthy calls. There was an extension upstairs in the main bedroom, and Lydia toyed with the idea of going up there; at least she could loll on the bed and be more comfortable, and her grandmother wouldn't leave the drawing room yet.

As she hesitated, the phone rang, and she quickly picked it up.

'Quinta,' she said, pleased. 'I was just going to ring you.'

'Oh, good,' said Quinta. 'I'm dying to have a chat, I haven't spoken to you for ages. It's all been a bit busy here.'

'Meet me for coffee, tomorrow. Or are you at work?'

'No, I'm not. Why don't you come here?'

'I'd rather not, too many people about.'

It would be wonderful to escape for an hour or two, thought Quinta.

'Good, I'll see you at half past ten,' said Lydia. 'I'll seize a table for us.'

'Where?'

'Flora's.' She held a hand over the mouthpiece. 'Yes, grandmother, I'm just coming. Sorry, Quinta, just grandmother going on at me, you see why I can't really talk on the phone. See you tomorrow, bye.'

'Ooof,' said Quinta, plonking herself down on a padded bench in a secluded corner. 'What a relief.'

'I thought we'd be better off down here than upstairs in the goldfish bowl, visible to all,' said Lydia. 'I've ordered coffee, and the waitress is bringing the trolley. It's laden with goodies, wonderful.'

Quinta made a face. 'It's all very well for you, Lydia, it doesn't matter what you eat, whereas I become more and more round.'

'Tell,' said Lydia. 'What's happening about Alban? How is he? How are you coping?'

'Badly,' said Quinta.

'He's sprained his Achilles tendon, hasn't he?' said Lydia. 'Painful. He'll have to do a lot of work on it when it's healed; not just the physio, but going to a gym and really getting his strength back. You must tell him.'

Quinta laughed. 'Alban won't listen to me, and, frankly, I don't think anything would get him near a gym. I won't mention it at the moment, in any case, because at present he mostly just moans.'

'It must be agonizing,' said Lydia, her voice full of sympathy.

'I suppose so,' said Quinta doubtfully. 'Although he's taking a lot of painkillers, and the doctor says that now it's properly in plaster, and he is keeping it up, it shouldn't be hurting so very much.'

'People's pain thresholds are different,' said Lydia. 'Alban's an artist, after all; maybe he's more sensitive than the rest of us. Well, you just have to be firm with him, Quinta, or he'll never get better.'

'Mmm,' said Quinta, unconvinced.

'Thank you,' Lydia said to the waitress as she put their coffee on to the table. She inspected the trolley, finally choosing the most sumptuous of the cakes on offer. Quinta, who loved chocolate, succumbed to a rich, dark slice of chocolate truffle cake.

'What's his mother like?' said Lydia indistinctly, her mouth full of cream and almonds.

'Lucy is terrific – as a person, I mean.'

'Is she helpful, or does she expect you to wait on her hand and foot as well?'

'No, no, she's not at all like that.'

'Then why do you sound doubtful about her?'

'Do I? I don't mean to.' Quinta hesitated, and shook her head. 'I don't want to be disloyal, because they've both been so kind to me, but actually, they argue a lot, which is a bit of a strain. She isn't as sympathetic as he would like, he says she's a hard woman. But she says he's moaned and groaned about every little thing since the moment he was born, so she can't take him very seriously now.'

'Oh, dear,' said Lydia. 'Just what you need. What does Phoebe think about all this?'

'She's quite enjoying herself,' said Quinta. 'She gets on very well with Lucy, who is super with her.'

'How are you going to manage with Alban when Lucy goes back and Harriet's moved into her own house?' asked Lydia. 'If he can't walk, he'll be at home all the time. That's going to be very difficult for you.' She was silent for a moment, thinking of practicalities.

How kind Lydia is, thought Quinta, not finding her cake so delicious now that she had been reminded of all the arrangements she was going to have to make. Asking about my problems, when she's got worries of her own.

'Of course,' went on Lydia, 'his studio is on the ground floor, that's something.'

Quinta made a face. 'Yes, but you know how up and down the house is, everything on a slightly different level. It's a nightmare for a wheelchair.'

She sighed. 'Lucy did suggest that he should find a more suitable place – just temporarily – but of course, that threw him into a terrible temper, "A sick man needs his home . . . How could he work? . . . Was she trying to drive him into insanity . . .?" Anyway, a carpenter is supposed to be coming today, to put ramps up all over the ground floor, so that he can move around in his wheelchair. We've put a bed for him in what was the morning room – it's never used, and it's right by his studio, so that's fairly convenient. He doesn't like it in there, though. Says it's a poky little room, and the panelling makes him feel claustrophobic.'

'He's obviously feeling rather tetchy,' said Lydia. 'You don't want to let him get away with that; it could easily become a habit.'

'You could say that,' agreed Quinta. 'Then Lucy, who I have to say does stir him up rather, said that if he didn't stop finding fault with everything that everyone had done for him, he'd feel really claustrophobic because she'd put a black cloth over his head.'

Lydia shook her head. 'That's not the way to handle him; you'd think she'd know better, being his mother.'

'I don't think she's got the patience she must have had when he was little.'

Lydia wiped her mouth with a paper napkin and sighed contentedly. 'I wonder if I could manage another cake; just a small one.'

'Certainly not. That would be pure greed. May I join you?'

'Hello, Titus,' said Quinta, strangely pleased to see him. 'What are you doing here?'

He took Lydia's lazy smile for agreement and pulled up a chair to the table. 'Oh, I've been out and about, doing the things one does on a Saturday morning, and I thought I would drop in here for a cup of coffee. There are some ghastly university people upstairs, so I fled down here for peace and quiet.'

'We're gloomy rather than peaceful or quiet, down here,' said Lydia. 'I've got problems with my home life and my love life, which we haven't got round to discussing yet, and Quinta's in the thick of it with Alban being as awkward as he knows how.'

Titus looked at Quinta's face. The dark shadows were back under her eyes, and she looked strained. She shouldn't look like that, not at her age, he thought with sudden anger.

Lydia looked from one of them to the other, then quickly lowered her eyes. He cares about her, she thought in a moment of revelation. He really minds about her. And Quinta? Difficult to tell, she always had such a guard on her feelings, especially where men were concerned.

Do you good, Titus, Lydia said to herself, to really fall in love, and with someone younger than you. And Quinta couldn't find a nicer man; very good-looking, too, and plenty of brain. Much better for her than Alban, Lydia decided. Alban needed someone much tougher than Quinta, someone who would stand up to him. Like me, she thought, wondering whether Titus was really falling in love with Quinta . . . Not that it would do any good; Quinta clearly wasn't going to fall in love with anyone, not with her past hanging round her neck.

Titus was enquiring politely about her problems. Charm, he has more than his fair share of charm, thought Lydia as she told him about Adam and her grandmother and the terrible twins. He took a keen interest, he enjoyed other people's lives and relished knotty personal problems. 'As long as I don't have to get involved,' he said. 'The advice is free, but no comebacks if I get it wrong. Leave it with me, Uncle Titus will mull over your separate imbroglios and come up with a brilliant solution.'

Quinta grinned at him. 'Practical applications of working with chaos, is that what makes you an expert?'

'Of course it is,' said Titus. 'Let me order you some more coffee.'

Lucy Praetorius greeted Harriet with warmth. 'It seems such a long time since I saw you, and here you are, coming to live in Eyot, Quinta tells me.'

'Yes, and it's been so kind of Alban and you to let me stay in your house while I've been house-hunting. I've been in Cambridge, but I heard about Alban, so I came back to see if there was anything I could do.'

'Hello, Harriet,' said Quinta, coming into the room with a harassed expression on her face. 'Lucy, Alban says someone has been at his papers and he can't find anything.'

'Leave him to me,' said Lucy briskly.

'Having a hard time of it?' said Harriet sympathetically. 'Can I help?'

Quinta slumped into a chair and pulled a face. 'You are kind, but you've got your new house to sort out, and you must be starting work at the school any minute now.' She sat up. 'It sounds ungracious, because you know how kind Alban was to me when Phoebe was born, but goodness, he is being difficult.'

She ruffled her hair vigorously, making it stand up in wild disarray. 'It's just about manageable while Lucy's here, she's a tower of strength, and very firm with him. But she can't stay much longer, and then I don't know what's going to happen.'

'He'll have to have a nurse,' said Harriet firmly. 'He's insured, isn't he?'

'Yes, I suppose the insurance would cover a nurse, but would a nurse put up with him? He isn't really that ill, just demanding and bad-tempered.'

'Nobody in their right mind would put up with him,' said Lucy, joining them. 'What a fuss about nothing, he can't remember where's he's put a piece of paper, so he has to have a scene, blame everyone else for it; dear me, I'd forgotten how tiring he is.'

'I know,' said Quinta with a wicked look on her face, 'let's invite Hermione from London to come and look after him. If she dotes on him the way you say she does, then she'd probably love to push him around in his wheelchair and wait on him hand and foot.'

'Hermione-from-London?' asked Harriet.

'His London girlfriend,' said Quinta cheerfully. 'Me here, Hermione in London. Quite a neat arrangement, don't you think?'

Harriet raised her eyebrows. 'Different, anyway.'

'Where's Phoebe?' said Harriet. 'I can't hear her. Is she doing her homework? She must have started back at school this week.'

'Yes, she has,' said Quinta. 'Today, in fact. She has a friend, Louise, who isn't at that school any more, she's going to your school, Harriet. Her mother picked Phoebe up today and took her back to play with Louise, who's still on holiday. You don't start for a few days yet, do you?'

'Next week,' said Harriet. 'Did you go and talk to the school about Phoebe?'

Quinta shook her head. 'I couldn't, I didn't have time, not with all the upheavals over Alban. But I wrote to the head, saying I'd taken her advice and Phoebe had been to see a psychologist; here was the report, and perhaps the problems weren't what she had thought. So I hope that clears things up.'

'Must be a fool, that headmistress,' said Lucy. 'Anyone can see that Phoebe's got all her wits about her. It's a pity she can't go to your school, Harriet, you'd know what to do with her.'

'Yes,' said Harriet. 'I'd love to teach Phoebe, but I'm sure in the end she'll do well wherever she goes.'

Lucy looked unconvinced. 'I think she'd be better off at your school, Harriet. Did you know that Alban has offered to pay the fees?' She gave Quinta a quizzical look. 'Apparently Quinta won't let him.'

'No,' said Quinta. She got up. 'Why don't I make some tea?'

There was a bang at the door. 'Oh, that must be Phoebe; she's back early.'

To her surprise, it wasn't Phoebe who came into the kitchen, but Maria Latimer. Looking tanned, well-groomed and rich, thought Quinta enviously. Why don't I ever look like that?

'Hello, Maria,' she said. 'Is everything all right? Where's Phoebe?'

'She's gone to her room. No, don't worry, she's been fine with us,' she added, seeing the worried look on Quinta's face. 'You know we love having her, but I've just popped in to warn you that I think something's wrong at school, and she's rather upset. She thinks you're going to be cross with her. She's been in the wars a bit, too. I must rush, Louise is waiting in the car, and she'll be creating if I leave her any longer.'

'Oh, Maria,' Quinta began, but Maria had given a wave to the assembled company and gone. Quinta looked at Harriet and Lucy.

'Better go and see what's up,' said Harriet sensibly. 'It won't be anything major, you know how dramatic children are about little things at that age.'

Quinta vanished, nearly colliding in the passage outside with Alban, who was manoeuvring himself along with difficulty in his wheelchair.

'I'll never get the hang of this bloody thing,' he grumbled. 'What are you all doing? Sitting in the kitchen gossiping, I expect, and there's Phoebe bawling her eyes out.'

Quinta ran to Phoebe's room. The door was shut, but Quinta could hear her crying inside. 'Phoebe,' she said, pushing at the door. It remained shut. Quinta was taken aback, Phoebe's door didn't have a lock, whatever had she done?

Phoebe had pushed her chest of drawers across the door on her side, and it took the combined efforts of Harriet and Lucy to coax her into removing it. A woebegone little face peered round the door when they finally persuaded her to open it.

'Phoebe!' cried Quinta, horrified. 'Your eye!'

'Don't say a word,' hissed Harriet, seeing that Phoebe was about to retreat into her room again. 'Come on Phoebe, it's all right. Whatever it is, Quinta won't be cross with you.'

Lucy held out her arms to the child, and Phoebe hurtled into them, burying her wet face in one of Lucy's best cashmere jumpers.

'Here's a handkerchief,' said Harriet. 'Have a good blow, and then come and tell us what's the matter. Look, here's Alban, he's so worried about you, he's come out of his room, all by himself.'

## 18

'Well,' said Harriet, after a calmed down and happier Phoebe had finally been dispatched to bed.

'She's asleep,' said Quinta, coming back into the room, her face strained. 'Alban, she's perched that Spanish hat on the end of her bed, and she's clutching your doll in a firm grasp. Perfect timing.'

'I'd forgotten that I'd bought them,' said Alban with honesty. 'I knew she'd like the hat, but I was doubtful about the senorita, knowing how she feels about dolls generally.'

'Yes, but it's hardly a doll, is it, with that exotic face and those amazing clothes.'

'I got her some castanets, too,' said Alban.

Quinta pulled a face, and he winked at her, in a better humour than he had been since he came back. 'I'll save those for the time being, perhaps.'

'Now, Quinta,' said Lucy in a no-nonsense voice. 'What are you going to do about that child? You can't say this school is the best place for her, not after this.'

'I don't know how that horrible woman could do such a thing,' said Quinta. 'Keeping her back a year, so that's she's in a class with children much younger than she is, and her friends all in the next class up. I thought they always kept them in their year group! And after I'd sent her that report as well. And why didn't she ring me, to discuss it?'

'She'll say she tried,' said Harriet dryly. 'And how the decision was taken by all the staff, with Harriet's best interests in mind, and how they don't believe in IQ tests . . . and so on and so on.'

'You can't send her to school tomorrow,' said Lucy, who was shocked to the core to see Phoebe's puffy eye and bruised legs. 'Not if she's going to come home like that.'

'I expect she lost her temper,' said Quinta. 'Then she'd lash out at anybody who said anything. And if they said she was stupid, and called her a baby, because she's in a class with younger children, then I'm not surprised she was furious.'

'Bloody awful school,' said Alban. 'If I didn't have this stupid leg in plaster, I'd go round there myself tomorrow and tell those idiot teachers what I think of them.'

'At least we're spared that,' Quinta whispered to Lucy.

'Lucy's right,' said Harriet. 'Phoebe can't go back there until all this is sorted out. I'm afraid it's all going to be very difficult for you, Quinta, you may have to lodge a formal complaint, and the whole business is cumbersome and very trying.'

'Can't I just send her to another school?' said Quinta wearily. 'It seems the simplest solution.'

Harriet shook her head. 'Not so easy. The way things are, she'd go labelled difficult or maladjusted, no school wants pupils like that. You may be sure that the school will present their handling of this whole affair in a way that puts you and Phoebe in the wrong. You could have a problem trying to persuade another school to take her.'

What do I do? thought Quinta desperately. I can't afford to pay for her, I can't let Alban or my parents pay her fees somewhere; my parents would take her over, and if Alban did it, then I'd never be able to get away from him. And I think he wants me to stay at home and look after him while he's laid up, and that means I'd lose my job, Gustav would have to employ someone else, the work couldn't wait. I wouldn't be able to finish the double-bass, or make Phoebe a cello; not that I can afford lessons for her, whatever Sylvester says about not charging. Oh hell.

'Someone at the door,' said Alban. 'Come on, Quinta, we'll sort things out, look at all the people you've got gunning for young Phoebe. We won't let those nasty little bureaucrats walk all over her.'

Quinta began to struggle to her feet, but Lucy pushed her back into her chair.

'I'll see who it is,' she said. Quinta gave a wan smile. She felt drained, beyond thinking about anything any more.

'Too late for that tea you were going to make,' said Harriet. 'Alban, where do you keep your wine? And none of us has eaten; I'm going to go to Gumble's, they're open late tonight, aren't they? Someone told me they do delicious spit-roasted chickens there.'

'Did I hear the magic word Gumble's?' said Titus, following Lucy into the room. 'Hello, Harriet. How's the great clean-up of the Augean stables going?'

'Augean stables?'

'The junior school.'

'It's not as bad as that,' said Harriet, taken aback.

'Just you wait and see,' said Titus knowingly.

He greeted the others, noticing Quinta's bleak face, but not commenting on it. 'I bumped into Simon just now,' he said. 'He's planning to come round and visit you.'

'Oh, no,' said Lucy and Quinta together.

Titus laughed. 'I told him not to. I said that Quinta had enough on her plate at the moment, without visitors, however familial, and that she was looking forward to a quiet evening.'

'Thank you,' said Lucy. 'That was very kind of you. What did he say?'

'He said, "Oh, bloody Tuesday, I suppose," and went off in a huff.'

'I'll ring him up later,' said Lucy. 'As you can see, Quinta is not having a quiet evening at all. Harriet is just going to Gumble's to get some food; have you eaten? If not, do join us.'

'No, I haven't eaten. I just dropped in to see if Alban would like to be wheeled to some suitable hostelry, but instead I will accompany Harriet to Gumble's and carry the bags.'

'Thank you,' said Harriet. 'Give Quinta a drink, we won't be long.'

'Well,' said Pauline. 'I've heard all about Phoebe's disgraceful behaviour at school; she hit Mrs Gridlock's granddaughter quite hard on the arm. She'll be lucky if the school takes her back; I'm not surprised that you've decided she's to stay at home for the time being. Really, Quinta, it's time you admitted that you can't bring up that child single-handed, and accepted that you need your parents' help. I told you right from the beginning that it wouldn't work, but of course, you've always been so obstinate. I feel for you, naturally I do; I can't imagine what it's like to have a backward child, of course mine are exceptionally advanced for their ages, we've been so lucky. But a stable home environment does count for a lot although it may be old-fashioned to say so.'

'Phoebe is not backward,' said Quinta with gritted teeth. She longed to put the phone down, cut off Pauline's quacking voice, but she knew that would only bring a temporary respite.

'Naturally, no mother believes her child is backward, all our geese are swans, aren't they? But you have to look facts in the face, Quinta, which is something you've never been very good at. I mean, that school she goes to isn't exactly very demanding academically, is it? The children who go from there to the Cathedral School always need extra help to bring them up just to an average standard, and of course they're nowhere near the level necessary for the scholarship class. They're at least a year behind in maths and English, so if Phoebe is a year behind that . . . well, I can't think what you're going to do with her.'

'As it happens,' said Quinta crossly, 'she's very bright, the educational psychologist I took her to said so.'

Silence.

'You never told me you'd taken her to an educational psychologist. I suppose the school arranged that for you, it's the first thing they do with problem children.'

'Phoebe is not a problem child.'

'Don't shout,' said Pauline irritatingly. 'You always lose your temper at the slightest little thing, and after all, I'm only trying to help you. Now, what I rang up about, was to ask if you could pick Peter up for me this afternoon? He'll be at the Cathedral; he's started as a probationer now, and is loving it. Gavin has to stay on for evensong, but Peter only does the practice, he won't sing evensong just yet. Although he's much further on musically than the other probationers; I'm sure Simon Praetorius will have him in the choir much sooner than anyone else. If you take him home and give him tea, I'll call round and pick him up when I collect Gavin at six fifteen. I can't pick Peter up earlier, because I'm going to Leeds for the day, I've got a committee meeting.'

Quinta didn't ask for details; Pauline was born on a committee, she thought savagely. She ran everything with remorseless efficiency and energy; grrr, thought Quinta.

'I'm sorry,' she said. 'I can't. Phoebe's got a music lesson, and I want to be there.'

'Nonsense, she can't have,' said Pauline. 'Simon Praetorius teaches her, doesn't he? I must say it's very kind of him to take the trouble, normally he only takes on very good pianists, you know. He'll be at the Cathedral this afternoon, with the boys, you must have got the day wrong.'

'It's a cello lesson,' said Quinta.

'Cello lesson! Since when is Phoebe having cello lessons? You can't afford cello lessons, and besides, it isn't fair on the poor child. She has no powers of concentration, and stringed instruments are very difficult to learn, my two have to work very hard at their instruments, and they're both very gifted musically.'

Quinta took a deep breath, and at the same time gave a piece of wood which was lying on the floor a hefty kick.

'None the less, Phoebe is having cello lessons, I can't change the time, because it has to fit in with when Sylvester is in Eyot, and . . .'

There was a minor explosion at the other end of the line.

'Sylvester? Sylvester Tate?' said Pauline incredulously. 'Teaching Phoebe? I never heard of such a thing.'

'As it happens,' said Quinta, 'he thinks this dim, backward child is very promising, and he suggested the lessons, not me. So, I'm sorry, but I can't have Peter this afternoon.'

Sam came into the workshop a few minutes later, to find Quinta angrily screwing up balls of paper and hurling them at the beam.

'Awkward phone call?' he enquired.

'Pauline,' said Quinta. 'Bludgeoning me into doing something for her as usual. Working out my timetable to the last minute, and then making me do whatever it is she wants. I don't want to pick Peter up from the Cathedral, I've got enough on my plate with Alban and Phoebe, but she won't listen, she just goes on until you give in from sheer desperation.'

'She should be in politics, your friend Pauline,' observed Sam.

'I hate her,' said Quinta vehemently.

'Oh, good,' said Sam. 'You're coming on, Quinta, you've never brought yourself to admit that before. Come and have a sandwich, it's lunchtime.'

Quinta always felt uneasy in the Cathedral. She was an outsider, she didn't belong. She shied away from a contemptuous canon who wafted past with an insincere smile pinned to his face and eyes that looked straight through anyone who crossed his path.

Oh dear, thought Quinta, diving behind a pillar. One of the waiting choir parents, someone she knew slightly, came up to her.

'Hello, Quinta, what are you doing here? Come to pick up Pauline's boy, I suppose. Why are you lurking behind that pillar, are you afraid of being seen? How's Phoebe?'

Quinta looked at her defensively, and then pulled herself together. Olivia's son had been at school with Phoebe before he went into the choir, and Olivia had always been perfectly pleasant. She mustn't let herself imagine that all choir parents were like Pauline. They couldn't be; Pauline was one in a generation.

'Phoebe's fine,' she managed to say in what she hoped was a normal voice. 'How's Alexander liking the choir?'

'It seems to be going all right, but,' and she lowered her voice, looking round to see if they could be overheard, 'but some of the other parents are a bit odd.'

'Pauline, for one,' Quinta whispered back.

'Yes, she's fairly hard going,' said Olivia. She paused. 'Um, I heard there's a spot of trouble with Phoebe at school.'

'News does travel fast,' said Quinta sadly.

'Don't let it get you down,' said Olivia. 'That head is a most peculiar woman. It was different when the previous head was there, Phoebe would have been quite all right with him. What I'm trying to say is, you should get Phoebe away from there. It isn't the right place for her.'

'No, I've come to the same conclusion. But I don't know where to send her.'

'The Cathedral School is just as peculiar in its own way, but of course, the children wear uniform and call the masters sir, so people just think how marvellous. We're disappointed, except for the singing, of course, but the buzz is that this new deputy head is going to make some fairly major changes.'

'Good,' said Quinta. 'I'm glad for Alexander's sake, but it makes no difference to me, I can't afford the fees.'

'No, of course not. Perhaps Phoebe can try for a scholarship when she's older, she's clever, isn't she?'

'The school doesn't think so, nor does Pauline.'

'Pauline! Nobody's clever in her book, except her own little darlings. Oh, here they come. Ring me up, Quinta. I know how busy you are, but there's no reason why we shouldn't meet one Saturday morning for a coffee.'

'Thank you,' said Quinta. 'I'd like that.'

And I mean it, too, thought Quinta, watching for Peter among the little boys straggling across the north transept. Olivia's quite genuine friendliness was refreshing; mustn't get paranoic, she told herself, there are plenty of people who think Phoebe's okay.

Peter came slowly towards her. 'Hello,' he said.

'Hello, Peter,' said Quinta cheerfully. 'Did your mum tell you I was going to pick you up today?'

'Yes, she said she'd ring you this morning to arrange it and tell you when to come. Can we go? Quite quickly would be best, because the proper choristers will be coming across into the Choir now.'

He grabbed her hand and almost dragged her out of the door. Then he walked silently alongside Quinta, looking at his shoes. When they rounded the corner, Quinta felt his little hand stealing into hers. She gave it a reassuring squeeze, feeling very sorry for him all of a sudden.

'Have you got any clothes to change into?' she asked when they got home and she could take in the full glory of his school uniform. 'Do you have to wear those shorts all year round?'

'Yes, until I'm eleven,' said Peter.

'They'll be cold in winter.'

'Yes,' he said. 'I've got some other clothes in my bag. Shall I go and put them on?'

'Yes,' said Quinta. 'You'll be more comfortable. Phoebe will be back in a minute, she went to the shops with Mrs Praetorius.'

'Is that Mr Praetorius's mother? Our Mr Praetorius?'

'Yes, it is.'

'Oh,' said Peter.

'Here they are, now.'

Quinta introduced Peter to Lucy. He shook her hand gravely. 'I know Mr Praetorius,' he told her. 'He's at the Cathedral.'

'Yes,' said Lucy. She looked down at his shorts, and frowned. 'What's happened to your leg, Peter? Have you hurt it?'

Quinta came over and knelt down to look. An angry red weal was visible all down the front of one of his shins. She cried out when she saw it.

'Peter, that must be so painful! However did you do it? Look, it's still bleeding, oh, and the inside of your sock has got blood on it.'

'I did it at school,' said Peter. 'It does hurt rather.'

'Didn't the nurse at school put anything on it?' asked Lucy.

'I didn't go to Sister,' said Peter, hanging his head. 'They said, if I did, they'd . . . they'd . . .'

His voice cracked and two tears dribbled down his face. He gave a heroic sniff. 'It's nothing.'

'Come on,' said Quinta. 'Out with it. You're not at school now, and you're going to have to tell your mother, she'll spot that at once.'

'I'll tell her I fell over,' said Peter.

'Did you?'

He shook his head. 'No,' he said. 'They do it to you in the choir. They've got shoes with metal bits underneath, some of them, and they hold you and scrape their shoe down your leg.' He swallowed valiantly. 'They said if I made a noise or told anyone, they'd do the other leg as well.'

Quinta gave Lucy a horrified glance. 'Come along, Peter,' she said. 'I'm sure we can find something in the bathroom which will make it feel better.'

Peter trotted off after her, as Phoebe came bouncing out of her room.

'Hello, Peter,' she said. 'Look at your leg! It's horrible.'

'So's your eye,' said Peter looking with interest at Phoebe's eye which was now turning a rich purple colour. 'How did you get that?'

'School,' said Quinta.

'Same here,' said Peter.

Lucy sat down with a cup of tea and opened the local evening paper. 'Listen to this,' she said to Quinta as she came back in. 'Child abuse on the increase, says NSPCC.'

'I can believe it,' said Quinta. 'And there's far more kinds of it than the NSPCC can possibly imagine.'

'You'd better tell Harriet about Peter,' said Lucy after a while.

'Do you think that's wise?' said Quinta.

'Yes. I don't think Harriet will stand for bullying, and it's obviously flourishing there.'

'Mmm,' said Quinta. 'Peter said that Gavin says they all have to go through it, and he can't wait to be a senior because then he's really going to lam into the younger ones.'

'You must definitely say something to Harriet,' said Lucy.

Phoebe pushed Peter in front of her into the room.

'Me and Peter are going to play that new game Harriet got me. Neither of us wants to do anything very jumpy, because of our wounds,' she added importantly. 'And Peter's going to tell me about the choir. He says the clergymen in the Cathedral are weird.'

Peter nodded. 'They are. They're all very excited at the moment, because they're cremating a Bishop in a fortnight.'

'In a fortnight?' said Lucy, surprised. 'Which Bishop has died? Isn't a fortnight a long time to wait for a funeral?'

Peter thought hard, and then his face lit up.

'They aren't cremating him, they're castrating him,' he said triumphantly.

Quinta and Lucy burst out laughing, and Peter looked rather hurt. 'It's a big service. In York Minster, the Archbishop does it.'

'You are stupid, Peter,' said Phoebe scornfully. 'They're *consecrating* the Bishop. I saw about it in the paper. Come on.'

Quinta and Lucy gave way to their laughter as the two children went off.

'It's the new Bishop of Eyot, of course,' said Lucy. 'Simon said the enthronement would be later this month, and of course, he'll have to be consecrated first.'

'Sylvester would prefer the other,' said Quinta. 'He has no time for Bishops.'

'Lord, isn't life in France going to be dull after this.' said Lucy.

It isn't going to be exactly dull for me, thought Quinta gloomily. What was she going to do without Lucy? Harriet had said she would help as much as she could, but she had her work, and then her running, two or three hours a day, she had told Quinta. It seemed madness to her, and Alban had exclaimed at the pointlessness of it, but Harriet just laughed, and said that some people got their kicks writing music, and others running and how boring it would be if we all chose to spend our time in the same way.

Alban had been more than usually troublesome, and when his mother tried to pin him down about getting a nurse, he had exploded.

'No, I will not have any bloody nurse, some silly woman I don't know, talking to me as though I was about five years old, telling me what I can do when . . . No, no and no. Quinta can stay at home and look after me, I need someone who understands about my work.'

'Quinta's got a job,' said Lucy.

'She can give it up. Phoebe's at home for the moment, Quinta can stay here and look after both of us, I can't see why you're making such a fuss about it.'

'Alban,' said Quinta, trying to be patient, 'I can't just give up my job like that. If I did, Gustav would get someone else, and there wouldn't be a job for me to go back to when you're on your feet again. What do I do then?'

'Marry me,' said Alban furiously. 'I don't know why, after all these years together, you're being so difficult about something that's so simple. You marry me, then you don't have to do your piddling little job. I earn a lot of money, you don't have to work, Phoebe can go to a proper school.'

'But I don't want to marry you,' screamed Quinta. She took

a deep breath and controlled her voice. 'And it may seem a piddling little job to you, but it earns me enough to live on, and I like doing it. Now that I'm starting to make instruments . . .'

'Oh, grow up,' said Alban irritably. 'Nobody will want to buy anything you make, cloud-cuckoo land is what you're living in. Okay, Lydia asked you to make her a bass, so what? She just felt sorry for you. I said your going to college was a waste of time, but you're so bloody obstinate. You always think you know best.'

'She does,' said Lucy calmly. 'She knows what's best for her; which isn't necessarily what's best for you. You're exactly like your father was, selfish to the bone. And no, being a composer does not excuse your terrible behaviour. I'm ashamed of you. If you won't find a nurse, then I will, but I will not have Quinta harassed like this.'

Both Lucy and Quinta knew that however many nurses Lucy might engage, Alban would get rid of them the moment she had gone back to France, and would nag or blackmail Quinta into giving up work.

Quinta tried reasoning. 'Phoebe isn't exactly at home all the time,' she reminded him. 'She goes to Mrs Maddox to do some maths and science every morning. And she says she can have her for one or two afternoons. That's only three or four afternoons to fix up for her; in fact she can come into the shop. Sam wouldn't mind.'

'Oh, very professional,' sneered Alban, 'taking your child into work with you.'

Quinta flushed. 'I am trying to organize things so that you will be all right. Mrs Gridlock is willing to come in at eight, so that I can get to work early, and . . .'

'I'm not having that gossipy old bag anywhere near me,' said Alban, 'so you can just cancel that arrangement.'

Quinta looked helplessly across at Lucy, who raised her eyes to heaven and gave an expressive shrug.

'We'll talk about it later,' she said, holding the door open for Quinta.

'We won't discuss it later, there's nothing to discuss,' Alban shouted after them.

They found Titus in the kitchen. 'Hello,' he said. 'You couldn't hear me because Alban was bellowing. The door was on the latch, so I let myself in. I hope you don't mind.'

'No, of course not,' said Lucy. 'Oh, Alban is impossible. He insists that Quinta leaves her job, for that's what it will mean, simply to be here and push him around in his wheelchair and fetch and carry for him. He says he needs someone all the time, he may have to go to London, it strains his arms trying to wheel himself around the house all day, what if he needs something and can't go out . . .'

'Yes, I'm afraid I overheard,' said Titus. 'Rather difficult not to,' he added dryly. He sounded courteous and pleasant, but inside he was seething. This time it hit him with even more of a shock; he couldn't bear to see Quinta going through all this. For the first time in his life, he was caught up in someone else's suffering, and it's much worse than my own, he thought, because what can I do about it?

He pulled out a chair for Lucy. 'Sit down,' he said. 'I've got an idea.'

'Brilliant, Titus is brilliant,' said Lydia with awe. She tied the telephone cord into a tight, curly knot. 'It's the perfect solution.'

'Isn't it?' said Quinta happily. 'Although you may not think so after a few days of Alban. Listen, I'll ring Titus and ask him to collect you, okay? He said he would. Will your grandmother mind?'

'Too bad if she does,' said Lydia darkly. 'She won't if Titus comes to pick me up. He's got such bags of charm that man, he can twist grandmama round his little finger.'

'Oh, good,' said Quinta. 'Well, I hope he hasn't got any of his older ladies with him.'

'He won't have,' said Lydia. 'Rumour has it that he's keen on the Bishop's wife . . .'

'Oh,' said Quinta, with a sudden pang. 'Faustina? She's very attractive.'

'Yes, but still too old for him,' said Lydia. 'Apparently, they're friends from way back; wonder what the Bishop thinks of it all. Anyway, it's probably just malicious gossip, I think she looks far too sensible to do anything silly in a place like Eyot, might as well send all the info straight to the *News of the World*. I'll go and break the good news to grandmama, and I'll see you later.'

'Bye,' said Quinta.

'You're almost as untidy as I am, Lydia,' said Quinta later that evening, as she flicked open the catches of a bulging suitcase. The top sprang up, and several books slid on to the floor. Underneath were bundles of underclothes, more books, music and odd items of costume jewellery.

'And several pairs of woolly socks,' said Quinta, holding them up.

'I just threw everything in. I didn't want to waste time sorting things out, it only gets unpacked at the other end. Here, put that lot in a drawer, I can organize it all later.'

'Bet you don't,' said Quinta.

'I will when I want something and I can't find it,' said Lydia cheerfully. 'Oh, the luck, I can't believe it, away from grandmama, and somewhere that I can get to see Adam. Clever Titus for suggesting it!'

'You may live to regret it,' said Quinta.

Quinta was so relieved that Lydia was coming to take Alban off her hands that she didn't mind Lydia brooding about Adam all the time. As soon as Lydia escaped from her grandmother's house, Adam had reappeared. 'Which is a pity,' said Harriet cryptically.

Lydia wasn't completely sure that she wanted to be back on the same terms with Adam as before, but in a way she was pleased. 'You see!' she said triumphantly. 'I knew it! It was grandmama who was putting Adam off. She's from another age, she doesn't understand young people.'

'I thought she didn't like the look of Felix and Zoe,' said Quinta. 'Is that not understanding young people?'

'That,' said Lydia, 'is the perception and sound judgement that comes with the years.'

'Or, having your cake and eating it,' suggested Quinta.

'Threadbare sayings,' retorted Lydia. 'Anyway, there's no-one except Adam in my life at the moment, so I'm going to make the most of him. He's asked me to a party tomorrow night. I need something devastating to wear. A shopping expedition is called for, I think.'

She looked at Quinta's slightly alarmed face. 'No, Alban said he won't need me tomorrow night, and Harriet's coming in to give Phoebe an English lesson, so she won't need me to go through her homework for Mrs M with her.'

'I didn't mean that,' said Quinta quickly. 'I'm so grateful to you; you don't have to teach Phoebe.'

'I enjoy it,' said Lydia. 'I like doing history and geography with her. In fact, I think I might quite like to be a teacher, which is very surprising. Still, I daresay if I sit about for a bit, the urge will pass. My intentions and interests generally do.'

Quinta laughed. 'Don't belittle yourself, Lydia. You'll enjoy getting yourself something to wear.'

'Mmm,' said Lydia. 'And it's going to be outrageous. Adam says, be prepared for a slightly wild party.'

'Truly?' said Daphne. 'I hadn't heard that.'

'Nor had I,' said Marjorie, with the definite implication in her voice that what she hadn't heard about, wasn't true.

'She moved in yesterday, with a lot of her things. She had her double-bass, such a strange instrument for a young girl to play. She had bags, several boxes . . . Titus Croscombe collected her, helped her load it all into that smart car of his, and drove her to the Manor House.'

Marjorie shot a quick glance at Wyn, and snipped vigorously at a large branch of greenery. 'There,' she said, tossing the remains into a large green bin. 'Lucy Praetorius will be going back to France, so then Alban Praetorius will be alone in the house with those two young girls. *If* it's as you say.'

'It is,' said Wyn firmly. 'The nut on this stand is completely stuck, I wonder if any of the vergers are around? One of them might have some WD40.'

'What's WD40?' asked Daphne, who was busy at the sink, working her way through an army of large vases. 'That's the trouble when we have to do the really large displays, everything is dusty or stiff from not being used very often.'

'I gather the displays at the new Bishop's college at Cambridge were quite meagre,' said Marjorie. 'He'll see the difference, coming here.'

'WD40,' said Wyn, 'is a spray which loosens things. Ah, here's a verger.'

'More stands, ladies,' said the perspiring verger. He put them down with a clatter. 'Have you heard about Lady Wray's granddaughter? Done a bunk.'

'Hardly the way to describe it,' said Marjorie. 'Lydia has gone to stay with Quinta, who is an old school friend.'

'I know,' said the verger with a vulgar wink. 'The one that lives with the composer. Quite an eyeful she is, wouldn't mind her sharing my premises, I can tell you.'

He had gone too far, and he retreated somewhat hastily under the baleful gaze of three pairs of eyes.

'Well! Saying things like that, and in the Cathedral, too!' said Daphne.

'You see where loose living leads,' said Marjorie with satisfaction. 'It's like a contagion. Two people live together in an improper way, and then uneducated people like the verger think it's all right to make very unsavoury remarks . . . You can't tell where the plague may spread to.'

'Like a harem,' said Wyn dreamily, back in her Ottoman palace.

'Harem?' said Marjorie sharply.

'Yes, Alban Praetorius and two young girls . . . the prince and the virgins . . .'

'Wyn, I'm shocked at you! You see? Corruption, moral pollution, that's what it is. No-one is safe.'

'And I don't suppose they're virgins, not these days,' said Daphne. 'But I know what you mean, Wyn. Did you ever read that book, *Desert Princess*? Oh, it's a lovely story. I'll lend it to you if you haven't read it.'

'Daphne!' Marjorie's bark of disapproval echoed round the small flower room. Daphne gave a guilty start and a sniff, apologized, and scrubbed twice as hard at the vases, sending rivulets of dirty water over the side of the sink.

Marjorie sniffed. 'I think we'd better stop to have some coffee, and perhaps then go to the Bishop's Chapel for a quick prayer before we commence work on the flowers,' she said. 'It is a very sacred occasion in any Cathedral when a new bishop is enthroned, and I think the flowers should be arranged only by those who are secure in the purity of their minds.'

'It could be a very bare Cathedral in that case,' said Wyn to herself.

'What was that?' demanded Marjorie. 'What did you say? Speak up?'

'I said I think I'll have two lumps of sugar today, thank you, Marjorie. I need to keep my strength up.'

•

## 19

Lydia propelled Alban at great speed over the cobbled streets. He hung on grimly, shouting to Lydia to slow down, and for God's sake to watch where she was going. Lydia took no notice.

'If I slow down we'll be late for your appointment, and the doctors and physios have better things to do than hang around waiting for you.'

'Shows you've never been ill; the boot's on the other foot entirely. It's the patients who hang around for hours, not the hospital staff,' said Alban furiously.

With a final flourish, Lydia shot the wheelchair through the swing doors of Eyot General Hospital and trundled Alban towards the reception counter. The biddy on duty was an Alban fan, and she beamed at him.

'How nice to see you again, Mr Praetorius, and punctual to the minute for your appointment. Aren't you a good boy?'

Speechless, Alban glowered at her, and she nodded sympathetically at Lydia. 'Feeling the pain a little, I expect, well, it's physiotherapy today, isn't it? That'll make you feel much better.'

'He has an appointment with the doctor first, I think,' said Lydia, suppressing a very natural desire to giggle.

'Yes, you're right, dear, he has. Are you going to stay with him?'

'No,' said Lydia. 'I'm afraid I've got things to do.'

'That's right,' said Alban crossly. 'Leave me in the lurch, just when I'm most helpless.'

'Nonsense,' said Lydia. 'No problems here, plenty of people to wheel you around, if you need help. But you can manage perfectly well by yourself. You've got a book, haven't you, in case you have to wait anywhere?'

'Of course I'll bloody have to wait, spend the whole day waiting. You can buy me a paper before you go.'

'Please,' said Lydia under her breath, while smiling sweetly at him; she wasn't going to lose face in front of the woman behind the desk.

'Pick him up at about five,' the woman said. 'And don't worry, we'll look after him for you.'

'I'm sure you will,' said Lydia.

Lydia adored shopping, and although the shops in Eyot didn't offer the scope of London or Oxford, she still had a blissful day. She wanted something stunning to woo Adam away from that ghastly little Zoe; having found it, she pottered about for several hours looking for bits and pieces to go with it.

It was a humid day, with a heavy warmth in the air. Thunder, thought Lydia, as dark clouds began to gather over the city with astonishing rapidity. And help, as fat drops of rain began to bounce off the pavement.

She made a dash for the Cathedral, along with several other people suspicious of the dark clouds and thickening raindrops, and made it up the steps to the west door just as the skies opened in a cloudburst.

Lydia slipped into the quiet darkness of the nave. She could hear the rain drumming on the roof far above. A steward, sitting behind a desk with a large welcome sign on it, looked up and glared at her. Lydia beat a hasty retreat down the aisle, swerving to avoid a party of bemused Japanese tourists being filled in on the more seemly details of Guillebert's life.

She looked around for somewhere to sit down, but the seats in the nave were all roped off. She wandered on, and a more friendly verger advised her that the choir was open, very fine misericords in there, miss, they all want to see them.

Lydia, with an architect for a father, knew all about misericords, and had no intention of looking at them. However, where there were misericords there were seats, and so she slipped into the choir. The canons' stalls up at the back looked inviting and secluded, and she installed herself in a dark corner, glad to rest her feet, and quite happy to gaze up at the soaring vaults.

Lost in a reverie, she missed the bustle of the verger returning to clear the tourists out before choir practice and she didn't come out of her trance until the organ rumbled into action. She came to with a start, and sat up, as a horde of little boys in their cassocks came squabbling in to take their places in the choir stalls. A piping, bossy voice rang out as the head chorister rebuked a very small boy for having a loose cincture on his cassock.

The men wandered in, elegant and dignified in their dark red robes. Quinta should be here, thought Lydia, Titus looks terrific in red. He should have a dressing gown like that, very dashing. As though aware of being watched, Titus suddenly looked up from the music he was sorting and caught Lydia's eye. He raised an eyebrow at her, winked, and returned to his music. Simon came briskly in and placed his music on the stand.

'We'll start with the first psalm for this evening, gentlemen,' he said, raising his hand as a signal to the organist.

Lydia watched and listened, fascinated by the professionalism of it all as the little boys transformed themselves before her eyes into trained singers. From time to time, one of them would bang the ledge in front of him, and raise his hand, while they chanted on. They do that if they know they've made a mistake, Lydia realized. How amazing.

'No,' shouted Simon. 'No and no and no. Concentrate. You've just sung "The Lord is grey and his mercy is everlasting." The skies may be grey, my hair may be grey, of course it is, working with you lot; but the Lord is GREAT. T-T-T-T. Again!'

Entranced, Lydia heard them finish work on the psalms and sing the Magnificat through. Seconds after the amen to the Gloria had faded away, they were all opening a new piece of music, whipping through the pages and finding the places in less time than Lydia would have believed possible. Four boys hurried out of the choir, taking their music with them. Off to the loo, thought Lydia.

A series of discords on the organ announced a change of mood, an eerie voice rang out in a strange, fragmented kyrie, and first one side and then the other added urgent cross rhythms. What was it? Lydia was electrified, she had never heard such exciting music in a church. A fanfare from a trumpet rang out; startled,

Lydia looked up to the organ loft where a solitary musician stood, trumpet in hand. Four treble voices floated across the choir; those four boys hadn't gone to the loo at all. They were standing in a little gallery below the triforium, watching Simon Praetorius intently. Perfection, thought Lydia.

Not so Titus. He gestured to Simon, who angrily waved to the singers to stop. 'Now what?' he demanded. 'Must you interrupt? We don't have enough rehearsal time for this as it is.'

'Tempo,' said Titus briefly. 'I don't think this tempo works very well.'

'I set the tempo,' said Simon, glancing down at his score.

Lydia saw one or two of the other men putting their heads together. One of the choristers laughed and was instantly quelled by a more senior boy standing next to him.

'I sang this with Alban,' said Titus. 'He took it much more quickly. And it is marked "a lot faster."'

Simon pushed his hair back from his forehead in a quick, nervous gesture. 'Oh, very well, have it your own way,' he said irritably. 'After all, I'm only the Master of the Choristers, let's have a democratic choir here, everyone have their say.'

He raised his hands again. 'From the beginning . . .'

Faster, it was better. Obviously Titus had been right, thought Lydia with part of her mind. The other part was in turmoil: Alban had written this? She felt overwhelmed. Of course, she had heard Alban's music before, on recordings, but this was different. Because she knew him? Or because it was so powerful, and she thought of Alban as an interesting man, yes, and a very attractive man, but of limited emotional strength and response.

Wrong she said to herself. You couldn't be more wrong.

'Sorry about that,' said Titus to Simon afterwards in the vestry as they robed up for evensong.

'No, it's okay,' said Simon sombrely. 'You were right. My mind wasn't on it. Don't know why the Precentor insisted we sing Alban's Venetian Mass, it's too difficult, and the congregation won't like it. And I loathe it. I loathe everything Alban's ever written.'

'It'll make them sit up, do them good,' said Titus. 'Anything in particular bothering you? Anything I can do to help?'

'No,' said Simon shortly. He fiddled with the white silk MA hood which was attached to the top of his robe. 'No, blast it. It's Quinta, I just can't stop thinking about her, it's driving me mad. And it's going to lose me my job if I go on like this.' He glanced at Titus. 'You're spending a lot of time there, aren't you bowled over by her?'

'I go to play chess with Alban,' said Titus evasively.

'Yes, and you can. I expect you're even allowed there on the sacred Tuesday and Thursday nights, when she sleeps with Alban. Oh, I can't bear it.'

'If it's any consolation,' said Titus, almost casually, 'I don't think those Tuesday and Thursday nights are happening.'

'Because of his leg?' said Simon. 'Well, that's one good thing, then.'

'More because I don't think Quinta wants to,' said Titus thoughtfully. 'And I think because Alban may have another interest.'

'What, a third one, to add to Quinta and Hermione?' said Simon bitterly. 'Wonderful. I don't want him to have anything to do with her, but I don't want him to toss her aside, either. I mean, what would she do? I'd go anywhere with her, look after her, whatever she wanted, but she won't have it. Goes on about me being a married man with children. Of course I am, but I don't believe that would matter if she felt for me half of what I feel for her. Or anything at all.'

'Quinta would have scruples about going off with a married man, I'm sure,' said Titus, thinking fleetingly about all the married women he had invited into his bed.

'She'll be homeless if she doesn't want to stay with Alban,' pointed out Simon. 'And there's Phoebe, she won't do anything that would hurt Phoebe. She earns a pittance, manages at the moment because she keeps house for Alban – but what's to become of her if all that falls through? You tell me that.'

'I don't know,' said Titus, adjusting his own hood. 'I can't imagine.'

It was a fine autumn morning, after the storm of the previous afternoon, and the colours of the changing trees were reflected in the still river waters as Titus strolled across the bridge into the old city. As he walked into St Wulfstan's Square, he saw a familar figure ahead of him.

'Good morning, Fausty,' said Titus, shortening his stride to match hers as he caught up with her. 'Why are you out and about so early?'

'I've just taken Milo to school,' said Faustina. 'Now I'm going shopping.'

She smiled and murmured a greeting to a middle-aged woman who was passing, a neat round basket held over one arm, and a neat little dog on a leash in her other hand.

'Who's that?' said Titus. 'Seems familiar, have I seen her hanging round the Cathedral?'

'I expect so,' said Faustina. 'She's one of the canons' wives.'

'Ah, yes. I thought for a moment she was one of the Cathedral groupies.'

'Groupies?'

'Yes, you know, women of various ages who are for some inexplicable reason drawn to men in clerical garb. A black cassock sends them into a state of helpless admiration and a cope gives them frissons of delight. In fact, Fausty, I have to report that the sight of even the most uninspiring man in full canonicals arouses lust of a base and terrible kind.'

Faustina had to laugh. 'Titus, you get more and more ridiculous. I know all about women who admire the clergy, of course I do, Lennox always has several hangers-on. He's very good with them, though, handles them all beautifully.'

'Aren't you jealous, sharing your husband with so many?'

Faustina shot him a look. 'Hardly. Mostly they're not so young, so even if his position permitted it, he wouldn't be interested.'

'No,' said Titus thoughtfully. 'He always has gone for the young ones, hasn't he?'

'He's been better these last few years. Realized how close to the wind he was sailing, I suppose.' She stopped to press the button at a crossing.

'Which way are you going, Titus?'

'Your way,' said Titus promptly.

'I'm going to Marks and Spencers to buy Milo some new underpants. He's afraid he's got the wrong sort, and that the other boys will laugh at him in the showers.'

'Oh, lord, the horrors of being a schoolboy,' said Titus. 'Did it tear at your heart strings to leave him at the school gate?'

'Not at all,' said Faustina cheerfully. 'I like Milo, but the summer holidays are far too long for both of us.'

'And where after M & S?' enquired Titus.

'A music shop,' said Faustina.

'Good,' said Titus. 'Gustav's is the one you want, and I'm on my way there myself.'

'What for?' said Faustina suspiciously.

'To browse,' said Titus blandly. 'And we can say hello to Quinta, and perhaps she'll show us how Lydia's double-bass is coming on.'

Faustina thought how lucky Titus was to enjoy life in the easy way he did. Nothing seemed to ruffle him, he had no particular worries. With a first-class mind, interesting work, a happy knack of getting on with people and a lively interest in everything that went on, his life ran on pleasant lines. She told him so, and he laughed.

'Ah, you don't know about the dark doubts that torment my soul in the early hours of the morning. Now, if you were there then, Fausty, to soothe my anguished brow . . .'

'That's all very well, Titus,' said Faustina, suddenly serious. 'But it can't go on.'

'Why ever not?' said Titus, disconcerted for once.

'Because you can't go back,' said Faustina. 'As the philosopher says, you can't step twice in the same river.'

'I am deeply suspicious of what philosophers say.'

'I know you can easily find another woman, Titus, of uncertain age, but is that what you really want? Don't you get lonely, leading the rather strange life you do?'

'Always,' said Titus promptly, 'when you aren't there.'

'No, don't be frivolous. Think about it. Of course, it's fine now, but how about in ten years' time? Are you going to be bedding women in their late fifties? Are they going to be interested in you if they're that way inclined? Aren't they likely to prefer a delicious toyboy in his early twenties, with rippling muscles and firm everything?'

'I am not a toyboy,' said Titus, seriously put out.

'No, not really, but it's getting that way.' Faustina paused to admire a particularly ravishing evening dress in a shop.

'That would suit you,' said Titus, hoping to change the subject.

Faustina wasn't going to be distracted. 'Don't you think that perhaps you would like to have a wife, a family?'

Titus pulled a face. 'I suspect that the harassed life of a father is not for me. I admire children from a distance, but I have noticed that at close quarters they are very wearing.'

'You'll be swept off your feet one day,' warned Faustina. 'By someone young enough to have hordes of children, and then all your civilized dalliances with women of a certain age will be a forgotten memory. And,' Faustina went on ruthlessly, 'you may already be a father. How would you know, with your neatly compartmentalized love life?'

Titus looked at her thoughtfully.

'Here we are,' said Faustina.

'I will go and buy my newspaper,' said Titus politely, 'and then wait for you here. Do you mean underpants literally, or do you actually want to spend an hour or so wandering round looking at this and that?'

'Underpants literally,' Faustina assured him.

'Then I will be here.'

They paused on the bridge and looked down the river, past the Palace and the school playing fields beyond to the distant line of hills.

'Lovely,' said Faustina, with a deep sigh, as they walked on. 'I adore these little cobbled streets, I hope they never tear them up.'

'Eyot was lucky, the sixties mania for redevelopment didn't reach the heart of the city,' said Titus. 'Even the university has very little concrete nastiness to show for that profoundly unsatisfactory period of destruction and brutalism.'

'It's a backward place, I suppose.'

'If its backwardness has preserved its cobbled streets, then I'm all for it,' said Titus.

'Don't you feel restricted here?' asked Faustina. 'After America, or even Cambridge?'

'Not at all,' said Titus. 'I find there's a surprising amount of life going on here, what with the Cathedral, the university and the town. You would have to be a dull man not to enjoy it.'

He stopped in front of the violin shop. 'Here we are. This is Gustav's,' he said, opening the door for her.

The bell tinkled and clanged as they went into the shop. Sam looked up from the counter, and gave them a welcoming smile.

'This is Faustina Lennox–Smith,' said Titus. 'She's going to be starting a course at the university, so you have to be nice to her; think how good a customer she'll be.'

Faustina was grateful to Titus for not introducing her as the Bishop's wife. She suspected that Sam knew very well who she was, but it would be a relief for even a few minutes to be just a music student, and not an episcopal appendage.

'Is Quinta in?' asked Titus.

'I don't think so; she went out a few minutes ago. There's something special she needs, some chemical or other.'

'That's a pity; we wanted to see Lydia's bass.'

Sam enthused. 'It's nearly finished, such a strong, masculine instrument, with a magnificent scroll. Of course, you can't tell how good it is until it's played, you don't know until then what the sound will be like. But I have faith in Quinta, I think the sound will match its looks. Go up and see it when you're ready, Quinta won't mind.'

Titus lounged against the counter chatting to Sam as Faustina consulted her list.

'Are things going better for Quinta now Lydia is staying at the Manor House and acting as wheelchair attendant to the great man?'

'Yes, because otherwise work would have been such a problem, and she shouldn't give up this job. Work in her line isn't so easy to find these days, even here in Eyot where we have quite a few dealers.' Sam paused and shook his head. 'On the other hand, I wouldn't say she's her usual cheerful self. There are the worries about Phoebe, and then in the longer term, she feels she can't stay with Alban . . .'

Faustina watched them out of the corner of her eye. 'What gossips men are,' she said. 'Far worse than women.'

'No harm in gossip,' said Sam seriously. 'It's a good thing to take an interest in your friends' lives.'

'Do you think so?' Faustina said doubtfully. 'Perhaps it depends what kind of an interest you're taking.'

'As long as it isn't spiteful or unkind, it's beneficial,' said Sam.

'Unfortunately,' said Faustina, 'in my experience, most of it is both spiteful and unkind.'

'I'd never be spiteful about Quinta,' said Sam firmly. 'I'm too fond of her.'

'And you, too?' asked Faustina, looking at Titus in a slightly calculating way.

Sam wondered what she was plotting. He had often seen a similar look on the faces of his mother and sisters, all of them forceful and formidable women.

'Of course,' said Titus easily.

'Mmm,' said Faustina. 'I've found what I need, have you finished?'

Titus joined her. 'Upstairs, then, to see Quinta's bass, if Sam is sure Quinta won't mind.'

'No, of course she won't,' said Sam. 'You go and see the dragon bass.'

'Dragon bass?' said Faustina as she followed Titus up the stairs. 'What are you talking about?'

And then, as she reached the top and went through the door she saw exactly what he was talking about.

'That is superb,' she said. 'I had no idea Quinta was such an artist.'

Titus walked silently round the bass, which was propped up on a stand in the centre of the workshop.

'It's inspired,' he said at last. 'I wonder just what was going on in her mind while she was making this?'

Sam had come into the workshop after them, anxious to see their reactions.

'I can tell you that,' he said. 'Quinta read something by Joseph Campbell, about each of us having to slay our own dragons. Not external dragons, of course, not many of those about in Eyot. Internal dragons; fears, lack of confidence and so on, which prevent us doing what we ought to do. Quinta felt like that about her instrument making; she thought that she couldn't really do it, not professionally. So when she finally plucked up the courage to make something, she carved the scroll as a dragon's head.'

He ran a hand lovingly over the gleaming wood. 'This will always be a very special instrument for Quinta, and it's a blessing that it's going to a friend, she won't want to lose it for good, you see. And I think it's going to sound wonderful, once it's set up. It must do, with so much heart in it.'

'Not a very scientific assumption, that,' said Titus. 'Since sound is a matter of physics, rather than art.'

'Both,' said Faustina firmly. She was looking at the sketch Quinta had done of a bishop's head, which was pinned to a board. 'Titus, look at this.'

'Reminds me of someone,' said Titus.

'Yes,' said Faustina. 'Lennox.'

'Lennox?' said Titus with surprise. He stood back and looked at it again. 'Good lord, you're right. She must have seen a picture of him, and she's drawn him as he will be after his enthronement, be-mitred.'

'Yes,' said Faustina again. 'Or she's met him.'

'She could have,' said Titus. 'I doubt it, though. She doesn't get about very much.' He laughed. 'It's very, very clever, Faustina. You ought to buy it and get it framed, give it to Lennox for Christmas.'

'I don't think Lennox would like to see himself as a gargoyle,' said Faustina in a slightly abstracted voice.

Titus glanced at her. 'I believe the correct term is a grotesque. Unless it's a water spout.'

'Grotesque is more appropriate,' said Faustina.

As they went towards the door, she stopped and looked

again at the double bass and at the sketch of the bishop's head.

'I wonder,' she said. 'Titus, how old is Quinta?'

'About twenty-six, I suppose,' said Titus. 'Must be, because Phoebe's eight or so. It's difficult to tell from the way she looks, you notice her merriness and her personality rather than her age. She has a very unvacuous face for a young woman, though. Much more interesting than Lydia's.'

'Lydia is a beauty,' said Faustina. 'Quinta is an original. Goodness, so young, and able to make that. I envy her, you know. Despite all that she's been through.'

'I don't really know what you're talking about,' said Titus amiably, 'but I agree with you. I am definitely one of Quinta's admirers.'

Faustina flashed him a warm smile. 'One of many, I should imagine.'

'Oh,' said Titus. 'Do you think so?'

'Yes,' said Faustina.

They said their goodbyes to Sam and walked back towards the bridge.

'Quinta is bound to get married,' said Faustina. 'Not to Alban, she has too much sense to do that. She needs a man nearer her own age, although not too young, and someone who is less self-centred than Alban.'

'Lucky man, whoever he is,' said Titus lightly.

'Oh, yes,' Faustina agreed. 'A very lucky man.'


Quinta exclaimed when Lydia came into the kitchen dressed for her party: the prospect of an evening with Adam added an extra glow to her formidable beauty.

Quinta was wholehearted in her admiration, telling her she looked marvellous. Alban merely grunted. He didn't approve at all of her going out when he had to stay in, and had voiced his disapproval at length and at full volume.

'Good thing you weren't asked,' he said to Quinta. 'You couldn't have gone.'

'I would have gone,' said Quinta at once. 'I would have asked Harriet to come in and look after you and Phoebe – or Mrs Gridlock,' she added evilly.

Titus came round later for his game of chess. He insisted on being in Quinta's sitting room off the kitchen, which he said was much more pleasant than Alban's austere and untidy studio. He overruled Alban's objections, saying that there would be no more chess if Alban was too disagreeable.

Quinta waited for the outburst of bad temper at such a provocative remark, but Alban merely grinned and threatened Titus with reprisals once he was on his feet again. They bickered their way amicably through several games, until, just as Titus had checked Alban, the phone rang.

'Hello,' said Quinta. The two men paused and looked up from their game as Quinta held the phone away from her and shrugged her shoulders.

'I think it must be a nut. There's a tremendous row going on, someone's shouting, music . . . Hello? Yes, this is Quinta, who . . . what? Oh, Lydia!'

She turned to Titus and Alban, puzzled. 'It's Lydia, at least I think it's Lydia. I can't make head or tail of what she's saying. Do you think she's drunk?'

'Bring the phone here,' said Alban.

'Lydia?' he bellowed into the phone. 'Yes? What? Yes, of course, immediately.'

He slammed the phone down. 'Go and get her,' he said tersely. 'Quinta, find some clothes for her.'

'Clothes?' said Quinta in bewilderment. 'What sort of clothes? Why does she need clothes?'

'I don't know, but she said to come and get her, and bring some clothes, so stop arguing and just find her some clothes.'

'Okay,' said Quinta. 'I won't be a minute. What's the address?' she added as she shot out of the room.

Alban looked at Titus, and banged his forehead with his hand. 'Bugger it, I never asked.'

Quinta was back in a matter of minutes, thrusting a pair of trousers and a sweatshirt into a carrier bag.

'Quinta,' said Titus. 'Do you know where Lydia is?'

Quinta looked at him in surprise. 'At a party. I'm not sure where. Didn't she say?'

'I didn't ask,' said Alban. 'Surely you know . . . She walked there, didn't she?'

'Yes, of course she did,' said Quinta, relieved. 'It can't be far, then.'

'Lots of houses around here,' said Titus unhelpfully. 'No ideas at all? Who's giving the party? I mean, is it Adam? Only his house isn't really in this area.'

'No, I think she was meeting Adam there. Hold on, I can't remember the address, but the party was being given by a Mrs . . . Mrs . . . It was slightly strange name . . . Dixon? No, not Dixon, but something like it.'

Titus stared at her. 'Not Mrs Doxyn, by any chance?'

'Doxyn! That's it, Mrs Doxyn,' said Quinta triumphantly. 'Do you know her?'

'I know of her,' said Titus rather grimly. 'And by good luck I know her house, because it was pointed out to me only the other day. If Lydia really is there, I think I'd better go right away. Hand over those clothes.'

'No, I'm coming too,' said Quinta.

'Better not,' said Titus. 'From what I know about Mrs Doxyn and her parties – which is strictly hearsay – it could be unsavoury.'

Alban frowned. 'Unsavoury? Then what on earth is Lydia doing there?'

'She didn't know, of course.'

'Quinta had better go with you, Lydia may want her,' said Alban.

'I don't mind,' said Quinta, not appearing to notice that Alban clearly felt more protective about Lydia than he did about her. 'But shouldn't someone stay here with you?' said Quinta.

'No,' said Titus. 'Alban's right; Lydia may need some moral support. We shan't be long.'

Titus set off down the street at a tremendous pace, leaving Quinta to jog behind him.

'What's so urgent about all this?' she panted.

'You'll see,' he said, stopping in front of a very smart black front door. 'This is it.'

After a few perfunctory knocks, he pushed open the door.

'They leave it open at parties like this,' said Titus. 'Until they've got a full house.'

'Parties like what?' said Quinta.

'You'll see,' he said again.

## 20

Once inside, it was like a scene from a bad film about ancient Rome. As Quinta's eyes became accustomed to the murky lights, she started to make out what was going on. She froze, and closed her eyes. 'Come on,' said Titus. 'We've got to find Lydia.'

'What kind of a party is this?' said Quinta, as a tall, middle-aged man, stark naked, shot past them in a state of considerable arousal. He gave a quick look at Quinta, but Titus barred his way and he dived into one of the rooms that led off the big hall.

'What was he doing?' said Quinta.

'Looking for somewhere to park his prick, what do you think?' said Titus crossly.

Quinta stared fascinated at a writhing pair on a spindly sofa; Titus grabbed her hand and pulled her through into one of the rooms.

'Lydia could be anywhere,' he muttered in her ear. 'Keep your eyes peeled.'

'I don't think I want to,' said Quinta, imagining where anywhere might be. Titus stepped over a pair of naked buttocks busily humping up and down on an indeterminate body. Quinta stepped too, anxiously avoiding some thrashing limbs, and mumbling 'Sorry, sorry,' as she felt something give underfoot.

'Not in here,' said Titus. 'Let's try upstairs.'

The next room smelt, Quinta thought, very peculiar. It had the dimmest of lights, and an extremely pornographic scene was playing on a huge video screen at one end of the room. There were fat, heavily tasselled floor cushions scattered over the floor, several of them occupied by couples variously engaged; one held a threesome, a stunned Quinta noticed.

'How do they manage to get themselves into those, um, places, all at the same time?' she whispered to Titus.

'Can't imagine,' he said. 'I've never tried it.' He went out on to the landing. 'This is all so bloody vulgar,' he said.

'Why are all the men old?' said Quinta. 'When the girls are mostly quite young.'

'That's why the men are here, randy old goats, they should have better things to do with their evenings,' said Titus with distaste as a high court judge he knew went flaccidly past, his hand firmly grasping the bare behind of a girl with long dark red hair who looked about fifteen.

'That's Zoe!' said Quinta in amazement.

Titus didn't seem very surprised. 'Didn't you see Felix downstairs? Or perhaps you wouldn't recognize him, not unless you were familiar with his bare backside.'

'How did you recognize him?'

'He stopped what he was doing for a moment and looked up at me,' said Titus. 'Gave me a wink; nasty piece of work, that guy.'

'There's a dog in here,' said Quinta opening another door. 'It must belong to the owner, poor thing, shut away.'

'A big dog?' said Titus, pushing past her.

'Yes,' said Quinta, as Titus firmly shut the door in her face. 'Not in there, I don't think,' he said.

Their attention was caught by some muffled noises coming from a small door at the end of the passage. By this time Quinta was past being shocked, and was beginning to get the giggles.

'I think that's the loo,' she said. 'I just cannot begin to think what they might be doing in there.'

'Sssh,' said Titus. He banged on the door.

'Go away, go away,' came a screech from the other side.

'Lydia!' said Quinta. She bent down and tried to speak through the keyhole. 'Lydia, it's Quinta. Open the door.'

'Quinta?'

The door opened an inch or two, and Lydia's scared face peered through the crack at them.

'Thank God,' she said. 'Have you brought my clothes?'

'Here you are,' said Quinta, passing the bag through.

Two minutes later a dishevelled Lydia emerged from the lavatory.

'Will they let us out?' she said. Quinta took her arm, she could feel her trembling.

'Yes,' said Titus. 'I know a lot of these people, all I have to do is call one or two of them by their names, or just say, "Good evening, judge, your lordship, archdeacon, doctor" . . . half of them will be in a terrible panic that they've been recognized.'

He started down the stairs, brusquely shouldering aside some people carrying whips who were coming up the steps.

'There's what they call an SM room up there,' said Lydia in a strangled voice.

'Very uncivilized,' said Titus calmly. 'Quickly, now, you two.'

They made their way to the hall, only impeded by a large man with a blonde wig who put out a hand towards Quinta.

'Lovely tits,' he said with a ghastly leer. 'And is your pussy as red as your hair? Take your clothes OFF, darlings, that's the rule here. Do it yourselves, or I'll call up some of the boys and they can help.'

Titus administered a hard knee in a very painful spot, and pulled Quinta and Lydia out of the front door.

'What a horrible place,' said Quinta. 'The smell!'

'Drugs, hormones and sweat,' said Titus. 'Not very pleasant. Lydia, walk a bit more quickly, warm yourself up, you're shivering.'

'Fright, not cold,' said Quinta. 'Are you all right, Lydia?'

Lydia nodded. 'I locked myself into the loo just in time,' she said.

'Where's your lovely dress?' said Quinta suddenly. 'You can't leave that there.'

'I can,' said Lydia firmly. 'Nothing would make me go back there.'

'Where was Adam?' asked Quinta, walking alongside Lydia and putting a supporting arm round her.

'He wasn't there,' said Lydia quickly. 'I must have misunderstood his directions and gone to the wrong party.'

Quinta opened her mouth to point out to Lydia that if Felix and Zoe were there, Adam probably was as well, but she saw Titus shake his head slightly at her, and coughed instead.

'Here we are,' said Titus, leading the way indoors. 'Alban, where do you keep your brandy? Here's Lydia, come back from an orgy, and I think she needs a strong drink.'

'Orgy?' said Alban in tones of strong disapproval. 'In Eyot? What on earth were you doing there? Did you enjoy it?'

'No, it was completely horrible and I was scared stiff,' said Lydia, and burst into tears.

Their night of adventure wasn't over yet. Alban blew up into the worst temper that Quinta had ever seen him exhibit; she realized how rarely she had crossed him during her long friendship with him, and was grateful. She wouldn't have liked to have been on the receiving end of that outburst. Lydia was much better able to cope with it, giving as good as she got and refusing to give in to his forceful condemnation of her sense and morals.

Quinta finally managed to deflect Alban, with Titus's help, and got an exhausted Lydia to bed with a hot drink and a soothing book. Then she sank into her own bed, too tired to read or listen to the radio or do anything but sleep.

An hour later, she was aroused from a deep sleep by strange noises at the window. Bemused, she sat up and looked round the room. It happened again; she wasn't dreaming, there was a noise at the window.

She opened the window and looked down. To her utter astonishment, she saw Zoe, clad only in a shower curtain, and clutching a small evening bag. She smiled up at Quinta.

'Hello,' she said. 'Did I wake you up? You took ages to come to the window.'

'Yes, you did wake me up,' said Quinta. 'What do you want? Why are you throwing things at my window?'

'Not things, peppermints,' said Zoe. 'I always have some in my bag, your breath can get a bit funny at parties, don't you find? Can I come in?'

'No,' said Quinta.

'I might begin to make more noise,' said Zoe calmly.

'Oh, all right,' said Quinta furiously.

She found her dressing gown, and padded downstairs and

through the dark cloisters, hoping that Alban wouldn't wake up. She drew back the bolts on the main door, and Zoe came in on quick light feet.

'I was at a party,' she said.

'I know,' said Quinta.

'Oh, were you there? I wouldn't have thought it was quite your scene. Anyway, I had to leave in rather a hurry when the cops came.'

'Wearing a shower curtain,' said Quinta.

'Yes, I left by the bathroom window,' said Zoe. 'I was in the bath with some gynaecologists, and . . .'

'Some gynaecologists?' said Quinta incredulously.

'Yeah, you always get those guys at these parties, they've got kind of a funny attitude to women. That's why they go in for gynaecology.'

'All of them?' said Quinta, fascinated despite herself.

'No, of course not, but mostly they're pretty weird, haven't you noticed? Anyway, I got out okay, don't know what happened to them. Can I sleep here?'

'No, certainly not,' said Quinta.

'Okay. Can you lend me some clothes, then? I don't look exactly respectable walking the streets dressed like this.'

'Oh, I'll find you something,' said Quinta, exasperated by Zoe's casual assumption that what she had been doing was nothing out of the ordinary, and that even mere acquaintances would help her.

'Can I fix myself a drink?' said Zoe, moving towards the brandy and some other bottles which had been left out on a tray.

'No,' said Quinta again. 'In fact, whatever you want, the answer's no. Just stay here, don't move, and I'll get you something to wear.'

She was back in no time and thrust some garments at Zoe. 'You'll have to go barefoot, nobody in this household has got feet that small.'

Zoe looked complacently down at her tiny feet.

'They are small, aren't they?' she said. 'I wear kid's shoes. What about Phoebe, can't I borrow a pair of her trainers or something?'

Over my dead body does she wear anything of Phoebe's, thought Quinta.

'No,' she said. 'She has very big feet, English size five.'

'Hey, that's big for a kid that age,' said Zoe. 'You ought to do something about that, men don't like big feet.'

'Short of binding them, there isn't much I could do about it even if I wanted to, which I don't,' said Quinta. 'There's the cloakroom, please put on those clothes and go.'

Zoe came out a few minutes later, twisting her long hair round with a supple hand.

'Do you have a hair clip?'

Quinta dived into the drawer of the hall table and pulled out one of her hair clips.

'Here,' she said.

'Thanks, great,' said Zoe. 'Could you use this shower curtain?'

'No,' said Quinta. This was becoming surreal.

Zoe shrugged. 'I guess I've no use for it, so I'll just leave it here. See you!'

And with a breezy wave of her hand she was gone.

Quinta let out a long breath. 'Well,' she said. 'I can't wait to tell Titus about this, he's going to crease up.'

And she turned the hall light out and went back to bed.

'We did very well, ladies,' said Marjorie, beaming with pride. 'Everyone said, they never saw such beautiful flowers.'

'And the Bishop liked them too,' said Daphne. 'Seeking us out especially to thank us.'

'He's a splendid man, splendid,' said Marjorie. 'But Wyn, dear, why didn't you tell us that you knew the Bishop's wife?'

'It was a long time ago,' said Wyn. 'And I never knew her very well.'

'She obviously wants to keep up with you, that could be very useful,' said Marjorie approvingly.

Wyn said nothing. She looked forward to seeing Faustina again; it was quite a few years now since she had been a secretarial assistant to the bursar of a theological college and had by chance struck up an unlikely friendship with the lonely and harassed Warden's wife. Faustina had put up with a difficult life with good humour and resilience, but Wyn had been sorry in some ways when a legacy freed her from the drudgery of that kind of work and she had left Cambridge to come and live in Eyot.

Now she felt they could pick up some of the old threads, but there was no way any hint of gossip about Faustina or the Bishop's household would reach Marjorie or Daphne through her. In fact, she thought, she could be quite helpful; disinformation, that was what the thriller writers called it.

'We may be a mere northern Cathedral, nothing to compare with our smarter southern foundations, but I defy anyone to put on a better show,' went on Marjorie.

'I wasn't too sure about the Bishop's cope,' said Daphne. 'What was that rather strange bird supposed to represent?'

'It looked like a phoenix,' said Wyn. 'A symbol of resurrection and new life.'

'I never thought of the phoenix as a Christian bird,' said Marjorie. 'It was probably meant to be a dove. As far as I'm concerned, it looked more like the Bishop's Christmas goose. I don't hold with these very modern copes, we are a traditional congregation here, and I think he should have chosen something a little less outré.'

'Blaze of colour,' said Wyn.

'I don't suppose he'll wear it again,' said Daphne, in a placatory way. 'They often just put them away, don't they? And he'll find so many wonderful robes here, he'll hardly need to use that one.'

'Very true, Daphne,' said Marjorie. 'Now, we must get on. Wyn, you go and check all the flowers, we'll need to take out anything that's faded and several of the displays will need freshening up. Daphne, Mrs Jonquil should have the new flower roster. You fetch that, and we'll have a good look at it to see who's doing what. That Mrs Norris said that she'd asked for the school to have another week, and I just want to make sure that nobody's taken any notice of her.'

They moved in a wedge formation out into the south transept, Marjorie surging in front, with Daphne and Wyn slightly behind her. They paused for a moment to listen to the choir at morning rehearsal.

'The boys were in fine voice for the enthronement,' said Marjorie. 'Ours is certainly one of the best choirs in England.'

Except that some of them hadn't seemed to know the difference between F natural and F sharp, Wyn, who had a good ear, said to herself. And one boy appeared to have been singing the words of quite a different psalm from all the others, and she had, with her own eyes, seen the deputy head chorister land a nasty kick on the shins of the little probationer standing next to him during the Prayer of Humble Access.

'They looked very sweet,' she said diplomatically.

'Pity most of them can't sing,' said a sarcastic voice behind them.

'Oh, Mr Praetorius, you startled us,' said Marjorie, bridling at his remark. 'Just like you to make a joke about your clever choristers.'

'Put them all in sacks and dump them in the river, if I had my way,' said Simon morosely. 'Listen to them, all over the place. Oh, God, that's Tomkins, doesn't matter how many times I explain it to him, he can't see any difference between a crotchet and a minim. "But was it in tune, sir?" is all he can say.'

Simon hurled himself through the choir screen, yelling at the unsuspecting Tomkins. 'The filled-in black ones with straight stems are crotchets, corncrake. The ones with the empty middles are MINIMS, Tomkins, MINIMS.'

'Yes, sir,' said the hapless Tomkins.

'And they last twice as long as crotchets, Tomkins!'

The assistant organist climbed back into his loft and Simon began another day's routine.

'The life of a Cathedral is very special, isn't it ladies?' said Marjorie complacently. 'Everyone working in harmony, to the greater glory of God. And we pay our humble part; flowers may not seem much, but it is our little service and offering, and nothing is too small to escape God's notice. Now, to our tasks, dears.'

'And the ones with little tails, Tomkins, are QUAVERS . . . .'

Faustina dived from Leofric Street into one of the numerous little alleyways that ran off it. In her haste, she bumped into a woman, and began to apologize.

'Don't worry,' said Harriet. 'Who were you escaping from?'

'Was it so obvious?' said Faustina. 'Mrs Dean.'

'An actual Mrs Dean, or the Dean's wife?' enquired Harriet, who had a precise mind.

'The Dean's wife. An admirable woman, but goodness, she is keen on committees and groups. I do what I can, but really, I hate that kind of thing.'

Harriet was standing in front of a newly-painted dark green front door. 'Come in,' she said, putting a key in the lock. 'Come in and have a cup of coffee, if you aren't too busy.'

'No, I'm not, and I'd love to,' said Faustina, who realized that this was the house Harriet had just moved into and was consumed with house-curiosity. 'This is very old, nobody gets these houses, how on earth did you manage it?'

'Oh, I heard about it on the grapevine, and staked a claim. It is very old, some of it is the same date as the Cathedral. And it's got a little walled garden at the back, which is amazing in the heart of the city.'

Faustina exclaimed with pleasure at the low, panelled rooms, the old fireplaces and the ancient wooden staircase. Harriet led the way upstairs, 'I use this as a sitting room, because there's more light.'

Faustina sank into a deep and extremely comfortable sofa. 'How unusual,' she said. 'Not many single women of an academic disposition seem to give much thought to creature comforts. But all this is wonderfully comfortable.'

'Yes, I appreciate it when I come home exhausted from running.'

'I do admire you,' said Faustina. 'I was never sporty.'

'Musicians seldom are, in my experience,' said Harriet. 'Good thing, or all the best running places would be chock-a-block.'

'I never thought of that,' said Faustina, laughing at the thought of towpaths and parks crammed full of athletic musicians.

She bit appreciatively into a ginger biscuit. 'Quinta,' she said. 'I wanted to ask you about Quinta.'

She noticed a slightly wary look on Harriet's face, and reassured her. 'No, it's not vulgar curiosity. It's just an idea I've had. She interests me, and I can see that her life is rather a struggle at the moment what with one thing and another. I may be able to help.'

Harriet relaxed. 'It is hard for her,' she agreed.

'She was at school with Lydia, wasn't she?' Faustina went on.

'Yes, at Grisewood. A very good school, though I can't imagine it ever suited Quinta.'

'It's very disciplined, isn't it?' said Faustina. 'And in such a remote place. I've only been there once, when Lennox was working near by, and I went down to see him. A nightmare journey; I took my son, who was fifteen or sixteen then, and I remember he complained all the way, and was sick several times.'

'A memorable journey,' said Harriet, pouring more coffee.

'Thank you,' said Faustina, in an abstracted voice. And then, 'I wonder . . . Harriet, how old is Quinta? She can't be more than twenty-two or twenty-three, can she?'

Harriet looked at Faustina. 'No, she isn't, but she says she's older for Phoebe's sake.'

'I thought so,' said Faustina. She put her cup down on the table. 'Thank you,' Harriet. I'm sure I can do something for her and Phoebe, it's just the best way to go about it.'

'I hope you can,' said Harriet. 'Although I don't think you're the only one concerned about Quinta's well-being just at the moment.'

'Ah, no, perhaps not,' said Faustina. 'And I don't suppose you're talking about Simon.'

'I am not,' said Harriet with a grin.

Faustina sighed. 'No, but until Quinta gets rid of all that emotional baggage, it may not be much use. My help will be practical rather than emotional; I know what a strain an eight-year-old child can be, particularly with no father around. Of course, she should have had help from the father all along.'

'Men!' said Harriet with feeling.

'I must get back to the Palace,' said Faustina. 'We've got those dreadful twins staying at the palace with us; goodness, how I wish they'd go. Even Lennox isn't very happy about them, although to begin with, of course, he was delighted to have a young and pretty girl about the place.'

'Just let me put these in the kitchen and I'll come part of the way with you,' said Harriet, carrying the things off into her tiny, immaculate kitchen. 'I promised Quinta I'd take Phoebe off her hands for an hour or so.'

'Shouldn't you be training?' said Faustina, taking a quick look up and down Leofric Street to make sure the coast was clear.

'Later,' said Harriet.

She was very surprised when the door to the Manor House was opened by Lucy.

'Hello, Lucy,' said Harriet, as they brushed cheeks in greeting. 'I didn't know you were back in England.'

'Just a fleeting visit to see how Alban is doing, and to give a hand with my grandchildren. Evie has broken some ribs, she collided with a row of dustbins while walking along doing spiritual exercises. So typical of her; I've no patience with all this churchy nonsense. I've sorted her out, told her to pay more attention to Simon or he'll disappear with a floozy, found a dim cousin to give her a hand while she's tied up in sticky plaster, and come round here to recover.'

Quinta called to Harriet to come in.

'I can't come to the door,' she said, 'Alban's wheelchair has jammed, and I'm trying to fix it.'

'Very inefficiently,' said Alban, peering down at the wheel.

'Where's Lydia?' asked Harriet, used to seeing her with the wheelchair.

'Off wheelchair duty,' said Lucy. 'Just while she goes on an errand to the Palace for her grandmother, who isn't well.'

'Let's hope she doesn't come across that ghastly pair Felix and Zoe while she's there,' observed Quinta.

'Is Lady Wray not well?' asked Harriet, kneeling down beside the chair to help Quinta. 'Look, I think that nut there is the problem. Have you got a pair of pliers?'

'She's housebound at the moment with an arthritic hip,' Lucy explained as Quinta found the pliers.

'Oh dear. Does Lydia feel she ought to be looking after her grandmother rather than Alban?'

'She does feel a bit guilty,' said Quinta, 'but her grandmother is apparently even more irascible and naggy than usual when her hip is hurting, and Lydia says she's got a job here, looking after Alban, and that comes first.'

Lucy's eyebrows rose. 'I shouldn't think that goes down very well with Wilhelmina.'

'Actually, Mrs Gridlock goes in and gives her a hand, which is much better. Lydia hasn't got a clue about looking after sick people.'

'You're telling me,' said Alban with feeling.

'You aren't ill,' said his unimpressed mother. 'Just temporarily maimed. I know just how Wilhelmina feels, a young and vigorous person dancing attendance on one when one isn't feeling very well is quite exhausting. Now, tell me why those Titian-haired twins are staying at the Palace.'

'Drains, I think,' said Quinta vaguely, as she watched Harriet give the nut a final, determined wrench. 'Adam's got problems with his drains – nasty smells, Lydia says. Lady Wray wouldn't have them again, so they've gone to their uncle's.'

A door banged. 'There's Lydia,' said Quinta. 'It didn't take her long.'

She put her head round the door and called along the passage. 'Lydia? Is that you?'

'Goodness,' said Lucy, as Lydia came slowly into the room. 'What is the matter with you, child? You look as though you've seen a ghost.'

'I didn't know whether to say something, or laugh or cry, or what,' Lydia confided to Quinta later. 'I have to say, the Bishop behaved with considerable *savoir-faire*. "So sorry to interrupt you," he said to them. "Do finish what you were doing."'

Lydia's face crumpled. 'It's funny, I suppose, Quinta, but I feel devastated. How could I have trusted that man? Why couldn't I see what kind of a man he was? I mean, people knew! The Bishop and his wife had a good idea of what he was like, and Titus has been dropping heavy hints about how his name is mud in Cambridge because of what he's been up to.'

She sniffed. 'And, apparently, he was nearly flung out of Eton because of what he got up to with Felix – and other boys. He wasn't, because if they threw everyone out for that I gather they'd be half empty. And he was clever, so he survived . . .

Oh, Quinta, I've been such a fool. I'm never going to get it right with men. There was Angus, deceiving me like mad, and then I go and get involved with Adam. You're right, you said at the dig that he was a monster, and that's exactly what he is. And as for Zoe and Felix . . .!'

Lydia drew breath and shook her head in disbelief. 'Brother and sister! Incest! It is completely disgusting. The only good thing about it – apart from me finally seeing what Adam's really like – is that that awful pair will have to go. The Bishop was very contained about it, I think so as not to upset me, but you could see he was seething. He'll have them out of there in no time. It's very difficult for him, a man in his position, and his nephew and niece, there in the Palace. It would cause the most tremendous scandal if it came out, and I suppose bishops can't have so much as a breath of any sexual hanky-panky about them or their families.'

'What exactly happened?' said Quinta. 'Come on, out with it. What were they doing?'

'It was a sandwich,' said Lydia. 'The Bishop gave me the book for grandmama, and then he said, hadn't I been on the dig, because his nephew and niece were staying with him, would I like to say hello? I couldn't really say no, so he went along to this room, and opened the door, and there they were. Sandwiched!'

'Doing what?' said Quinta, puzzled.

'Oh, sharpen your wits,' said Lydia. 'Think about it. Zoe on the bottom, then Felix, and then Adam on top. All of them totally naked, needless to say!'

Quinta looked at Lydia with huge round eyes, trying to keep a straight face. In vain; her mouth twitched and she let out a peal of laughter. 'Oh, oh, I know it's horrible, and so immoral it doesn't bear thinking of, but Zoe must have been so squashed.'

'Serve her right,' said Lydia viciously. 'Hope she's got several broken ribs, like Alban's sister-in-law.'

She paused. 'Quinta, Adam was at that party the other night, wasn't he?'

Quinta nodded. 'Titus said later that he'd seen him there.'

'I thought so,' said Lydia. 'How stupid I've been. I asked him when I saw him again, and he was a bit furtive. He had the nerve to accuse me of being a prig, said he didn't suppose the party was half as shocking as I made out, and I should loosen up, let go of my inhibitions.'

'Now you know what he means by letting go of inhibitions, I'd stick to yours,' said Quinta, trying to pull herself together. 'Goodness, the things people get up to. It makes me feel quite old. Well, Lydia, you can't say your time in Eyot has been uneventful.'

'No,' said Lydia. 'No more men for me, that's one thing I'm certain of.'

Quinta laughed. 'Until the next one comes along.'

'He hasn't come along for you, has he?' said Lydia.

'No,' said Quinta.

'You're still in love with Phoebe's father, aren't you?' said Lydia.

'I suppose I am,' said Quinta ruefully. 'A one-man woman.'

'No-one alive is that,' said Lydia. 'If you want my opinion, which you don't, I think that all that side of you froze when everything happened and he ditched you, and you've been living in the fridge ever since. One of these days something else will happen to break the spell. Then you'll come out into the sun, wonder what you ever saw in him, and get on with a normal life. With another man, and I don't mean some strange relationship like the one with Alban.'

'Perhaps,' said Quinta, unconvinced. 'But Alban's over. Quite, quite finished. No more Tuesdays and Thursdays.'

'Mmm,' said Lydia. 'I'd gathered that.'

'Do you live here?' Faustina asked as Titus opened the door of the Manor House. 'You were here yesterday, I know, because I met one of the three graces, on my way here, and she told me all about it. Oh, look, more callers, here comes Sylvester.'

'You know Sylvester, I gather?' said Titus.

'Oh, yes, I've known him for years. And Lily, what heaven.'

Sylvester greeted Faustina warmly. 'Playing butlers, Titus?' he enquired civilly as he filled the hall. 'Quick, move along there, what a crowd, I can hardly breathe.'

'That's your fault, not ours,' said Lily. 'What's going on here, is it a meeting?'

'No, Lily,' said Titus. 'I came to play chess with Alban, my charity work, you know. I try to get here most days, it keeps him amused. However, today the bird has flown, taking Lydia with him.'

'Gone to London, has he?' said Sylvester, expanding into a large armchair. 'I will say this for Alban, he has some decent-sized furniture.'

'It would be better if he had some decent-sized friends,' said Lily.

'I will ignore that remark,' said Sylvester.

'Yes, he's gone to London,' said Titus. 'Last-minute decision, so I gather, there's a recording of some of his music being done. He originally said he couldn't go, not in the wheelchair, but late last night he changed his mind. I think it's an attempt to cheer Lydia up, take her mind off her broken heart, which is unusually kind of him.'

'I expect his suffering has made him into a finer person,' said

Sylvester. Lily looked sceptical, and said that if no-one was at home to offer them a cup of tea or coffee, then she would do something about it.

'Where's Phoebe?' said Faustina. 'Out with that woman who teaches her in the mornings, I suppose.'

'No, actually not today,' said Titus, gracefully skirting round Lily and reaching for cups and saucers. 'Lucy Praetorius is here on a brief visit, and she's taken Phoebe out with her. Quinta's here, though. She's working in the bathroom.'

The others stared at this extraordinary pronouncement; only Sylvester looked unsurprised. He nodded knowledgeably.

'Varnishing, is she? Is that the double-bass? Nearly finished, then.'

'In the bathroom?' said Faustina.

'You fill it with steam. That takes all the dust out of the air, so the varnish can be flawless. Old trick.'

'Very pongy,' said Titus. 'I spoke to her through the bathroom door; I must say, I shouldn't care to be in there.'

'If she's finished, tell her I've made coffee,' said Lily. 'I hear it's a beautiful instrument, and I daresay Lydia will like it, although I can't be doing with those huge instruments myself. Cellos are quite enough trouble.'

Quinta sat down gratefully to the glass of water which Lily had proffered when she saw her red face dripping with perspiration. She was wearing an old T-shirt, which was wringing wet, and a pair of Alban's shorts, which came to just above her knees.

Titus regarded her with awe. 'You look like a demented boy scout,' he said finally. 'I can see why you choose to work at home; you'd frighten all the customers away from Gustav's if they saw you looking like that.'

'Very professional,' said Sylvester approvingly. 'If not altogether becoming.'

Isn't it strange, thought Quinta as she gulped her water down, how little I care what I look like. Is it lack of hormones? Is Lydia right? Have all my normal feelings been frozen? More likely vanished for good, she thought gloomily.

'Back to work,' she said, stretching.

'Going well, is it?' asked Sylvester.

'I hope so,' said Quinta.

'Come out again by one o'clock and I'll treat you to lunch,' said Titus.

'No, you won't,' said Sylvester. 'I will.'

'We can all go out to lunch,' said Lily.

'I think I'd better get back to work as soon as I've finished this,' said Quinta. 'Thank you all the same.'

'No, I insist,' said Sylvester. 'If Gustav cuts up rough, which he won't, because he isn't here, then you can tell him I took you out to discuss a new commission. There now!'

Quinta smiled at him, and headed back to the bathroom.

'Are you going to buy a cello from Quinta?' said Faustina.

'Not for me, but Phoebe needs a decent one, or soon will. Gustav ought to be ashamed of himself, the one she's got is the best of his rental ones, and it's dire. I shall have to have a word with him about it.'

'Are small cellos expensive?' asked Titus.

'More than Quinta can afford. I know of a small German one, lovely instrument, that would just do for Phoebe now, then Quinta could be making her the next size up. But it's too much, I don't suppose Quinta could afford half of it.'

'The most important thing for Phoebe is for her to get back to school,' said Lucy, who had just come in with Phoebe. 'This staying at home is doing her no good; she's more of a handful than ever.'

'Course she is,' said Sylvester. 'She needs her cohorts to boss around. I'm working on it, I had a go at the headmaster, that fool Poughley, a couple of days ago. Said he ought to offer a music scholarship other than the choral ones. He blustered in his usual way, and then admitted that there is something called the Bishop's Fund, which is supposed to be used to help non-choristers, but he's always handed over the loot to some favourite in the choir.'

'Can he do that?' asked Lucy.

Sylvester shook his head disapprovingly. 'Probably not, but he has. It's just the behaviour you would expect from a headmaster closely connected with the Church. I thought that since he'd been rumbled we might have been able to shame him into doing something sensible with it, like giving Phoebe a scholarship. However, he says the money in the fund would barely cover music lessons, never mind school fees.'

'Someone will come along and top it up,' said Lily with certainty.

'Seen it in the tea leaves, have you, Lily?' said Titus, amused.

'Don't mock,' said Sylvester. 'I've never known Lily wrong. If she reckons there's going to be enough money from somewhere to send Phoebe to a suitable school, then you can bet there will be.'

'The three graces are very worried about Phoebe,' said Faustina.

'Three graces?' said Sylvester.

'Those flower women,' said Titus. 'Frightful gossips, know everything. One of them isn't too bad, but the other two, oh, lord!'

'Wyn is quite reasonable,' agreed Faustina. 'I used to know her in Cambridge. She's inquisitive, likes to know what's going on, but she's quite capable of keeping her mouth shut. Those other two aren't, though.'

'Who are they?' said Titus. 'Apart from being the mainstay of the Cathedral flowers. Are they put away in the vestry every night? Do they have any existence outside the Cathedral precincts?'

'Marjorie Jessop is married to a man who mostly works abroad,' said Lily. 'You can hardly blame him. Daphne lost her husband some years ago.'

'Mislaid him in a flower arrangement, did she?' said Titus flippantly.

'And Wyn inherited some money from an aunt,' Lily went on. 'Together with a house up here. She works part time in a charity shop.'

'How do you know all this?' said Titus.

'Lily knows everything,' said Sylvester. 'Well, if there's no Alban to cheer up, I'll be on my way. Tell Quinta to join us at the Vicenza, Titus, at one. You too, of course, Faustina.'

'Not me this time, thank you all the same,' said Faustina getting up. 'I've still got rooms full of boxes to unpack. I only came over this morning to see how Lydia was.'

'Don't tell me she's ill, too!' said Sylvester.

'No,' said Faustina. 'She had a nasty shock, yesterday, that's all. Found her young man *in flagrante* at the Palace, heavily involved with my nephew and niece, who seem to have no sense of decorum whatsoever.'

'I don't believe for a moment that that girl's your niece,' said Lily unexpectedly.

'Well, Felix is my nephew, I'm sure of that,' said Faustina. 'And he has a twin called Zoe, although I have to admit I haven't seen her since she was about two years old. And this girl is so like Felix, she must be his twin.'

'No,' said Lily firmly. 'That pair have been out to shock, they're laughing up their sleeves at you. Ring the Bishop's sister in America, I think you might be surprised.'

Faustina looked thoughtfully at Lily. 'I think I will,' she said slowly. 'I must say, I'd be very glad if you were right; it could defuse a potentially very embarrassing situation.'

'Plenty of those about without starting any more,' said Lily. 'Come along, Sylvester, we've got a lot to do before lunchtime.'

'I don't know why I put up with your bullying,' grumbled Sylvester. 'You made me come, I could be at home working . . .'

'Bye, Quinta,' Faustina called through the bathroom door. 'Don't expire in there, and let me know how Lydia is.'

Lydia was at that moment wheeling Alban into the studio in London. She retreated into the background as he was swept up in a flurry of technical and musical talk. The musicians pottered up to him, patted him on the shoulder, commiserating with him before they settled into their places.

Lydia was awed to see a very famous conductor wander in and pounce on Alban, score in hand. The irritable, self-centred man she knew was before her eyes transformed into a professional. I feel a waste of space, she thought.

Alban was calling for her.

'Lydia,' he said peremptorily. 'I've left some pages of music in my flat, I thought I had them here. Pop into a taxi, will you? Hermione will be there, the papers are in my desk, she'll find them for you. Tell her it's for my new suite. She'll know.'

He turned away, immersed once more in discussions. Lydia found her way out of the maze of passages and hailed a passing cab. Goodness, she thought, sitting down with a bump as the taxi lurched away from the pavement, I wonder if Quinta realizes what a big noise Alban is? And I wonder what this Hermione is like? I suppose Quinta won't really be interested. How could she have lived with Alban for all that time, gone to bed with him twice a week, without ever feeling more than mild affection for him? How could you feel mild anything for a man like Alban?'

Fortunately, Alban had handed her the key to his flat, because Hermione wasn't in. In fact, Lydia very quickly realized, Hermione had gone for good. And had obviously been gone for several days, thought Lydia, recoiling as she opened the fridge.

She looked around the flat, which was in a terrible mess. Hermione had clearly had a lot of possessions there, and had taken them all with her, judging by the empty shelves and drawers, the gaps on the wall and the generally unlived in look of the place.

Alban isn't going to like this, thought Lydia as she opened the large scroll topped desk. Inside was a sealed envelope addressed, in a flowery hand, to Alban. Lydia looked at it, wondering whether to leave it where it was, but after a moment's hesitation, she picked it up and put it in her bag. Alban would presumably want to know why Hermione had done a flit.

She rummaged through the papers in the desk. There was very little music there, just a slim folder without a name on it, that must be it. She tucked it under her arm and let herself out of the flat.

Alban seized the folder with a quick thanks. Lydia just had time to ask him how long he would be; good, she thought. Shopping. Several blissful hours all to herself.

She had reckoned on catching the six o'clock train, but by half past eight that evening, she knew that they wouldn't be back in Eyot at all that night. She rang Quinta, so that she wouldn't expect them, and told her all about Hermione's departure.

'He hasn't read her letter, yet,' she said.

'How do you know?'

'Because I haven't given it to him. He's completely absorbed in his music, honestly, I don't think he'd notice if the world ended while he's in there. And they must be paying a fortune in overtime, you know what musicians are like about working to the second.'

'They always overrun on Alban's recordings,' said Quinta. 'They're used to it. Where are you going to stay?'

'I don't know,' said Lydia. 'I've got a key, we can go back to my house, I don't think Mum would mind.'

'I expect Alban will have his own ideas,' said Quinta.

Alban did. 'Perfectly good flat of my own,' he said. 'There's a sofa bed you can camp on, Hermione won't mind.'

'Um,' said Lydia. 'I don't think Hermione will be there.'

'Of course she'll be there,' said Alban. 'She's always there.'

'She's gone,' said Lydia firmly.

'Oh, balls,' said Alban. 'Where could she possibly have gone to?'

He soon found out as he read her letter with growing rage. 'She's gone to America, if you please. With some miserable percussionist. Percussionist! She might as well run away with the second trumpet; what an idiotic woman!'

He was even more annoyed when he got to his flat. 'It looks like a pigsty,' he said. 'Was it like this when you were here this morning?'

'Yes,' said Lydia.

'Well, why didn't you tidy it up?' he demanded.

'Why should I?' said Lydia equably. 'I went shopping.'

'Went shopping? You aren't paid to go shopping!'

'No, I'm paid – very little, I may add – to wheel you about. You didn't need wheeling, they didn't want me in the studio, so I went to do some things of my own. I am certainly not paid to clear up after you and your sluttish girlfriend.'

If Alban hadn't been in a wheelchair, he would have paced. As it was, he could only glare, and Lydia took no notice.

'I don't mind sleeping here tonight, since it's late, but if you're staying over tomorrow night, then this place must be cleared up.'

'Ah, you've come to your senses, good.'

'No, if by that you mean that you think I'm going to clear it up. Of course I'm not. I'll ring one of those cleaning agencies, they can send somebody round.'

Alban looked at her calm face and realized he was beaten. 'All right,' he conceded. 'It'll cost a fortune, though.'

'You can afford it, judging by the size of the royalty cheque lying in your desk.'

'Oh, that's where I left it, is it?' said Alban.

He looked around the room and pulled a face. 'It's a bit desolate, isn't it. It'll be lonely, too, in that big bed. I don't suppose . . .'

'I,' said Lydia firmly, 'am sleeping on the sofa. Tonight, you may take me out to dinner, because I'm not eating here. And don't get any ideas about me being a successor to your Hermione or to Quinta, because I am not an adoring flautist with a case of arrested development, nor do I owe you a debt of gratitude the way Quinta felt she did. If you want to go to bed with me, you'll have to work a lot harder at it than that.'

'Oh,' said Alban with a grin. 'Do you know, perhaps I don't like gratitude and flattery as much as you think I do.'

'What I think,' said Lydia, looking at him thoughtfully, 'is that it's time someone took you in hand. You've got away with far too much for far too long.'

'Are we celebrating?' said Alban, regarding her with mocking eyes from under his ferocious eyebrows. 'In that case, fetch me the phone, and I'll book us a table.'

'You'll be sorry you came back from London so soon,' Quinta warned Lydia.

'Lucy is insisting we all go to the service at the Cathedral. I haven't been to a service for nearly nine years; not since before Phoebe was born . . .

'And it's much against my will,' she muttered rebelliously, as she tried to persuade Phoebe that her collection of twenty-eight toy owls would not feel abandoned if they didn't accompany her to the service. She didn't bother to argue about the extraordinary hat which Phoebe chose to wear, nor the odd socks, nor the huge, old, black cardigan of hers which Phoebe had unearthed from the back of a cupboard.

Lucy, who was responsible for organising the outing to the Cathedral service, blinked when she saw Phoebe, but with great forbearance said nothing.

'I did warn you,' said Quinta. 'Why don't you go, and I'll stay here with Phoebe? I need to get lunch on in good time; after all, we're feeding thousands.'

Lucy and Alban had invited several friends to come and listen to the inaugural playing of Lydia's new bass.

'A double-bass party,' said Sylvester with enthusiasm. 'That's a first; of course I'll come.' He had turned down Lucy's suggestion that he join the group attending divine service with loud guffaws.

'Not me, Lucy, you know my opinion of that lot, bunch of hypocrites. No, definitely not for me.'

'So you see,' went on Quinta, 'it really would be better for me to stay here and get lunch ready.'

'You leave that to me,' said a voice behind Quinta.

It was Lily.

'No way are you getting me to a service,' she said. 'And Sylvester will be coming in about an hour, he can give me a hand. No, you don't need to show me where things are, Phoebe, I'll find everything I need.'

Lucy bundled a grumbling Alban, who had graduated from his wheelchair to crutches, into her car, together with a yawning Lydia, a noisy Phoebe and a reluctant Quinta.

'You're mad, mother dear,' said Alban. 'I haven't been to a service for years.'

'I daresay,' said Lucy. 'All the more reason to go today. It's the Bishop's first sermon, so it's a courtesy to Faustina. Also, they're singing your Venetian Mass, Alban.'

'Oh, no, spare me that,' said Alban. 'It'll be a dire performance, Simon hasn't a clue.'

'Don't be so arrogant,' said Lydia. 'Simon's just as highly thought of in his field as you are in yours. I'm looking forward to it.'

Alban slumped down in his seat with his arms crossed. 'Families,' he said.

'Lucky you to have so much family,' said Phoebe disapprovingly. 'And all you do is moan and complain.'

Lucy laughed. 'You tell him, Phoebe.'

Phoebe was excited at the thought of going to the service. 'Do we get to sit in the front row?' she asked. 'I want to be somewhere where I can see Gavin and especially Peter, and then I can make faces at them.'

'You will not make faces at anyone,' said Quinta. 'Any trouble, even a hint of trouble, and you're out of there. I told you, Lucy, this is a bad idea.'

'Nonsense,' said Lucy bracingly. 'It'll do us all good.'

Quinta was relieved to find that, although they were in good time, the nave was already filling up, and they were nowhere near the front. She showed Phoebe the hymns in her hymn book.

'I don't know any of these,' said Phoebe, disappointed.

'It doesn't matter,' said Alban. 'Hymn tunes are all the same, you'll pick it up as you go along.'

'Why are they all the same?' said Phoebe with interest.

'Lack of imagination,' said Alban. 'Dreary words, dreary tunes.'

'Why don't you write an undreary one?' said Phoebe. 'Anyway, they aren't all dreary; look, they've got carols in this hymn book. I like carols.'

'Some carols are all right, if you like that kind of thing,' said Alban grudgingly. 'Lydia, if you keep on craning your neck like that, you'll turn into a giraffe.'

'I'm just looking round to see who's here that we know,' said Lydia. 'Oops, there's grandmama, look, she's sitting with Sybil Stixwould, they must be friends again. I'd better go over and say hello.'

'Not now,' said Alban, restraining her. 'I think it's about to begin. Come on, Phoebe, stand up.'

'Why?' said Phoebe, dragging her hat off her head and carefully hanging it on the little hook on the chair in front. 'Look, a hat hook.'

'Because you do when they all come in,' said Harriet, slipping into the empty seat beside her. 'Watch over there, and you'll see the choir in a minute.'

Quinta cast Harriet a look of thanks; if anyone could restrain Phoebe's wilder frolics, it was Harriet. I suppose she has to come every week, thought Quinta, part of the job.

She rose with the rest of the congregation, then had to bend down to retrieve all the books which Phoebe had sent flying in her excitement at seeing Gavin and Peter process in.

Phoebe hadn't seen them robed before, and she was entranced. She tugged at Harriet's sleeve. 'Look,' she said urgently. 'Those are my friends.'

'I know,' Harriet whispered back. 'I teach them.'

Quinta stood up with the last of the fallen books and turned round to put them back in their place just as the Bishop reached them. He had a bland, welcoming smile that went no further than his mouth; the polite duty face of a man about his serious business.

Then he saw Quinta. For a second his eyes passed indifferently over her, then they focused with startling intensity. He was transfixed, then his gaze flashed to Phoebe's flaming red head alongside her. The Bishop's Chaplain twisted round to see why the Bishop had halted, and his cross waved dangerously. Behind the Bishop, the rest of the procession was piling up into itself as the rear kept moving until it finally bumped into the stationary group of clergy and servers.

With enormous self control the Bishop swept his gaze across to the people on the other side of the aisle, found, thank God, a familiar face, bestowed a generous smile in its direction, and moved off again.

It was superbly done. No-one, thought Harriet, would have noticed how thunderstruck the Bishop had obviously been to see Quinta – and Phoebe. The Introit came to an end, and the weedy voice of Canon Feverfew rose in the Collect for the day. Harriet, who was thinking furiously, paid no attention to the mellifluous words. Quinta beside her was motionless. Pale, breathing heavily as though she had had a tremendous shock.

And she has, thought Harriet grimly. But what self-control, she thought, as Quinta leant mechanically towards Phoebe to find her place in the order of service.

Harriet looked down the nave to where Faustina was sitting with Milo. Her face was serene, reserved and gave nothing away, but Harriet would have been prepared to bet that she had seen the Bishop falter. Then, startled by a powerful bass voice which rang out over the congregation, Harriet's eyes flicked across to the singer. Titus. Then she looked back again at little Milo, fiddling with his prayer book as he sat, patently bored, beside his mother.

Titus.

Titus. Milo. Faustina. The Bishop. Quinta. Phoebe.

Oh my goodness, thought Harriet. What a tangled web.

Phoebe reached behind Quinta and pulled at Alban's coat. He leaned towards her. 'A major,' said Phoebe in her normal voice. 'It's in A major.'

Alban's eyebrows went up, but he nodded, and put a finger to his lips. Phoebe's eyes narrowed as she listened to the music. Out of the corner of her eye, Harriet could see that she was about to say something else, and she swiftly put a restraining hand over Phoebe's mouth.

'Phoebe,' she said in a low voice. 'You mustn't talk. If you behave well, I'll buy you a little fluffy owl I saw in the National Trust shop.'

Phoebe's eyes brightened and she clenched her lips together firmly.

Although Harriet's mind was spinning with her revelation, her teacherly self noticed the boys in the choir. How nervous Peter looks, thought Harriet. Lucy's tale of Peter's bullying had come as no surprise to her. As she said to Lucy, bullying was endemic in the school; possibly worse in the choir, but fairly bad everywhere. Mr Poughley disagreed. He had told her magisterially that there was no bullying in the school, none at all, only children inventing incidents just to make mischief and draw attention to themselves.

'We are a Christian foundation,' he said in his most solemn tones. 'Bullying has no place in such a school.'

Looking at the smallest boys in the choir, Harriet wondered, not for the first time, why seemingly responsible adults treated children so appallingly. Far too many parents, teachers, social workers; anyone, in fact, who had any power over children thought of the wretches as things, not human beings.

Was that most children's lot? thought Harriet. To be born to be manipulated and abused by the very people who should most care for them? Did parents really ever do what was best for their children? Harriet cynically thought not. They always did what suited them personally; bolstering their own egos; hiding their inadequacies. How seldom we ask children themselves what they feel about it, she thought sadly, and would they tell us if we did ask?

And what effect did it have on all of us when we finally grew up and got away, she asked herself, thinking of Quinta, so badly let down by all those responsible adults when she had been hardly older than the biggest boy singing in the choir here this morning.

She felt Phoebe poking her painfully in the ribs, and realized that she alone was standing; the rest of the congregation were seated for the sermon. A biddy in a grim hat glared at her, and she quickly sat down. She looked past Phoebe to Quinta; she was leaning back in her seat with her eyes closed.

As the Bishop began to preach, expounding on his theme of how we carry old sins into our new lives unless we admit to them, face up to them, confess them to others and make reparation so that we can ask for forgiveness, Quinta slowly opened her eyes and looked up at him, aloft in his pulpit. The expression on her face was hard to read. Harriet nudged her. 'Are you all right?' she whispered.

'What?' said Quinta. 'Oh, yes, yes, of course.'

Harriet looked at Quinta's rigid body. Alban didn't seem to have noticed. Lucy, further down the line, was listening attentively. Phoebe was engrossed in plaiting and unplaiting the tassels on the hassock hanging on the chair in front.

The sermon wound to its conclusion and as the Bishop made his way back to his seat, Quinta's eyes never left him.

The service continued. Harriet stood up and knelt automatically, her mind not at all on the words of the service. Nor, she told herself with a flash of humour, was she the only one not attending. She was sure that the woman over there in a peculiar pink hat was fast asleep, and, judging by the look on his face, the man in the crumpled linen suit was thinking of nothing more spiritual than the roast beef he was going to have for lunch.

Harriet stood up to go forward to receive communion with Lucy. Alban stayed resolutely where he was, and so did Quinta.

Phoebe made faces and pointed to the order of service where it stated that children could go to the altar rail to be blessed. Harriet took her hand, to take her up with her, but Quinta shook her head, and gestured for Harriet to go up without Phoebe. As Harriet went past Alban, she saw him looking surreptitiously at Quinta, his thick eyebrows drawn together in a look of intense concentration.

He knows, thought Harriet.

The service went on its stately way, the last hymn was sung, the blessing given, the banners and crosses were hoisted into the air, and the long procession started back down the aisle.

Harriet looked at Quinta as the Bishop came towards them. She looked drained, calm and completely self-possessed. She gazed straight at the Bishop with clear, cool, appraising eyes. He bit his lip and looked away.

The choir turned to process into the north aisle, and began to sing a soaring version of the 150th psalm. It was the custom at some cathedrals, though not at Eyot, but the Bishop had specially requested that they sing it at his first Eucharist there.

'Praise him for his mighty acts: praise him according to his excellent greatness,' they sang. 'Praise him with the sound of the trumpet: praise him with the psaltery and harp.'

# Epilogue ∫

As they came out of the great west door and began to go down the steps, Quinta stopped and looked back. Her face broke into a huge smile, and she gave a wild and exuberant wave at the west front towering above her.

'Hi, God,' she said. 'Remember me?'

She jumped down the remaining steps, and then saw Phoebe's disapproving face gazing at her.

'Why are you so happy, Q?' she asked.

'Oh, just because,' said Quinta. 'You go on, I'll wait for Titus and walk back with him.'

'Yes,' said Alban. 'You do that, Quinta. No, Phoebe, no arguing, you come with us. Your ma needs a few minutes to herself, you leave her be.'

Faustina found the Bishop sitting in a blue study at his desk.

'I've just been unpacking some more boxes,' she said cheerfully. 'I found this charming charcoal sketch of a child. It's your aunt when she was little, isn't it? Your aunt Leonora. So strange, it's remarkably like Quinta's little girl. You haven't met her, have you? No, of course not. You may have noticed her in the Cathedral this morning, though; so striking with that flaming red hair.'

Faustina put the sketch down on a little table near the Bishop's desk. 'Except your aunt was dark, but of course with a charcoal sketch you can't tell. I don't think I'll hang it up, though, attractive though it is.'

The Bishop said nothing.

'Talking of your aunt,' Faustina went on in the same chatty

tone. 'We never did decide what to do with the money she left you. It's quite a lot, isn't it, even after taxes and so on? I know you were planning to put it into a pension or perhaps to buy another house with it, but do you know, I don't think we really need it. I've had an idea, there's a Bishop's Fund at the Cathedral School here. It's supposed to provide a non-choral scholarship for a musical child at the school, but there's nowhere near enough money for that at the moment.'

Faustina ran her hands over the keys of the open piano.

'It's a pity, because Quinta's little girl is very musical, and her mother can't afford to pay for proper lessons, or for her to go to a school like the Cathedral School where she might do better than she has at the primary school. Now, the thought occurred to me that if there were some more money in the Bishop's Fund, perhaps generously provided by the new Bishop, then Phoebe – that's what the child is called, Phoebe – she's just the same age as Milo, what a coincidence; then Phoebe could have a scholarship. And perhaps a trust fund, for when she's older. Sylvester thinks she may make a musician one day, and if that's what she wants, well, it can be expensive.'

The Bishop still said nothing.

'And by the way, I never spent the money you so kindly gave me to buy myself something for my fortieth birthday. I put it into shares, and it's increased quite a lot. I've now decided what I'm going to do with it. I'm going to buy a cello. Not for me, in case you're wondering, but for Phoebe. She needs a good instrument, and I don't need the money so . . .'

She went over and kissed the Bishop on the top of his head. 'And I think perhaps we'll have a few days in London quite soon, there's someone there I'd like you to see. There's a cold lunch laid for you in the dining room. I'm going to Alban's for lunch, and Milo's invited, too. I'll see you later, have a good brood.'

Quinta walked round to the north entrance, revelling in the warmth of the sun on her face. She felt light-headed, light-hearted, and quite different. The friendly verger was on duty at the entrance. Quinta wasn't surprised to see him there; on a day like this, it wouldn't be the glaring one.

'Do the lay clerks come out this way?' she asked.

The verger looked at her lovely smile and remembered sunny days of his own youth. 'You hop along inside, miss,' he said. 'They'll be getting changed in there.'

Quinta stood and looked down the aisle where the verger had pointed; in the distance she could see Titus's tall figure, his long white surplice draped over his arm. He saw her and came at once.

'Quinta.'

'I thought we could walk back to the Manor House together,' said Quinta.

'Wait here, I shan't be a sec.'

True to his word, he was with her in a very few minutes, taking her arm and leading her out through the Chapter House entrance. 'Quicker this way,' he said.

'I don't want to be quick,' said Quinta. 'I'm enjoying the sun. I want to go the long way, along the river, and over the Martyr's Bridge.'

'Then we shall go that way,' said Titus, wondering why she looked so radiantly happy.

'I had a revelation this morning,' said Quinta, as they walked peacefully along. 'I saw someone I haven't seen for a long time.'

'Someone?' said Titus.

'Him, of course,' said Quinta. 'Phoebe's father. Do you know, I've been imagining for nearly nine years that I was still in love with him.'

She paused.

'It's the Bishop, isn't it?' said Titus.

'Yes,' said Quinta. 'Only he wasn't a Bishop then.'

'Didn't you realize, when you heard his name again?'

'No. Everyone calls him Lennox, you see. When I knew him, he called himself Jon. Jon Smith.'

'Of course,' said Titus. 'He was the Rev. J L Smith in those days. I was surprised when I came back from the States and found he'd hyphenated his name.'

'What a ridiculous thing to do,' said Quinta dispassionately. 'Thought it sounded better for a man heading for a bishopric, I suppose.'

'And are you still in love with him, now you've seen him again?'

Quinta turned and looked at Titus, her eyes thoughtful.

'No, of course I'm not. I was. It was a real passion then, and I don't regret it, now, because to love someone that much is worth doing however little they feel for you. You see, I had never loved anyone before him.'

'What, not even your family?' said Titus, surprised.

'No,' said Quinta, shaking her head. 'They didn't love me, and I didn't love them.'

'What's your real name?' said Titus. 'It isn't Simpson, is it?'

'No, I changed it when I came here, so that my parents couldn't find me. It's Malplass.'

'Do you have a brother called George?'

Quinta stared at him. 'Yes, I do. How did you know?'

'Because I knew him slightly. At Cambridge. He told me that he had a younger sister who had run away and his parents had been pretty beastly about the whole affair. He looks very like you.'

'Yes, he does,' said Quinta slowly. 'Or did, I haven't seen him for a long time. Why didn't he get in touch with me?'

'As you said, you'd changed your name. Did your parents trace you in the end?'

'Yes. It took a little while, but they did. I should have changed my first name, of course. Quinta is too unusual. But that would have been like becoming a non-person, giving up almost the only thing I had left, you see.' She looked down into the river, almost blue today, with the clear sky above it. 'Perhaps they never told George they'd found me.'

'I daresay not,' said Titus grimly. 'He didn't seem to have much contact with them. You could get in touch with him yourself, you know.'

Quinta stopped and gazed at Titus. 'Of course I could! And I will. It would be lovely to have a brother again.'

Titus smiled at her almost childlike delight at the thought of finding her brother again.

'I got a shock this morning, too,' he confided.

'Oh?' said Quinta.

'Yes,' said Titus, taking a deep breath. 'I discovered I'm a father.'

Quinta felt as though the sun had gone in.

'You, a father?' she finally said, in a reasonably normal voice.

'Me, a father. Faustina's boy. Milo. We had an affair. Some time ago. Nearly nine years ago, to be precise.'

'Didn't you know before? That he was your son?'

Quinta was fascinated, despite herself. It seemed so strange, grown-up people living as dangerously as she had.

'No. I went to America. I heard that Faustina had had another child, but I never suspected . . . Then, a few days ago, Faustina said something which made me wonder. And today, when I saw Milo sitting beside her in the Cathedral, I suddenly realized that he is very like my mother.'

Quinta pulled at her lip. 'Is . . . I mean, are you and Faustina . . .?'

'No,' said Titus, looking away from her. 'No. I thought perhaps . . . she is a very attractive woman, and I'm very fond of her . . . But no, you can't go back. And besides, there's someone else.'

'Another older woman?' said Quinta. 'Oh, Titus, you are a disgrace!'

'And so are you,' said Titus. 'Do you still like older men, Quinta? What about me? Would I be old enough for you?'

Quinta looked up at him. 'Am I old enough for you, if it comes to that?'

'Exactly right,' said Titus, his voice muffled by her red hair.

Lunch at Alban's house was a good deal livelier than the Bishop's. The double-bass, finished, shining, majestic, was played to the assembled company.

'Excellent,' said Sylvester. 'Beautiful tone, Quinta, you are a clever girl. I didn't recognize the music, what was it?'

'Alban wrote it for me,' said Lydia, loosening her bow.

'As an engagement present,' said Alban, half proud, half embarrassed. 'She won't have me on any other terms, so . . .' He hobbled over to her side, and put a possessive arm around her.

'I'm only marrying you because you're so tall,' said Lydia.

'As good a reason as any,' said his mother. 'Well, Lydia, we shall get on a lot better than I do with my other daughter-in-law.'

'It'll do you good to be married,' said Lydia to Alban. 'You'll have to behave much better than you're used to. No walking all over people, and certainly no more strange floozies in your London flat. I shall soon put a stop to anything like that.'

Faustina had a quiet word with Titus as they sat together on a little sofa, champagne in hand.

'I have a toast for you, Titus,' said Faustina quietly. 'To your son.'

'Ah,' said Titus. 'Yes. Milo.'

'You guessed, then.' said Faustina.

'I'm sorry,' said Titus. 'I didn't know, not until today, when I thought how unlike Lennox Milo is, and how he reminds me of my mother. Does Lennox know?'

Faustina laughed and shook her head. 'Goodness, no, and he never will. You don't think I'm going to give up the moral high ground now I'm firmly installed on it? Definitely not. The Bishop's reputation will be balanced on a knife edge now; everything he and I do must be above reproach.'

'Ah, he knows about Quinta.'

Faustina nodded. 'He's always known, of course, but he was too cowardly to do anything about it. He's paid a very high price, and may have more to pay yet, it depends how much gets out. He could be lucky, he's been lucky in the past. However, I've forced him to do something about Phoebe's education; it's the least he can do. And I shall make him see a man in London who I think will be able to help him with his little problems.'

'Good,' said Titus. 'And what about Zoe and Felix?'

Faustina laughed. 'Do you know, Lily was quite right? I rang Lennox's sister in California; of course Zoe is there. She is indeed a lawyer, and very busy. This creature of nature turns out to be a distant cousin, hence the same Titian hair. A long time girlfriend of Felix's.'

'Are they staying in Eyot?'

'I gather not,' said Faustina. 'Not enough scope for them, Felix says; I can quite believe it.'

Titus laughed, and his eyes strayed to the other side of the room, where Quinta was laughing with Sylvester. Her high spirits were as frothing as her glass of champagne.

'I think Quinta has got over her fascination with older men,' he said.

'One older man,' said Harriet as she went past.

'Mmm,' said Titus, getting up.

Lily appeared at his elbow. 'Fixed things with Quinta, have you?' she asked.

Titus gave her a quizzical look. 'Is it that obvious?'

'To those that know,' said Lily. 'Don't waste any time. Now Quinta's made that bass and lost an eight-year millstone from round her neck, there'll be no stopping her. Don't forget, she'll need a roof over her head. Find a decent house, plenty of room for her and Phoebe, and her pesky instruments. She won't be happy in those rooms of yours at the university, too many prying dons about.'

Titus laughed, and made his way to Quinta's side, slipping an arm round her waist. 'Lily tells me I must buy a house,' he said in his most velvety voice. 'You'll have to choose it.'

Quinta gave him a ravishing, happy smile. 'Listen,' she said. Phoebe, who had an excellent voice, was putting Milo right about the 150th psalm. 'No,' she said. 'It finishes on a top G, like this, "Let everything that hath breath praise the Lord",' she sang.

'I hope the Bishop's listening,' said Faustina.

*Now available in hardback from Sceptre, Elizabeth Pewsey's third novel in the Mountjoy series:*

# Unholy Harmonies

A wild and wicked autumn wind howls off the fells through the country town of Unthrang, bringing with it a mysterious stranger who is destined to upset the settled lives of its residents. Justinia FitzOdo, for one, who has left her job and London to move North with her husband. But her new life doesn't bring her contentment and Justinia finds ever more irksome repression in her marital lines, until she is forced back on to the path of her vocation as a singer.

Others, too, are bemused to find their lives dramatically changed as the charismatic newcomer Issur intervenes: Sadie, abandoned by her husband for the milkman; the beautiful Roxane, who maintains a grand seventeenth-century house with no visible means of income; and Merle, whose writings about country life have proved very wide of the mark.

The local clergy are not spared by the wanton wind of change. Goings-on in Unthrang Church are echoed by unholy machinations in the dignified precincts of Eyot Cathedral, where the evangelical Succentor is hell-bent on destroying centuries of musical tradition. It takes the combined efforts of composer Alban Praetorius, cellist Sylvester Tate and singer Alexia Wryston to re-establish harmony in this discordant world.

**For £2.00 off Unholy Harmonies, see voucher at end of following extract**

"Justinia, how nice. What are you doing in Eyot?"

Oh, no. Pauline Norris. Justinia looked around as though some means of escape might suddenly appear.

"Hello, Pauline," she said in what she hoped was a friendly voice.

"Isn't it ridiculous? We both live in Unthrang, and hardly see each other, and then we bump into each other in Eyot. Of course, I'm so busy, it's hard to keep up with my friends."

I'm not a friend, thought Justinia.

"Shopping?" said Pauline, her sharp eyes boring into Justinia's big leather bag.

Justinia's defences went up; she's not going to prise anything out of me, she said to herself. Uninteresting though the contents of her bag were, she wasn't revealing them.

"Such a busy time, when one's moved into a new house, especially when there's a lot of work to be done," Pauline went on in her relentless way. "I expect you're picking up swatches of fabric, wallpaper samples. Really, I quite envy you."

"Toothpaste," said Justinia resignedly. You always gave in to Pauline, quicker and easier, really, to get it over with.

"You should support the local shops," said Pauline instantly. "Of course, Nigel and I do a big shop at Sainsbury's, well, you have to, don't you, one appreciates the variety . . . But things like a tube of toothpaste, well, we'd always go to Morton's in Unthrang for that."

"It's a special kind of toothpaste that Digby uses," said Justinia. "Morton's don't have it, so I have to come to Eyot for it."

"Special toothpaste? Does Digby have trouble with his teeth?

Bad gums, perhaps?" Her bright eyes, eager for information, searched Justinia's face.

Justinia was giving nothing away. "He just likes the taste," she said.

"You mustn't let men get away with their little foibles," said Pauline with a sharp laugh. "How long have you been married?"

None of your business, thought Justinia crossly.

"It's nearly four years, isn't it? And now this splendid house you've bought, I expect you'll soon be shopping for things for the nursery."

Justinia gave her a ravishing smile, thinking of the packet of contraceptive pills sitting in the bag with the toothpaste.

"A good idea, to start a family," Pauline persisted. "After all, with Digby up in London and you here . . . Well, men can get lonely, in that way. That's where children make a difference; they're a great tie for a man."

"Digby is too busy to be lonely," said Justinia firmly.

"Ah, I didn't mean anything, you know, you mustn't take offence. But I've been married quite a while, and of course, I'm older than you, and I know what men are like. Naturally, you feel sure that Digby wouldn't look at another woman, but perhaps you ought to know . . ."

"Justy!"

Rescue.

"Lydia, I'm sorry I'm late, I was just chatting to Pauline. You know Pauline, do you?"

"Yes," said Lydia without enthusiasm. "How are you, Pauline?"

Pauline longed to know Lydia better, since her husband was such a very distinguished composer. In truth, Lydia was one of the few people who could make Pauline feel uneasy, so with a few final remarks she excused herself and went on her way, hoping to meet someone else so that she could mention her chat with Lydia Praetorius; an old friend, you know, wife of Alban Praetorius, the composer.

"What was all that about?" asked Lydia. "Why were you making faces at me? What are you doing in Eyot? Why aren't you beavering away in the museum? Why were you talking to ghastly Pauline?"

"Lunch," said Justinia. "Let me take you to lunch, I feel in need of refreshment."

"All right," said Lydia. "But a quick one, although I long to chat. Alban's gone to London for the day, so I have masses of things to do while his back is turned."

"A lover?" asked Justinia with interest, as they joined the queue at the food counter in Horatio's Bar.

"Of course not," said Lydia, laughing. "Cleaning his studio, throwing out all the food he's been hoarding in the fridge – you know how he hates to throw anything away – that kind of thing. Very wifely. Very domestic. How's Digby?"

"Fine," said Justinia.

"So why aren't you in London, working? Have you taken time off to fix the new house?"

"I've given up my job in London," said Justinia. "Too difficult, now that we've bought this house in Unthrang. It's too far, and it's very stressful, hurtling down for Monday morning, and then fighting one's way back on Friday night."

"Won't you be bored?"

"Probably, but once the house is straight, I'll see if I can find a job here, in Eyot. Plenty of museums about, there must be something I can do."

"Not the same as the British Museum."

"No," agreed Justinia, squeezing her chair up to a little round table in the corner.

"Is Digby in London very much these days?"

"He's there today," said Justinia. "Usually, he goes into his office here, but he goes up to London once or twice a month."

"Business booming?"

Justinia nodded, her mouth full of luscious linguine. "This is good. Yes, it's all doing very well. People travelling more and more, at least the kind of people he arranges travel for."

"A select group, are they?"

"I wouldn't say select. Targeted. Particular types of business, and he's getting into other kinds of group travel: orchestras and so on."

"Lucrative?"

"Mmm, not too bad."

"You could work for his company. You know a lot about music, don't you? Do you still sing?"

"A bit. No, I wouldn't like to work for Digby, best to keep one's private and professional lives separate."

"I expect you're right. And Digby's probably difficult to work with, he's very bossy, isn't he? Still, don't let him get too involved with his work. You don't want to find yourself stranded out in Unthrang."

"While I languish into motherhood?" asked Justinia.

"No need to bite, such an idea wouldn't occur to me. I don't think you could languish. You look as though you could with your dreamy eyes and pre-Raphaelite hair, but that doesn't deceive anyone who knows you."

"Do you think Digby knows me?"

Lydia was sitting back, relaxed and peaceful, but she shot Justinia a very sharp glance from under half-closed eyes.

"I don't suppose he does. Men seldom do, they're constantly being surprised by their wives."

"Do you surprise Alban?"

"Nothing surprises Alban. He's far too wrapped up in himself and his music to be surprised. Annoyed is the furthest he'd go, and that only if it was something that directly affected his comfort or his work."

"You're very lucky, you know," said Justinia thoughtfully. "Being married to a musician."

Lydia looked hard at her cousin. "What an extraordinary thing to say. I'm married to Alban because he's Alban, not because he's a composer."

Justinia explained. "You live in a musical world. I don't. I think I should like to have been a musician, you see."

"Yes, you were very musical, weren't you? That lovely voice, I always thought you were destined to be a singer."

"It would have been difficult. My parents didn't approve of music as a career, and it didn't seem sensible to train at the time."

"Musicians never bother about those things," said Lydia with chilling directness. "They just go ahead and do it, because they have to. Not because it's sensible or convenient."

"No, well," said Justinia, "I never had the drive, so I suppose my mother was right. I have a degree, and qualifications for museum work; much more practical and useful."

"Yes," said Lydia. "And Digby isn't fond of music, is he?"

Justinia laughed. "Not at all. Likes what he calls a jolly good tune, which means one that he can whistle a few bars of, and that's his lot. I took him to the opera once or twice before we were married, but I can't say he took to it."

"There's a good Music Society Choir here," said Lydia. "Alban's brother Simon runs it. They're forming a Chamber Choir, too, the Eyot Camerata. Go and audition, you'd enjoy it, and you'd meet people."

"I've already met a lot of people," said Justinia darkly. "Unthrang is full of people."

"Interesting people?" asked Lydia.

"No, I don't think so. There's Pauline, of course."

"Ugh," said Lydia. "Well she and Nigel must be the worst of it."

"I suppose so. There's a strange old woman who lives in a big house with a tower. She's called Zephania Zouche, I'm told; I haven't met her; she keeps herself to herself and wears a strange flat hat. Then there's a woman, a young woman, called Roxane, who lives in a lovely seventeenth-century house on the green, Juniper House. I think she lives alone, but the woman at the shop told me that she lets the house out, and that a family are coming for the autumn."

"Then there's Sadie, she's all right; a widow I think – at any rate, there's no husband about. She lives in a funny little yellow cottage on the other side of the green. The vicarage contains the vicar, who's hearty and modern and evangelical. He gets on very well with Digby; Digby likes anything that's up-to-date. That's about it. Oh, and Sylvester is living in Crag End, while Midwinter Hall is having its works done."

Lydia looked pleased. "Sylvester? Well, never a dull moment if Sylvester's around. What about Lily? Is she with him? Is Gabriel in residence?"

"Lily's there, I think Gabriel is abroad. Anyway, those are all the ones I've met so far."

"There must be more than that. No country wenches to tempt Digby's roving eye?"

"Roving eye? What do you mean?"

Lydia shook her head, startled at the vehemence of Justinia's voice. "Calm down, it was an idle phrase, no more. Have some pud."

"Sorry," said Justinia, as a passing waiter waved a hand towards a table laden with ruinous and creamy things. "It's just Pauline was making some silly remarks. Why does everyone suppose that if you've been married for more than five minutes and you don't have children, then your husband must be off having affairs?"

"Which Digby isn't."

"No, he isn't," said Justinia, stabbing at a quivering crème caramel. "He isn't that sort, and besides, we're still in love, strange though that must seem."

"Doesn't seem strange to me," said Lydia. "Now, stop fretting and eat up. I'll be seeing Simon this evening, I'll ask him about his choirs. You're a soprano, aren't you?"

Justinia nodded. "I'd like that, as long as it's a convenient evening; Digby doesn't like me being out when he's at home. But he often works late, so it shouldn't be a problem."

They parted affectionately, Lydia promising to come and see the house. "And I'll bring Alban, too; although he always grumbles about my horrible Mountjoy relations, I think he's got rather a soft spot for you. Says you're too damn beautiful to miss."

Justinia laughed, and the tension which Lydia had noticed all through lunch vanished from her face.

I can't return the compliment, Justinia thought as she made her way through the tourists in the crowded streets towards the car park. Digby isn't very keen on any of my Mountjoy relations; I wonder if he knew what they said when we got married. Oh well, we've proved them wrong, our marriage is a success, more than you can say for some of them.

"Shock Sale," said the screamer in the window. "Swimsuits from France, ridiculous prices."

Justinia hesitated, eyed a particularly appealing costume which looked good even on the twig-like physique of the dummy in the window, and pushed open the door of the shop. Roxane had invited her to swim in her indoor pool at Juniper House. "It doesn't get enough use; you'd mostly have it to yourself."

Thinking that she would be glad to get out of the Old Rectory and that she could do with some exercise now she was no longer going to work every day, Justinia had searched in vain for her swimsuit. It had been lost or mislaid in the moves, first from her flat in London to Digby's larger one, then to their London house, and now up here to Unthrang.

A tiny, vivacious assistant emerged from behind the counter. "Is it a swimsuit you're after?"

Justinia smiled and said it was.

"Lovely, they are. From France, genuinely, not one of these signs some shops put up just to attract customers. We wouldn't do that. Did you see one you liked in the window?"

"Yes," said Justinia, pointing it out.

"Beautiful, these colours." The assistant fixed dark, sparkling, expert eyes on Justinia. "Thirty-six, is it? This should be all right."

She escorted Justinia to a minute changing room, pulling the curtain across with a flourish. "I'll go and check if we have other sizes, or perhaps you'd like to try on one or two different models."

Her heels clicked smartly as she went back into the main part of the shop, while Justinia took off her jacket and began to undo her shirt.

"I'll help you with your bra," said the assistant, coming back with an armful of brilliantly coloured costumes. "Lovely ones you've got, are they natural?"

Justinia laughed. "Yes, my own."

"Smashing," said the girl with a sigh. "I"ve got practically nothing up top myself, all artificially bolstered, that's the advantage of working in lingerie. But you'd be surprised at what some women have done, they go to America for it. Very realistic, but too firm. I only asked because you've got such a small waist, lucky you to have a figure like that."

Justinia pulled on the swimming costume, which turned out on inspection to cost an alarming amount, even in the Shock Sale, but the assistant's admiration was wholehearted and Justinia knew that Digby would appreciate it. As she was starting to get dressed again, the assistant reappeared, whisked away the costumes, with coos of delight at the one that Justinia had chosen, and delivered some wisps of underwear to the little table in the changing room. "Look lovely on you, these would," she said winningly. "Get your lover really excited."

"Lover?" said Justinia. What was this, why was everybody talking about lovers today?

"Must be a lover," said the girl. "You're married, you've got rings on, a good one too, it must have cost, that one. But the way you look at yourself, you're thinking of some man admiring you in that costume, I can tell."

"And why shouldn't it be my husband?" said Justinia, laughing.

"Never is," said the girl wisely. "Someone else's husband, perhaps, but not your own."

"Well, you're wrong." said Justinia, looking at the pile of lace. "It is for my husband."

"Never mind," said the girl with great cheerfulness. "Looking the way you do, it won't be for long, must be any number of men willing to have a fling, you with a figure like that, not to mention your looks. I see them all in here, women wanting to look sexy for their lovers, then ten minutes later, their husbands are in here – buying pretties for their mistresses of course, not for their wives."

"You're very cynical," said Justinia, hunting for her cheque book.

"Come back soon, when that lover turns up," said the girl with a wicked look as Justinia left the shop. "Tell me all about him, I shan't breathe a word!"

# Children of Chance

## ELIZABETH PEWSEY

In the sultry heat of an uncommonly hot English summer, young Prue Pagan heads north to take up her holiday job at Mountjoy Castle. Newly released from the confines of her convent school, she tastes the pleasures – and dangers – of her new position with innocent abandon. At nearby Minwinter Hall, Prue's more worldly friend Cleo is also working for the summer. And while Prue is stalked by Lord Mountjoy's irascible heir, Cleo pursues her own quarry. Nothing is quite what it seems, however, and many secrets lie hidden between castle, hall and village. By the time the summer is out so are most of the secrets, and Prue is not the only one wiser in the ways of the world.

'A deliciously wicked tale of the shedding of innocence'
*Company*

SCEPTRE